The Complete Works of
COUNT TOLSTÓY
Volume XXIV.

Tolstóy and His Wife

Photogravure from a Photograph

LATEST WORKS ℒ LIFE GENERAL INDEX ℒ BIBLI-OGRAPHY ℒ ℒ ℒ ℒ

Tolstói, Lev Nikolaevich

BY COUNT LEV N. TOLSTÓY

Translated from the Original Russian and Edited by

LEO WIENER

AMS PRESS
NEW YORK

Reprinted with permission of J. M. Dent and Sons, Ltd.
From the edition of 1905, London
First AMS EDITION published 1968
Manufactured in the United States of America

Library of Congress Catalogue Card Number: 68-57229

AMS PRESS, INC.
New York, N.Y. 10003

CONTENTS

LIST OF ILLUSTRATIONS

THE SLAVERY OF OUR TIME

1900

THE SLAVERY OF OUR TIME

INTRODUCTION

ALMOST fifteen years ago the census taken in Moscow evoked in me a series of thoughts and sentiments which I, as well as I could, expressed in a book, entitled *What Shall We Do Then?* Toward the end of last year, the year 1899, I had occasion once more to reflect upon the same questions, and the answers at which I arrived were the same as in the book, *What Shall We Do Then?* but as it seems to me that in these fifteen years I have been able more calmly and at greater length, in connection with the now existing and popular doctrines, once more to reflect upon the subject which was discussed in the book, *What Shall We Do Then?* I now offer my readers new proofs, which bring us to the same answers as before. I think that these arguments may be useful to people who are sincerely striving after an elucidation of their position in society and to a clear determination of the moral obligations which arise from this position, and so I print them.

The fundamental idea, both of that book and of the present article, is the rejection of violence. This rejection I learned and came to understand from the Gospel, where it is most clearly expressed in the words, " An eye for an eye . . . that is, you have been taught to use violence against violence, but I teach you to offer the other cheek, when you are smitten, that is, to endure violence, but not to offer it." I know that these great words, thanks to the frivolously perverse and mutually concordant interpretations of the liberals and of the church, will for the majority of so-called cultured people be the cause why they will not read the article, or why they will read it with a bias; none the less I place these words at the head of the present article.

I cannot keep people who call themselves enlightened from regarding the Gospel teaching as an obsolete guidance of life which was long ago outlived by humanity. It is my business to point out the source from which I drew the knowledge of the truth which is still far from being cognized by all men, and which alone can free people from their calamities. And this I am doing.

June 28, 1900.

1

A WEIGHER serving on the Moscow-Kazán Railway, with whom I am acquainted, told me, in a conversation which I had with him, that peasants who load freight on his scales work for thirty-six hours in succession.

In spite of my full confidence in the truthfulness of my interlocutor, I could not believe him. I thought that he was either mistaken, or was exaggerating, or that I had not understood him correctly.

But the weigher went on to give me such details about the conditions under which this work takes place, that no room for doubt was left. According to his story there are 250 such freight-hands on the Moscow-Kazán Road. They are divided into parties of five, and work by contract, receiving from one rouble to one rouble and fifteen kopeks per thousand puds of freight loaded or unloaded.

They come in the morning, work a day and a night unloading, and immediately after the end of the night, in the morning, start to load up, and thus work for another day. Thus they sleep but one night in forty-eight hours.

Their work consists in throwing out and taking away bales weighing seven, eight, and even ten puds. Two men hoist the bales on the shoulders of the other three, and these carry the load. By such labour they earn one rouble per day, out of which they have to feed themselves. They work continuously, without holidays.

The weigher's story was so circumstantial that it was impossible to doubt it, but I none the less decided to verify it, and so went to the freight station.

Upon finding my acquaintance at the freight station,

5

I told him that I had come to look at what he had told me.

"Nobody to whom I tell it is willing to believe it," I said.

"Nikíta," the weigher, without answering me, turned to some one in the shed, "come here!"

Out of the door stepped a tall, slim labourer, in a torn coat.

"When did you begin working?"

"When? Yesterday morning."

"Where were you during the night?"

"Where else, but at the unloading?"

"Did you work at night?" I asked this time.

"Of course, I worked."

"And when did you come here to-day?"

"In the morning, — what a question!"

"And when will you get through with your work?"

"When they discharge me, — then shall I get through."

Four more labourers, out of a party of five, came up to us.

They were all without fur coats, in torn undercoats, although it was twenty degrees Réaumur below zero.

I asked them about the details of their work, evidently puzzling them with my interest in what to them was so simple and natural a thing as thirty-six hours' work.

They were all villagers, for the most part my countrymen, from the Government of Túla; there were also some from Orél and others from Vorónezh. They live in Moscow in hired rooms, some with their families, but for the most part alone. Those who live alone send their earnings home.

They board singly with their landlords. Their board comes to ten roubles per month, and they eat meat at all times without keeping the fasts.

They are at work, not thirty-six hours in succession, but always more, because they lose more than half an hour in going from their quarters and coming bac¹·, and, besides, are frequently kept at work for more than the set time. With such thirty-seven hours' work in succession they earn twenty-five roubles per month, out of which they have to pay for their board.

In reply to my question as to why they do such convict labour, they answered:

" What else shall we do ? "

" But why work thirty-six hours in succession ? Can't you arrange it in such a way as to work by relays ? "

" That's what we are told to do."

" But why do you consent ? "

" We consent, because we have to make a living. If you do not want to, — go ! If you are an hour late, you get your discharge, — and march ! There are ten other men who are ready to take your place."

The labourers were all young people ; only one of them was older, somewhere above forty. They all had emaciated, careworn faces and weary eyes, as though they had been drinking. The slim labourer with whom I had first begun to speak struck me more especially by this strange weariness of his look. I asked him whether he had not had something to drink that day.

" I do not drink," he answered, as without thinking always answer people who really do not drink.

" And I do not smoke, either," he added.

" And do the others drink ? " I asked.

" Yes, they do. They bring it here."

" It is no light work. It will give you strength, all the same," said a middle-aged labourer.

This labourer had had some liquor on that day, but he did not show it at all.

After some further talk with the labourers, I went to take a look at the unloading.

After passing between long rows of all kinds of merchandise, I came to some labourers who were slowly moving a loaded car. The shifting of the cars and the clearing of the platforms from snow, as I later learned, the labourers are obliged to do without any remuneration. It even says so in the contract. These labourers were as ragged and as emaciated as those with whom I talked. When they had rolled the car up to the place wanted, and stopped, I went up to them and asked them when they had begun working, and when they had had their dinner.

I was told that they had begun to work at seven o'clock and had just had their dinner.

"We had to have dinner after work was through, — they did not let us go."

"And when will they let you go?"

"Any time. It may be as late as ten o'clock," replied the labourers, as though priding themselves on their endurance in work.

Seeing my interest in their condition, the labourers surrounded me, and, speaking several at a time, apparently taking me for a chief, informed me, what evidently formed their chief grievance, that the quarters where at times they could warm themselves or fall asleep for an hour, between the day and the night work, were narrow. They all expressed great dissatisfaction with the crowded quarters.

"Some hundred men gather there, and there is no place to lie down in; it is crowded even under the benches," several voices said, with dissatisfaction. "Look at it yourself, — it is not far from here."

The quarters were crowded indeed. In the room, which was about twenty feet square, about forty men could find places on the benches.

Several labourers followed me into the room, and all of them, interrupting one another, angrily complained of the crowded condition of the quarters. "There is even no place to lie down under the benches," they said.

At first it seemed strange to me that all these men, who in a cold of twenty below zero, without fur coats, for the period of thirty-seven hours carried ten-pud weights on their backs, who were not allowed to go to dinner and supper when it was time to, but when it so pleased the authorities, and who, in general, were in an infinitely worse state than the dray-horses, should complain of nothing but the crowded condition of their warming-place. At first this seemed strange to me, but, when I reflected on their condition, I understood what an agonizing experience it must be for these men, who do not get enough sleep and are frozen, when, instead of resting and warming themselves, they crawl over a dirty floor under the benches, and there feel only weaker and more tired in the close, infected atmosphere.

No doubt, they only in this agonizing hour of a vain attempt at sleeping feel painfully the whole terror of their thirty-seven hours' work, which ruins their lives, and so are more especially provoked by this seemingly unimportant circumstance, — the crowded condition of the quarters. After watching several of their parties at work and speaking with some of the labourers, and hearing one and the same thing from all of them, I went home, fully convinced that what my acquaintance told me was the truth.

It was true that for money, which gives nothing but their sustenance to men who consider themselves free, these men find it necessary to hire themselves out for work to which in the times of serf law not one serf-owner, even the most cruel, would have sent out his slaves. Why, not even a hack-owner would send out his horse, because his horse cost money, and it is not profitable to shorten the life of a costly animal by means of thirty-seven hours of the hardest kind of work.

2

It is not merely cruel, but even unprofitable, to make men work for thirty-seven hours in succession, without any sleep. And yet such unprofitable exploitation of human lives is taking place all about us without interruption.

Opposite the house in which I live there is a factory of silk articles, which has all the latest technical improvements. In it live and work about three thousand women and seven hundred men. Just as I am sitting here, in my house, I hear the continuous rumble of machinery, and I know, for I have been there, what this rumble means. Three thousand women stand for twelve hours at the looms, amidst a deafening noise, winding, unwinding, spinning silk threads for the production of silk stuffs. All the women, with the exception of those who have just come from the villages, have an unhealthy appearance. The majority of them lead a very incontinent and immoral life; nearly all the married and unmarried women immediately after childbirth send their children either into the country or into a foundling house, where eighty per cent. of these children perish; and the mothers, not to lose their places, go back to work one or two days after childbirth.

Thus, in the period of twenty years that I have known this, tens of thousands of young, healthy women have been ruining their lives and those of their children, in order to produce velvet and silk stuffs.

Yesterday I met a young beggar of a powerful build, whose spine was curved and who was walking with crutches. He had been working with a wheelbarrow, when he lost his balance and injured himself internally. He spent what he had with doctors and curing-women, and has been these eight years without a home, has been begging, and murmurs against God for not sending death to him.

How many such ruined lives there are, which we either know nothing of, or, if we know, do not notice, thinking that it is right as it is!

I know in a Túla iron foundry labourers at the furnaces, who, to have every second Sunday free, work twenty-four hours in succession. I have seen these labourers. They all drink liquor, to brace themselves, and, just like those freight-handlers at the railroad, obviously are rapidly losing not only the interest, but even the capital of their lives. And what about the wasting of the lives of those men who are employed in admittedly injurious labour, — the compositors, who poison themselves with lead dust, the workmen in mirror factories, in card, match, sugar, tobacco, glass factories, the miners, the privy-cleaners?

The statistical data of England say that the average length of the lives of the men of the higher classes is fifty-five years, but that the duration of the lives of workmen in unhealthy professions is twenty-nine years.

It would seem that, knowing this (it is impossible not to know this), we, the men who use the labour that costs so many human lives, if we are no beasts, could not for a moment remain at peace. And yet, we, well-to-do, liberal, humane people, who are very sensitive, not only to the sufferings of men, but of animals as well, continue to employ this labour, try to become richer and richer, that is, to use more and more of such labour, and remain completely at peace.

Having, for example, learned of the thirty-seven-hour work of the freight-handlers and of their bad quarters, we will immediately send there a well-paid inspector, will not allow any work above twelve hours, leaving the third of the labourers who are deprived of their income to live as they please, will even compel the railroad to build commodious and ample quarters for the labourers, and then we shall with absolutely calm consciences receive and transport goods by this road and receive a salary, dividends, rentals from houses, from land, and so forth. And, upon learning that women and girls, who live in

the silk factory, far away from their families and amidst
temptations, are ruining themselves and their children,
that the greater part of the laundresses who iron our
starched shirts, and of the compositors who set up enter-
taining books for us, grow consumptive, we shall only
shrug our shoulders and say that we are very sorry that
this is so, but that we are unable to do anything to prevent this, and we shall continue with an easy conscience
to purchase silk stuffs, to wear starched shirts, and to
read the newspapers in the morning. We are very much
concerned about the resting spells of commercial clerks,
still more about the overexertion of our children in the
gymnasia, strictly forbid the draymen to overload their
horses, and even so arrange the slaughtering of the
animals in the slaughter-houses that the animals shall
suffer as little as possible. What remarkable eclipse
shrouds us the moment we touch on those millions of
labourers who on all sides slowly and often painfully kill
themselves with that work which we use for our conveniences and pleasures!

3

This remarkable eclipse that the people of our circle
suffer from may be explained only by this, that when
people act badly, they always invent such a world-conception for themselves that their evil deeds may not
appear as evil, but as the consequences of invariable laws
which are beyond their power. In antiquity such a
world-conception consisted in this, that there exists God's
inexplicable and invariable will, which for some determined a low position and work, and for others a high
position and the enjoyment of the goods of life.

Upon the theme of this world-conception a vast number
of books were written and an endless number of sermons
delivered. This theme was worked out from the most
various sides. It was proved that God created different

kinds of men, slaves and masters, and that both ought to be satisfied with their situation; then it was proved that the slaves would be better off in the world to come; then it was made clear that, although the slaves were slaves and must remain such, their situation would not be bad, if their masters were merciful to them; then, after the liberation of the slaves, the last explanation was, that wealth was entrusted to some people that they might use part of it for good acts, and that in this case the wealth of some and the poverty of the others did not represent anything bad.

These explanations for a long time satisfied both the poor and the rich, especially the latter. But the time came when these explanations became insufficient, especially for those who began to understand their condition of poverty. Then new explanations were needed, and just at that time these new explanations made their appearance. These appeared in the form of science, — political economy, which asserts that it has found the laws according to which labour and the use of its productions are distributed among men. These laws, according to the doctrine of this science, consist in this, that the distribution of labour and the use of it depends on supply and demand, on capital, interest, wages, prices, profit, etc., in general on invariable laws which condition men's economical activity.

On this theme there were in a short time written not fewer books and pamphlets and delivered not fewer lectures than there had been written treatises and delivered theological sermons on the previous theme, and even now they incessantly write mountains of books and pamphlets and deliver lectures on the same subject; and all these books and lectures are just as misty and incomprehensible as the theological treatises and sermons, and, like the theological treatises, they attain their end, which is, to give an explanation of the existing order of things,

such as would make it possible for one set of men to be
at rest, and not to work, and to enjoy the labours of
other men.

The fact that for the investigations of this putative
science they did not take the condition of the men of the
whole world during all its historical existence as a model
of the general order, but only the condition of men in
small England, which has existed under exceptional conditions, at the end of the last and the beginning of the
present century, did not in the least interfere with the
recognition of the truth of the propositions arrived at by
the investigators, even as the endless disputes and differ-
ences of the leaders of this science, who cannot come to
any agreement as to how to understand rentals, increased
valuation, profit, etc., do not interfere with it at the present time. There is but one fundamental proposition of
this science which is recognized by all, and that is, that
human relations are not conditioned by what men consider good or bad, but by what is advantageous to the
people who are already in an advantageous position.

What has been accepted as an indubitable truth is
this, that, if in society there are bred a large number
of robbers and thieves, who take from the labouring
people the productions of their labour, this is not due
to the fact that the robbers and thieves act badly, but
because such are the unchangeable economic laws, which
may be changed only by a slow evolution, is determined
by science, and so, according to the doctrine of this
science, the men who belong to the class of the robbers,
thieves, or abettors, who enjoy the fruits of their robbery and stealing, may calmly continue to enjoy what
they have stolen and taken by violence.

Though the majority of the men of our world do not
know these soothing explanations of science, just as many
former men did not know the details of the theological
explanations which justified their position, — they none

the less know that this explanation exists, that the learned
and wise men have incontrovertibly proved that the existing order of things is just what it ought to be, and
that, therefore, we may calmly live in this order of
things, without trying to change it.

It is only in this way that I am able to explain that
remarkable blindness in which find themselves the good
people of our society who sincerely wish the animals
well, but with an easy conscience feast on the lives of
their brothers.

4

The theory that God's will consists in this, that one
set of men should rule another, for a long time eased
men's consciences. But this theory, in justifying the
cruelties of men, carried these cruelties to the utmost
limits, and thus provoked opposition and doubts as to
its truthfulness.

Even so now the theory that the economic evolution
takes place according to inevitable laws, in consequence
of which one set of men must hoard capital, while others
must work all their lives, to increase this capital, while
preparing themselves for the promised socialization of the
tools of production, — by provoking an even greater
cruelty of one set of men against all others, — is beginning now, especially amidst simple men who are not
stultified by science, to provoke certain doubts.

You see, for example, the freight-handlers, who are
ruining their lives by their work of thirty-seven hours'
duration, or the women in the factory, or the laundresses,
or the compositors, or all those millions of people who
live under grievous, unnatural conditions of monotonous,
stultifying slave labour, and you naturally ask : " What
has brought these people to such a state, and how can
they be liberated from it ? " And science answers you
that these men are in such a state, because the railroad

belongs to such and such a company, the silk factory to such and such a master, and all the plants, factories, printing offices, laundries, to capitalists, in general, and that this situation will improve if the working people, by uniting into unions and coöperative societies and by means of strikes and of participation in the government exerting an ever greater influence upon their masters and the government, will attain, at first a shortening of the work-day and an increase of the wages, and finally this, that all the implements of production will pass into their hands, and then all will be well; but now everything is going the way it ought to, and there is no need of changing anything.

This answer cannot help but appear very strange to unlearned men, particularly to unlearned Russians. In the first place, neither in relation to the freight-handlers, nor to the women, nor to the many millions of other workers, who suffer from the hard, unhealthy, stultifying labour, does the belonging of the implements of production to the capitalist offer any explanation. The implements of production in agriculture which belong to the labourers who are living now at the railroad have not been seized by the capitalists at all; these labourers have land, and horses, and ploughs, and harrows, and everything needed for the cultivation of the soil; even so the women who work in the factory are not driven to this work because the implements of production have been taken from them; on the contrary, they generally go away from home against the will of the elder members of the family, though their work is very much needed there, and though there are there all the implements of production. In the same condition are millions of labourers, both in Russia and in other countries. Thus the cause of the wretched condition of the working people can by no means be found in the seizure by the capitalists of the implements of production. The cause must be found in what drives them out of the village. So much in the first place. In the second place, neither the shortening of the work-day, nor the increase in wages, nor the promised socialization of the implements of production, can in any way free the working people from this state, even in that distant future, when science promises them that liberation.

All that cannot improve their condition, because the wretchedness of the position of the working people, upon the railroad, or in the silk factory, or in any other factory or plant, does not consist in a greater or lesser number of working hours (the agriculturists work, while quite satisfied with their lot, as much as eighteen hours a day and thirty-six hours in succession), and not in the small pay, and not in this, that the railroad or factory does not belong to them, but in this, that the working people are obliged to work under injurious, unnatural, and frequently dangerous and pernicious conditions of life, in city barracks, full of temptations and immorality, and to do slave work for other people.

Of late the hours of work have been reduced and the pay has been increased, but this reduction of the hours of labour and the increase of pay have not improved the condition of the working people, if we do not consider their more luxurious habits, — a watch and chain, silk kerchiefs, tobacco, wine, meat, beer, and so forth, — but their real welfare, that is, their health and morality, and, above all, their freedom.

In the factory of silk articles with which I am acquainted, twenty years ago there worked mainly men who worked fourteen hours a day and earned fifteen roubles clear a month, which they generally sent home to their families in the country. Now it is mostly women who work there: they work eleven hours a day and earn sometimes as much as twenty-five roubles per month, or more than fifteen roubles clear; they generally do not send the earnings home, but spend them here, chiefly on dresses, drunkenness, and debauchery ; and the reduction of hours of labour only increases the time passed by them at the inns.

The same, in a greater or lesser measure, takes place in all the factories and plants. Everywhere, in spite of the reduction of the hours of labour and the increase of pay, the health, as compared with that in agricultural work, is injured, the average length of life is diminished, and morality is lost, as, indeed, it cannot be otherwise, when we consider how they are removed from the conditions, most conducive to morality, of family life and free, healthy, varied, sensible agricultural labour.

It may be, as some economists assert, that with the reduction of hours of labour, the increase of wages, and the improvement of sanitary conditions in the factories, the health of the working people and their morality is improved as compared with the condition in which the factory hands used to be formerly. It may be even that of late and in certain localities the condition of the working people in the factories has in external conditions been better than the condition of the rural population. But this is true for only some localities and is due to this, that the government and society are doing, under the influence of the propositions of science, everything that can be done for the deterioration of the rural population and for the improvement of the condition of the factory hands.

If the condition of the factory hands is in certain localities — and that, too, only in external conditions — better than the condition of rural labourers, this only proves that with all kinds of oppressions it is possible to reduce to wretchedness a life which from external conditions is best, and that there does not exist so unnatural and bad a condition but that a man can adapt himself to it and remain in it for several generations.

The wretchedness of the condition of the factory hand and of the city workman in general does not consist in his working long and getting little for it, but in this, that he is deprived of the natural conditions of life in the midst of nature, is deprived of liberty, and is obliged to do monotonous slave work for another.

And so the answer to the questions as to why factory and city labourers are in a wretched state, and how to help them, can nowise consist in this, that it is due to the fact that the capitalists have seized the implements of production, and that the reduction of the hours of labour, the increase of wages, and the socialization of the implements of production will improve the position of the working people.

The answer to these questions must consist in the indication of the causes which have deprived the labourers of the natural conditions of life amidst nature and have driven them into the slavery of the factories, and in the indication of the means for liberating the working people from the necessity of passing from the free life in the country to the slave life in the factories.

Thus the question as to why the working people in the cities are in a wretched state includes first of all the question as to what are the causes which drove these people away from the country, where they or their ancestors lived and could live and with us in Russia still live, and what it is that against their will has been driving them into the factories and plants.

If there are such working people, as in England, Belgium, Germany, who for several generations have been living in factories, even these do not do so of their own free will, but because their parents, grandparents, or great-grandparents were for some reason obliged to change their agricultural life, which they liked, for a life in the city and in the factories, which presented itself to them as hard. The rural population was at first forcibly dispossessed of its land, says K. Marx, and driven out and reduced to the state of vagrancy, and then, by force of cruel laws, they were tortured with tongs, hot iron, scourges, for the purpose of making them submit to the demands of private labour. And so the question as to how to liberate the working people from their wretched condition would seem naturally to reduce itself to the question as to how to remove those causes which have driven several and now drive away the rest from that condition which these people have regarded as good and have driven them into a condition which they have regarded as bad.

But the economic science, though it in passing points out the causes which have driven the labourers away from the land, does not busy itself with the removal of these causes, but turns all its attention only to the amelioration of the condition of the working people in the existing factories and plants, as though assuming that the condition of the working people in these plants and factories is something unchangeable, something which must by all means remain for those who are already in the factories, and must become the condition of those who have not yet left the villages and agricultural labour.

Not only has the economic science become convinced that all the rural labourers must inevitably pass through the condition of the city workers in the factories, but also, despite the fact that all the sages and poets of the world have always looked only in the conditions of agricultural labour for the realization of the ideal of human happiness; despite the fact that all working people with uncorrupted habits have always preferred agricultural labour to any other; despite the fact that work in the factories is always unhealthy and monotonous, while agricultural work is most healthy and varied; despite the fact that agricultural labour is always free, that is, that the labourer

at his will alternates between work and rest, while work
in the factory, even though it all should belong to the
working people, is always slavish, in dependence on the machine; despite the fact that factory work is secondary,
while agricultural is basic, so that without it no factories
could exist, — despite all that, the economic science asserts that the country people not only do not suffer from
changing the country for the city, but even wish for it
themselves and strive for it.

5

No matter how unjust is the assertion of the men of
science that the good of humanity must consist in that
which is profoundly repulsive to human sentiment, in
monotonous, slavish labour in the factories, the men of
science have inevitably been led to the necessity of this
obviously unjust assertion, just as the theologians were
inevitably led to just as obviously unjust an assertion
that the slaves and the masters are different beings, and
that the inequality of their conditions in this world will
be requited in the world to come.

The cause of this obviously unjust assertion is this,
that the men who have been establishing the propositions
of science have belonged to the well-to-do classes, and
have been so accustomed to those advantageous conditions
amidst which they live that they do not even admit the
idea that society could exist outside these conditions.

But the conditions of life to which the men of the well-
to-do classes have become accustomed are that abundant
production of various objects necessary for their comforts
and pleasures which are obtained only, thanks to the now
existing factories and plants, as they are arranged at the
present time. And so, in discussing the amelioration of
the working people's condition, the men of science, who
belong to the well-to-do classes, always assume only an

amelioration such that the production of the factories will remain the same, and so the comforts of life which they will enjoy will also remain the same.

Even the most advanced men of science, the socialists, in demanding a complete transference of the implements of production to the working people, assume that the production of the same or nearly the same articles as at present will be continued in the same or similar factories with the present division of labour.

According to their conception, there will be only this difference, that then it will not be they alone, but also everybody else, who will enjoy those comforts which they are now enjoying all by themselves. They have a dim idea that with the socialization of the implements of labour they themselves, the men of science and, in general, the men of the ruling classes, will have a share in work, but for the most part in the shape of managers, — as draughtsmen, scholars, artists. But they preserve silence as to who will make white lead with muzzles on their faces, who will be the stokers, the miners, and the privy-cleaners, or they assume that all these things will be so perfected that even the work in the sewers and underground will form a pleasant occupation. Thus they present to themselves the economic life both in the utopias, like the utopia of Bellamy, and in learned treatises.

According to their theory, the working people, having all united into unions and societies, and having educated solidarity in themselves, will finally, by means of unions, strikes, and participation in parliaments, arrive at this, that they will get possession of all the implements of production, including the land; and then they will feed so well, will dress so well, will enjoy such amusements on Sundays, that they will prefer life in the city, amidst stones and chimneys, to the life in the country, in the broad expanse, amidst plants and domestic animals, and will prefer the monotonous machine work, according to the whistle, to the varied, healthful, and free agricultural labour.

Though this assumption is as little probable as the assumption of the theologians concerning that heaven which the working people will enjoy in the world to come for having worked so painfully in this world, intelligent and cultured men of our circle none the less believe in this strange doctrine, just as former learned and intelligent people used to believe in a heaven for the working people in the world to come.

The learned and their disciples — people of the well-to-do classes — believe in this, because they cannot help believing in it. They are confronted with a dilemma: either they must see that everything which they enjoy in their life, from the railroad to matches and cigarettes, is their brothers' labour, which has cost many human lives, and that they, by not participating in this labour, but enjoying it, are very dishonest people, or that everything which takes place is done according to invariable laws of economic science for the general welfare. In this is contained that inner psychological cause, which compels the men of science, wise and cultured, but not enlightened men, with assurance and insistence to assert such an obvious untruth as that it is better for the good of the labourers to abandon their happy and healthy life amidst nature and to go to ruin their bodies and souls in factories and plants.

6

But even if we admit the obviously unjust assertion, which is contrary to all the properties of human nature, that it is better for people to live and work in factories and cities, doing mechanical slave work, than to live in the country and do free manual labour, — even if we admit all that, the very ideal, toward which, according to the teaching of the men of science, the economic evo-

lution leads, contains such an internal contradiction as
can in no way be disentangled. This ideal consists in
this, that the working people, having become the masters
of all the implements of production, will enjoy all those
comforts and pleasures which are now enjoyed only by
well-to-do people. All will be well dressed and housed
and fed, will walk over an asphalt pavement under
electric lights, will attend concerts and theatres, read
newspapers and books, will go out driving in motors, and
so forth. But for all men to use certain articles, it is
necessary to redistribute the manufacture of desirable
articles, to determine how much time each working man
is to work: how is this to be determined?

Statistical data may determine (very imperfectly at
that) men's needs in a society which is fettered by capi-
talism, competition, and want; but no statistical data
will show how many and what articles are necessary for
the gratification of the needs of a society, in which the
implements of production will belong to society itself,
that is, where men will be free.

It will be absolutely impossible to determine the needs
in such a society, because the needs will in such a society
always be infinitely greater than the possibility of gratifying them. Everybody will desire to have everything
which the rich now have, and so there is no possibility
of determining the quantity of articles needed by such a
society.

Besides, how can people be made to agree to produce
articles which some of them will consider necessary,
while others will consider them unnecessary or even quite
harmful?

If it shall be found that for the gratification of the
needs of society it will be necessary for every person to
work, say, six hours a day, who will compel a man in a
free society to work these six hours when he knows that
some of the hours are used for the production of

articles which he considers unnecessary and even harmful ?

There is no doubt that with the present structure of
society they produce with a great economy of forces,
thanks to machines and, above all, to the division of
labour, extremely complicated, most varied articles, which
are carried to the highest degree of perfection, the production of which is advantageous to their masters, and the
use of which we find very convenient and agreeable ; but
the fact that these articles are in themselves well done
and with a small waste of energy, and that we find them
indispensable for ourselves, does not prove that free people
would without constraint produce the same articles. There
is no doubt but that Krupp with the present division of
labour makes beautiful cannon in a short time and in
an artistic manner, and that N—— similarly produces
coloured silk stuffs, and S—— perfumes, smooth cards,
face-powder, which saves the complexion, and Popóv
delicious whiskey, and so forth, — that this is very advantageous, both for the proprietors of the establishments
where they are produced and for the consumers of them.
But cannon, perfume, and whiskey are desirable for those
who want to conquer the Chinese markets, or like drunkenness, or are interested in the preservation of the complexion, and there will always be some people who will
find the production of these articles injurious.   And, to
say nothing of such articles, there will always be some
people who will find that exhibitions, academies, beer,
meat, are unnecessary and even harmful.   How are these
men to be compelled to take part in the production of
such articles ?

But even if people shall find a means for having all
men agree to manufacture certain articles, — though there
can be no such means except compulsion, — who will in
a free society, without capitalistic production, without
competition or supply and demand, determine upon what

articles the forces are chiefly to be directed ? what is to
be produced first, what later ?   Are they first to build a
Siberian road and fortify Port Arthur, and then lay out
a highway through the counties, or vice versa ?   Which
is to be provided for first, — electric lights or the irriga-
tion of the fields ?   And then again the insoluble question
in connection with the freedom of the working people as
to who shall do this or that work.   Obviously, it will be
most pleasant for all people to busy themselves with the
sciences or with drawing, rather than to be a stoker or a
privy-cleaner.   How can people be made happy in this
distribution ?

No statistical data will answer these questions.   There
can be but a theoretical solution to these questions, that
is, such a solution as that there will be men to whom the
power will be given to manage all that.   One set of men
will decide these questions, and other men will obey
them.

But, in addition to the question of the division and
direction of production and the choice of work in the
socialization of the implements of production, there appears
also the chief question, — as to the degree of the division
of labour which may be established in a society which is
organized on socialistic principles.   The present division
of labour is conditioned by the wants of the working
people.   A workman agrees to live all his life under
ground, or all his life to produce one-hundredth part of
a certain article, or all his life monotonously to swing his
arms amidst a rumble of machines, only because without
that he will not have any means of support.   But a workman who shall be in possession of the implements of
production, and who, therefore, will not be suffering want,
will only through compulsion agree to enter into conditions of the division of labour which dull and kill all the
mental capacities and under which people work now.
The division of labour is unquestionably very advan-

tageous and proper for people, but, if men are free, the division of labour is possible only to a certain narrow limit, which has long ago been crossed in our society.

If one peasant from preference plies the shoemaker's trade, while his wife attends to the loom, and another peasant ploughs, and a third peasant works in the smithy, and all of them, having acquired exceptional agility in their work, later exchange their products, such a division is advantageous for all of them, and free people will naturally thus divide their labour among themselves. But a division of labour under which a mechanic all his life produces one-hundredth part of an article, or a stoker in a foundry works in a temperature of fifty degrees Réaumur or in noxious gases which choke him, is disadvantageous for men, because, while producing the most trifling articles, it ruins the most precious article, man's life. Consequently the division of labour which now exists can exist only under compulsion. Rodbertus says that the division of labour unites humanity communistically. That is true, but it is only the free division of labour, that is, such that people of their own free will divide the labour, that unites humanity. If people decide to build a road, and one man digs, another hauls rock, a third breaks rock, and so forth, such a division of labour unites men. But if a strategic railway, or an Eiffel tower, or all those foolish things with which the Paris Exposition is full, are built independently of the desire and frequently even contrary to the desire of the working people, — and one labourer is compelled to mine the ore, another to haul coal, a third to smelt this ore, a fourth to cut down trees and square them, none of them having the slightest idea of the purpose of the articles prepared by them, such a division of labour not only does not unite them, but, on the contrary, disunites them.

And so, if people will be free in the socialization of the implements of labour, they will accept only such a division of labour that the good of this division will be greater than the evil which it will cause the labourer.

And since every man naturally sees his good in the expansion and diversity of his activity, the now existing division of labour will naturally be impossible in a free society.

And as soon as the present division of labour shall be changed, there will also be diminished (to a very great extent) the very production of those articles which we now use, and which, it is assumed, all society will use in the socialistic state.

The assumption that with the socialization of the implements of production there will be the same abundance of articles as is produced under the compulsory division of labour, is like the assumption that with the liberation of the serfs there would remain the same domestic orchestras, gardens, rugs, lace, theatres, which used to be produced by the serfs. Thus the assumption that with the realization of the socialistic ideal all men will be free and, at the same time, will enjoy everything, or almost everything, which the well-to-do classes now enjoy, contains an obvious inner contradiction.

7

The same is here repeated that existed in the times of the serf law. As then the majority of the serf-owners and of the well-to-do classes in general, though recognizing the condition of the serfs as not entirely good, proposed for its improvement only such changes as would not impair the chief advantage of the landed proprietor, even so the men of the well-to-do classes, though recognizing the condition of the working people as not quite good, now propose for its improvement only such measures as do not impair the advantageous position of the men of the well-to-do classes. As then a well-disposed

proprietor talked of paternal power and, like Gógol, advised
the proprietors to be good and to care for their serfs, but
did not even admit the idea of the emancipation which
presented itself to him as harmful and dangerous, so also
now the majority of the well-to-do people of our time
advise the masters to care more for the good of their
workmen, but equally do not even admit the idea of such
a change of the economic structure of life as would make
the working people entirely free.

And just as then the advanced liberals, recognizing the
condition of the serfs to be unchangeable, demanded of
the state the limitation of the masters' power and sym-
pathized with the agitation of the serfs, so now the
liberals of our time, recognizing the existing order as
invariable, demand of the government the limitation of
the capitalists and manufacturers, and sympathize with
the unions, the strikes, and in general the agitation of the
working people. And just as then the most advanced
people demanded the emancipation of the serfs, but in the
project left them in dependence on the landowners, or on
corvées and taxes, so now the most advanced men demand
the liberation of the working people from the capitalists, the socialization of the implements of production,
but with all that leave the working people in dependence
on the present distribution and division of labour, which,
in their opinion, must remain invariable. The teaching of
economic science, which is followed without a comprehension of its details by all the well-to-do people who consider themselves enlightened and advanced, at a superficial
glance appears liberal, even radical, in that it contains
attacks upon the rich classes of society, but in its essence
this teaching is in the highest degree conservative, coarse,
and cruel. In one way or another the men of science,
and with them all the well-to-do classes, want by all
means to retain the now existing distribution and division
of labour, which make it possible to produce the large

quantity of articles used by them. The existing economic structure the men of science, and with them all the men of the well-to-do classes, call civilization, and they see in this civilization — the railways, telegraphs, telephones, photographs, Röntgen rays, clinics, exhibitions, and, above everything else, all the appliances of comfort — something so sacred that they do not even admit the idea of changes which may destroy all that or even a small part of these acquisitions. Everything may, according to the teaching of that science, be changed, except what they call civilization. Meanwhile it becomes more and more evident that this civilization can exist only by compelling the working men to work. But the men of science are so convinced that this civilization is the highest good that they boldly say the very opposite of what the jurists used once to say : instead of " *Fiat justitia, pereat mundus,*" they now say, " *Fiat cultura, pereat justitia.*" They not only say so, but even act so. Everything may be changed in practice and in theory, except civilization, — except all that which takes place in foundries and factories and, above all things, is sold in shops.

But I think that enlightened men, who profess the Christian law of brotherhood and love of their neighbours, ought to say the very opposite :

" It is all very nice to have electric illumination, telephones, expositions, and all the Arcadian Gardens with their concerts and shows, and all the cigars, and matchboxes, and suspenders, and motors ; but may they go to perdition, and not only they, but also the railways and all the calico and cloth factories in the world, if for their production it is necessary that ninety-nine hundredths of men should be in slavery and should perish by the thousand in factories which are necessary for the production of these articles. If, to light London or St. Petersburg with electricity, or to erect the structures of an exhibition, or to produce beautiful dyes, or to get beautiful stuffs woven quickly and in great quantity, it is necessary that the smallest number of lives should perish or be contracted or ruined (and statistics show us how many of them perish), then let London and St. Petersburg be lighted by gas or oil, let there be no exhibitions, let there be no dyes, no stuffs, so long as there shall be no slavery and the ruin of human lives resulting from it."

Truly enlightened people will always prefer to return to travelling on horseback and on bales and even to digging the ground with sticks and hands, rather than travel on railways, which regularly kill so many people each year, only because the owners of the roads find it more profitable to pay damages to the families of the killed than to build the roads in such a way that they will not kill so many people, as is the case in Chicago. The motto of truly enlightened men is not "*Fiat cultura, pereat justitia,*" but "*Fiat justitia, pereat cultura.*"

But civilization, the useful civilization, will not be destroyed. People will never have any occasion to return to digging the ground with sticks and lighting up their houses with chips. Not in vain has humanity with its servile structure made such great progress in the technical arts.

If men shall come to understand that it is not right for their pleasure to exploit the lives of their brothers, they will find out how to apply all the discoveries of mechanics in such a way as not to ruin the lives of their brothers, will know how to arrange life in such a way as to use all the perfected instruments for the subjugation of nature they can use, without retaining their brothers in slavery.

8

Let us imagine a man from an entirely foreign country who has no idea about our history and our laws, and let us show him our life in all its manifestations and ask

him what chief difference he observes in the manner of
life of the men of our world.

The chief difference in the manner of life of the men
to which he will point will be this, that some — a small
number of men — with clean white hands are well fed,
clothed, and housed, work very little and at something
easy, or not at all, and only amuse themselves, wasting
on these amusements millions of hard working days of
other men; while others, always dirty and poorly clad,
poorly housed, and poorly fed, with dirty, callus-covered
hands, work without cessation from morning until evening, at times through the nights, for those who do not
work, but amuse themselves all the time.

If it is hard between the slaves and the slave-owners
of the present time to draw as sharp a line as the one
which separated the former slaves from the slave-owners,
and if among the slaves of our time there are such as are
only temporarily slaves and later become slave-owners, or
such as at the same time are slaves and slave-owners,
this mingling of the two at their points of contact does
not weaken the truth of the proposition that all the men
of our time are divided into slaves and masters, just as
definitely as, in spite of the twilight, the twenty-four
hours are divided into day and night.

If a slave-owner of our time has not an Iván whom he
can send into a privy to clean out his excrements, he has
three roubles which are so much wanted by hundreds of
Iv* ns, that he can choose any one out of a hundred Iváns
and appear as a benefactor to him, because he has chosen
him out of the whole number and has permitted him to
climb into the cesspool.

The slaves of our time are not merely all those factory
and foundry hands who, to exist, are obliged to sell themselves into the full possession of the masters of factories
and foundries; such slaves are also nearly all those
agriculturists who, without rest, work in other people's

fields, taking other people's corn to other people's granaries, or who work their own fields, only to be able to pay interest on unextinguishable debts to the bankers; and just such slaves are all those numerous lackeys, cooks, chambermaids, janitors, coachmen, bath servants, waiters, and so forth, who all their lives perform duties which are most improper to a human being and contrary to their own natures.

Slavery exists in full force, but we do not recognize it, just as at the end of the eighteenth century people did not recognize the slavery of serfdom.

The men of that time believed that the state of the people who were obliged to work the land of their masters and to obey them, was a natural, inevitable condition of life, and did not call that state slavery.

The same is true among us: the men of our time regard the state of the working men as a natural, inevitable economic condition, and do not call this state slavery.

And, as at the end of the eighteenth century the men of Europe began slowly to see that the condition of the peasants who were in the full power of their masters, though formerly it had seemed to be a natural and inevitable form of economic life, was bad, unjust, and immoral, and demanded a change, so now the people of our time begin to understand that the state of hired men and of working people in general, which formerly used to be regarded as absolutely legal and normal, is not such as it ought to be, and demands a change.

The slavery of our time is now precisely in the same phase in which the serf law was in Europe at the end of the eighteenth century, and serfdom in Russia and slavery in America were in the second quarter of the nineteenth century.

The slavery of the working people of our time is just beginning to be recognized by the advanced men of our society, but the majority of people are still fully convinced that there is no slavery among us.

The men of our time are supported in this wrong idea of their condition by the circumstance that we have just abolished slavery in Russia and America. In reality the abolition of serfdom and slavery was only the abolition of an obsolete, useless form of slavery, and the substitution for it of a more substantial form of slavery which embraced a greater number of slaves than formerly. The abolition of serfage and slavery was very much like what the Crimean Tartars did with their captives, when they decided to cut open the soles of their feet and fill the rents with chopped bristles. After performing this operation upon them, they took off their fetters and chains. Though the abolition of serfage in Russia and slavery in America did away with the older form of servitude, it was, indeed, accomplished only when the bristles in the soles had created ulcers, and there was an absolute certainty that the captives would not run away even without·fetters and chains, and would go on working. (The Northerners in America boldly demanded the abolition of the old slavery, because a new, the financial slavery, had already obviously taken possession of the people, while the Southerners did not yet see the obvious signs of the new slavery and so did not care to abolish the old slavery.)

With us, in Russia, serfage was abolished only when all the land was already taken up. If land was given to the peasants, taxes were imposed upon them, to take the place of the land slavery. In Europe the taxes which kept the people in slavery were abolished only when the people were deprived of the land, made unaccustomed to agricultural labour, and by means of an infection from city needs placed in complete dependence on the capitalists. It was only then that the corn taxes were abolished in England. Now they are beginning to abolish

the taxes on the labourers in Germany and in other
countries, transferring them to the rich, only because the
majority of the people are in the power of the capitalists.
One means of enslavement is abolished only when another
has taken its place.   There are several such means.   If
not one, another, a third means, or several together, keep
the people in servitude, that is, put them in such a condition that a few men have full power over the labours and
lives of a greater number of men.   In this enslavement
of the greater part of the people by a smaller part does
the chief cause of the wretched condition of the people
consist.   For this reason the means for ameliorating the
condition of working people must consist, in the first
place, in recognizing the fact that slavery exists among
us, not in any transferred, metaphorical sense, but in the
simple and direct sense of the word, — a slavery which
keeps one part of men, the majority, in the power of the
other, the minority, and, in the second place, having recognized this condition, in finding the causes of the enslavement of one set of men by others, and, in the third place,
having found these causes, in destroying them.

9

In what, then, does the slavery of our time consist?
What forces enslave one class of men to another?   If we
ask all the working people, in Russia, in Europe, and in
America, both in the factories and in all kinds of hired
occupations in the cities and the villages, what it is that
has compelled them to choose the condition in which they
are, — they will all say that they were brought to it by
this: either that they had no land on which they could
and would wish to live and work (all Russian working
men and many European ones will say so); or that taxes,
both direct and indirect, are demanded of them, and they
are not able to pay them unless they work for others; or,

again, that they are kept in the factories by the temptations of more luxurious habits which they have acquired and which they cannot gratify except by selling their labour and their freedom.

The first two conditions, the lack of land and the taxes, drive the men, as it were, into conditions of servitude, and the third, the unsatisfied increased needs, entices them into these conditions and retains them there.

It is possible to imagine, according to Henry George's project, the emancipation of the land from the right of personal ownership, and thus the destruction of the first cause which drives people into slavery, — the lack of land. We can equally imagine the abolition of the taxes, their transference to the rich, as is actually done in some countries; but with the present economic structure it is impossible to imagine such a state that amidst the rich people there would not establish themselves more and more luxurious, frequently harmful habits of life, and that these habits would not by degrees, as inevitably and as irrepressibly as the water is taken up by the dry earth, pass over to the working classes that are contiguous to the rich, and would not become so necessary to the working classes that the working people would be prepared to sell their freedom, in order to gratify them.

Thus this third condition, in spite of its arbitrariness, that is, in spite of the apparent ability of a man not to submit to the temptations, and in spite of the fact that science does not at all recognize it as a cause of the wretched condition of the working men, forms the most permanent and most ineffaceable cause of slavery.

Living near the rich, the working people are always infected by new needs and gain the possibility of always gratifying these needs, but only in proportion as they give the tensest labour for this gratification. Thus the working people of England and America, though occasionally receiving ten times as much as is needed for their support, continue to be the same slaves that they were formerly.

These three causes, according to the explanation of the working people themselves, produce the slavery in which they are ; and the history of the enslavement of the working people and the reality of their condition confirm the justice of this explanation.

All the working people are brought to their present state and are retained in it by these three causes. These causes, acting upon people from various sides, are such that not one man can get away from their enslavement. An agriculturist, who has at his command no land whatsoever or only an insufficient amount of it, will always be compelled, if he wants to be able to gain his sustenance from the land, to give himself into permanent or temporary slavery to him who owns the land.

If he in one way or another acquires as much land as he needs to be able to support himself upon it with his labour, taxes will be demanded of him in a direct and an indirect way, such that, to be able to pay them, he will be obliged again to sell himself into slavery.

But if, to free himself from the slavery of the land, he shall stop working the land and, living on somebody else's land, shall begin to ply some trade, exchanging his productions for commodities needed by him, on the one hand the taxes, and on the other the competition of the capitalists who produce the same articles as he does, but with improved implements, will compel him to sell himself into permanent or temporary slavery to the capitalists. But if, working for a capitalist, he should be able to establish free relations with him, such as would not necessitate his giving up his freedom, the habits of the new needs inevitably acquired by him will compel him to do so.

Thus the working man will in one way or another always be in the slavery of those men who possess the

taxes, the land, and the commodities needed for the gratification of his needs.

10

The German socialists have called the aggregate of conditions which subject the labourers to the capitalists, the
iron law of labour wages, meaning by the word "iron"
that this law is something invariable. But in these conditions there is nothing invariable. These conditions are
only the consequences of human enactments concerning
taxes, concerning land, and, above all things, concerning
commodities for the gratification of needs, that is, concerning property. But enactments are established and abolished by men. Thus it is not any iron, sociological laws,
but enactments, that establish men's slavery. In the
given case the slavery of our time is very clearly and very
definitely produced, not by any elementary iron law, but
by human enactments concerning land, taxes, and property. There exists an enactment about this, that any
amount of land may be the subject of possession by private individuals, may pass from person to person by inheritance, bequest, or sale ; there exists another enactment
about this, that every man must without murmuring pay
the taxes that are demanded of him ; and there exists a
third enactment about this, that any quantity of articles,
no matter in what way acquired, forms the inalienable
property of those men who own them ; in consequence of
these enactments slavery exists.

These enactments are so habitual to us that they present themselves to us as just such natural conditions of
human life, of the necessity and justice of which there
can be no doubt whatever, as in antiquity appeared to
be the laws about serfage and slavery, and we do not
see anything irregular in them. But, as there came the
time when men, seeing the pernicious consequences of
serfage, began to doubt the justice and necessity of the

enactments which asserted it, so now, when the pernicious consequences of the present economic structure are obvious, one comes involuntarily to doubt the justice and necessity of the enactments concerning land, taxes, and property, which produce these results.

As formerly they used to ask whether it is right that men should belong to others and that these men should not have anything of their own, but should give all the productions of their labour to their owners, so we should ask ourselves at present whether it is right that people should not be able to use the land which is considered to be the property of other men; whether it is right that men should give to others in the shape of taxes those portions of their labour which are demanded of them; whether it is right that people should not be permitted to use articles which are considered to be the property of others.

Is it right that men should not use the land, when it is considered to be the property of men who do not work it?

It is said that this law established itself, because ownership of the land is an indispensable condition for the success of agriculture, because, if there did not exist private property, which passes down by inheritance, people would be driving one another away from the land seized, and no one would work or improve the plot of land on which he sits. Is this true? The answer to this question is given by history and by the present state of affairs. History says that the ownership of land has by no means originated in the desire to secure the possession of the land, but in the appropriation of the common land by the conquerors and its distribution among those who served the conquerors. Thus the establishment of the ownership of land did not have for its aim the encouragement of agriculture. Now the present state of affairs shows us the groundlessness of the assertion that the ownership of land secures to the agriculturists the conviction that they will not be deprived of the land which they work. In reality the very opposite takes place everywhere. The right of the ownership of the land, which the large owners have enjoyed more than any one else, has had this effect, that all, or nearly all, that is, the vast majority of the agriculturists, are now in the condition of men who work somebody else's land, from which they may be arbitrarily driven by those who do not work it. Thus the existing right of the ownership of the land is by no means a protection of the agriculturist's right to the use of that labour which he puts on the land, but, on the contrary, a means for taking from the agriculturists the land which they work and for transferring it to those who do not work it, and so it is in no way a means for the encouragement of agriculture, but it is, on the contrary, a means for deteriorating it.

Concerning the taxes it is asserted that men must pay them, because they are established by common, though tacit, consent, and are used for public needs, and for the good of all.

Is that true?

The answer to this question is given by history and by the present state of affairs. History says that taxes have never been established by common consent, but, on the contrary, always in consequence of this, that certain men, having by conquest or other means gained the power over other men, have imposed tribute upon them, not for public needs, but for themselves. The same thing is done even at the present time. The taxes are collected by those who have the power to do so. If now a part of this tribute, called taxes and imposts, is used for public works, these public works are for the most part harmful, rather than useful, to the majority of men.

Thus, for example, one-third of the people's income is taken away from the people in Russia, but for the chief need, for the people's education, only one-fiftieth of the whole income is used, and this, too, for such education as rather stultifies and harms the people than does them any good. The remaining forty-nine fiftieths are used for things that are useless or injurious for the people, such as the arming of soldiers, strategic roads, fortresses, prisons, the maintenance of the clergy and the courts, salaries for military and civil officials, that is, for the support of those men who aid in the seizure of the money from the people.

The same thing takes place, not only in Persia, Turkey, and India, but also in all the Christian, constitutional governments and democratic republics: the money is taken from the masses of the people, — not as much as is wanted, but as much as can be taken from them, — and quite independently of the consent of the taxed (everybody knows how the parliaments are made up and how little they represent the will of the people), and is not used for the common good, but for what the ruling classes deem best: for the war in Cuba and the Philippines, for the seizure and retention of the wealth of the Transvaal, and so forth. Thus the explanation given that people must pay taxes, because they are established by common consent and are used for the common good, is as untrue as the other assertion that the ownership of land was established for the purpose of encouraging agriculture.

Is it right that people should not use articles which they want for the gratification of their needs, if these articles form the property of other men ?

It is asserted that the right of the ownership of articles acquired was established for the purpose of securing the working man against the seizure of the productions of his labour by any one else.

Is that true ?

We need only look at what is going on in our world, where such ownership is protected with especial care, to convince ourselves to what extent the actuality of our life does not confirm this explanation.

In consequence of the right of ownership of acquired articles, there is in our society taking place precisely what this right intends to avoid, namely, all the articles which have been produced by the working people are, in proportion as they are produced, constantly taken away from those who produce them.

Thus the assertion that the right of ownership secures to the working people the possibility of enjoying the productions of their labour is obviously still more unjust than the justification of the ownership of land, and is based on the same sophism. At first the working people are unjustly and violently deprived of the productions of their labour, and then the laws are enacted, according to which these productions, which were unjustly and violently seized from the working people, are recognized as an inalienable possession of the usurpers.

The ownership of a factory, for example, which is acquired by a series of deceits and rascalities committed against the working people, is considered to be a product of labour and is called a sacred ownership; but the lives of those working people, who perish in working in this factory, and their labour are not considered to be their property, but are, as it were, considered to be the property of the manufacturer, if he, exploiting the want of the working people, has bound them in a manner which is regarded as legal.

Hundreds of thousands of puds of corn collected by means of usury and a series of exactions from the peasants, are considered to be the property of the merchant; but the corn raised by the peasants on the land is considered to be the property of another man, if this man has received the land as an inheritance from his grandfather and great-grandfather, who took it away from the people. It is said that the law protects equally the prop-

erty of the owner of a factory, the capitalist, the landowner, and the factory hand and agricultural labourer.
The equality of the capitalist and the labourer is the
same as the equality of two fighters, when the hands of
one are bound, while a gun is put into the hands of the
other, and equal conditions are strictly observed for both
in the fight. Thus all the explanations of the justice and
indispensableness of those three enactments which produce slavery are as incorrect as were the explanations of
the justice and indispensableness of the former serfage.
All three enactments are nothing but the establishment
of that new form of slavery which has taken the place of
the older slavery. As formerly the establishment of enactments as to this, that men might buy and sell people and
own them, and might compel them to work, *was* slavery ;
so now the establishment of the enactments as to this,
that men cannot use the land which is considered to
be the property of another, must pay the taxes demanded
of them, and cannot use the articles which are considered
to be somebody else's property, *is* the slavery of our
time.

11

The slavery of our time is due to three enactments, —
concerning land, concerning taxes, and concerning property. And so all the attempts of men who wish to improve the condition of the working people are of necessity,
though unconsciously, directed to these three enactments.

Some abolish the taxes which weigh upon the working
people, by transferring them to the rich ; others propose
to do away with the right of the ownership of land, and
there have been made attempts at realizing this, in New
Zealand and in one of the States of America (an approach
to it is also the limitation of the right to dispose of the
land in Ireland) ; others again, the socialists, assuming
the socialization of the implements of labour, propose the

taxing of incomes, and inheritances, and the limitation of the rights of the capitalists, — the speculators. It would seem that those very enactments which produce slavery are being abolished, and that we may on this path expect the abolition of slavery itself. But we need only look more closely at the conditions under which the abolition of these enactments is accomplished and proposed, in order to become convinced that all, not only practical, but even theoretical projects for the improvement of the working men's condition, are only the substitution for one set of enactments, which produce slavery, of other enactments, which establish the new forms of slavery. Thus, for example, those who do away with the taxes and imposts levied on the poor, by first abolishing the enactments about the direct imposts, and later transferring these imposts from the poor to the rich, must necessarily retain and do retain the enactments about the ownership of land, implements of production, and other commodities, to which the whole burden of taxation is transferred. But the retention of the enactments about land and property, by freeing the working people from the taxes, turns them over into slavery to the landowners and capitalists. And those who, like Henry George and his followers, do away with the enactments about ownership, propose new enactments about a compulsory land rent. But the compulsory land rent will inevitably establish a new form of slavery, because a man, obliged to pay the rent, or single tax, will be compelled at every failure of crops and at every misfortune to borrow money from him who has it, and will again fall into slavery. And those who, like the socialists, in their project do away with the enactments about the ownership of land and the implements of production, retain the enactments about the taxes and, besides, are obliged to introduce enactments about compelling men to work, that is, again establish slavery in its primitive form.

Thus, in one way or another, all the practical and theoretical abolitions of one set of enactments which produce slavery of one kind have so far always been followed by new enactments which produce slavery of another, a new kind.

What is taking place is very much like what a jailer does, when he changes the chains from the neck to the arms, or from the arms to the legs, or when he takes them off, but fastens the bolts and bars.

All the ameliorations for the working people so far proposed have consisted in nothing else.

The enactments about the masters' right to force the slaves to do work have given way to enactments about the ownership of the whole land by the masters. The enactments about the ownership of the whole land by the masters has given way to enactments about taxes, the establishment of which is in the power of the masters. The enactments about taxes has given way to the strengthening of the right to own articles of use and implements of labour. The enactments about the right to own land, articles of use, and implements of production are now to be abandoned for the enactments about compulsory labour.

The primitive form of slavery was the direct compulsion to work. Having made the whole circle of the different latent forms, — ownership of land, taxes, ownership of articles of use and implements of production, — slavery now returns to its primitive form, though in a changed aspect, — to the direct compulsion to work.

Therefore it is obvious that the abolition of one of the enactments which produces the slavery of our day — either of the taxes, or of the ownership of land, or of the ownership of articles of use and implements of production — will not destroy slavery, but will only abolish one of its forms, which will immediately give way to another, as was the case with the abolition of personal slavery — serfage — for taxes. The abolition of even all three enactments together will not destroy slavery, but will only

provoke a new, still unknown form of slavery, which even
now is slowly manifesting itself in the enactment which
reduces the freedom of the working people, in the limitation of the hours of work, age, condition of health, in the
demands for an obligatory school attendance, in the reservation of a certain percentage to provide for the old and
the maimed, in all the measures of factory inspections, in
the rules of coöperative societies, and so forth.   All these
are nothing but advance enactments which are preparing
a new, still unexperienced form of slavery.

Thus it becomes obvious that the essence of slavery
does not lie in those three enactments on which it is now
based, and not even in any kind of enactments, but in
the fact that there are enactments, that there are men
who are able to establish enactments which are advantageous for them, and that, so long as men shall have this
power, there will be slavery.

Formerly it was advantageous for people to have direct
slaves, and so they established the enactment about the
personal slavery.   Then it became advantageous to have
land as property, to collect taxes, to retain acquired property, and corresponding enactments were made.   Now it
is advantageous for people to retain the existing distribution and division of labour, and enactments are introduced, such as would compel people to work with the
existing distribution and division of labour.   And so the
fundamental cause of slavery is enactments, — the fact
that there are men who are able to introduce them.

12

What, then, are enactments, and what gives men the
power to establish them ?

There exists a whole science, which is more ancient
and more deceptive and hazy than political economy, and
the servants of which have in the course of the centuries

written millions of books (which for the most part contradict one another), in order to answer these questions. But since the aim of this science, as of political economy, does not consist in explaining what is and what ought to be, but in proving that that which is ought to be as it is, we are able in this science to find very many discussions about right, about object and subject, about the idea of the state, and so forth, — about subjects which are obscure, not only to the students, but also to the teachers of this science; but there is no lucid answer to the question as to what an enactment is.

According to the science, an enactment is an expression of the will of the whole people; but since there are always more men who violate the enactments, or who wish to violate them but do not do so from fear of the punishments imposed for the non-fulfilment of the enactments, than those who wish to fulfil them, it is evident that the enactments can in no sense be understood as the expression of the will of the whole people.

There exist, for example, enactments about not destroying telegraph-posts, about showing respect to certain persons, about the obligation for every man to do military service or be a juror, or about not carrying certain objects beyond a certain line, or about not using the land which is considered to be the property of another, or about not making any monetary tokens, or about not using articles which are considered to be the property of some one else.

All these enactments and many others are extremely varied and may have the most varied motives, but not one of them expresses the will of the whole people. There is but one common feature to all these enactments, namely, this, that if a man will not fulfil them, those who established them will send armed men, and the armed men will beat, deprive of liberty, and even kill him who does not fulfil them.

If a man does not wish to give in the form of taxes

the portion of his labour demanded of him, armed men will come and take from him what is demanded, and, if he offers resistance, will beat him, deprive him of liberty, or even kill him. The same thing will be done with a man who will use the land which is regarded as somebody else's property. The same thing will happen to a man who will make use of articles considered to be the property of some one else, which he needs for the gratification of his needs or for work: armed men will come, will take from him what he has taken, and, if he offers resistance, will beat him, deprive him of liberty, or even kill him. The same thing will happen with a man who will not show respect to what it is enacted that respect shall be shown to, and with him who will not comply with the demand to become a soldier, or who will make monetary tokens. For every non-fulfilment of established enactments those who do not fulfil them will be punished: they will be subjected to personal injury, to the loss of liberty, and even to being killed at the hands of those men who have established these enactments.

Very many constitutions have been invented, beginning with the English and the American and ending with the Japanese and the Turkish, by which people are to believe that all the enactments established in their state are established by their own will. But all men know that not only in despotic, but also in assumedly free countries, in England, America, France, and elsewhere, the enactments are established, not by the will of all men, but only by the will of those who have the power, and so they always are such as are advantageous for those who have the power, — be they many, a few, or even one man. And the enactments are always and everywhere executed by the same means by which men have always and everywhere been compelled to do the will of others, that is, by means of personal injury, loss of liberty, murder, as, indeed, it cannot be otherwise.

It cannot be otherwise, because the enactments are the demand for the fulfilment of certain rules ; but people cannot be compelled to fulfil certain rules, that is, what is wanted of them, except by subjecting them to personal injuries, loss of liberty, and capital punishment. If there are enactments, there has to be the power which can make men fulfil them. There is but one power which can compel men to fulfil these rules, that is, the will of other men, and that is — violence, not simple violence, which is used by men against one another in moments of passion, but organized violence, which is consciously employed by men who have power, in order to compel other men to fulfil rules which are always established by them, that is, what they want.

Therefore the essence of the enactments is not at all the subject or object of right, not the idea of the state, nor the aggregate will of the people, and similar indefinite and confused conditions, but is this, that there are men who, in control of organized violence, are able to compel people to do their will.

Thus a definite, comprehensible, and indisputable definition of enactments will be like this :

Enactments are rules established by men who are in control of organized violence, for the non-fulfilment of which those who do not fulfil them are subjected to personal injuries, the loss of liberty, and even capital punishment.

In this definition is contained the answer to the question as to what gives men the power to establish enactments. What gives them the power to establish enactments is the same which secures the execution of the enactments, — organized violence.

13

The cause of the wretched condition of the working people lies in slavery. The cause of slavery lies in the enactments.   But the enactments are based on organized violence.

Consequently the amelioration of men's condition is possible only with the destruction of organized violence.

But organized violence is the government, and is it possible to live without any government ?   Without government there will be chaos and anarchy, all the progress of civilization will perish, and men will return to their pristine savagery.   "Just touch the existing order of things," we are generally told, not only by those for whom this order of things is advantageous, but also by those for whom it is obviously disadvantageous, but who are so used to it that they cannot imagine life without any governmental violence, "and the destruction of government will produce the greatest calamities, riots, pillage, murder, and in the end all the bad will rule, and the good will be enslaved by them."   But, to say nothing of the fact that all that, namely, the riots, pillage, and murder, at the end of which will come the kingdom of the evil and the enslavement of the good, has existed so far and exists now, the supposition that the violation of the existing order will produce troubles and disorder does not prove that this order is good.

"Just put your hand on the existing order, and the greatest calamities will result."

Just touch one brick out of a thousand bricks placed in a slender column of a number of yards in height, and all the bricks will fall down and break.   But the fact that the displacement of one brick or any push will destroy such a column and all the bricks does not at all prove that it is sensible to retain the bricks in an unnatural and unsuitable position.   On the contrary, it proves that the bricks should not be kept in such a column, but should be placed in such a way as to remain firm and admit of being used without destroying the whole structure.   The same is true with the present political structure. The political structure is very artificial and very frail, and the fact that the slightest push destroys it does not prove that it is indispensable, but, on the contrary, shows that, if it ever was necessary, it is now entirely unnecessary, and therefore harmful and dangerous.

It is harmful and dangerous, because with this structure all the evil which exists in society is not only not diminished and mended, but also strengthened and confirmed. It is strengthened and confirmed, because it is either justified and clothed in attractive forms, or concealed.

All the well-being of the people as presented to us in the so-called well-managed states, which are governed through force, is nothing but seeming,— a fiction. Everything which can impair the external decency, all the hungry, sick, monstrously corrupt are hidden away in places where they cannot be seen, but their not being seen does not prove that they do not exist; on the contrary, there are the more of them, the more they are concealed and the more cruel to them those are who produce them. It is true, every violation, much more every cessation of the governmental activity, that is, of organized violence, will impair such external decency of life, but this violation will not produce a disorganization of life, but will only reveal the one that has been concealed, and will make it possible to mend it.

Men have thought and believed until recently, until the end of the present century, that they cannot live without any government. But life goes on, and the conditions of life and people's views change. And, in spite of the efforts of the governments, which are directed toward retaining people in this childish condition, in which it seems easier for an injured man when he has somebody to complain to, people, especially workmen, not only in Europe, but also in Russia, more and more come out of their childhood and begin to understand the true conditions of their life.

" You tell us that without you we shall be vanquished by the neighbouring nations, by the Japanese, the Chinese," now say the people from the masses, " but we read the newspapers and know that no one is threatening us with war and that only you, the rulers, for some reasons which are unknown to us, enrage one another, and then, under the pretext of defending your nations, ruin us with taxes for the support of fleets, armaments, strategic railways, which are needed only for your ambition and vanity, and start wars with one another, as you have just now done with the peace-loving Chinese. You say that you protect the landed property for our good, but your protection has resulted in this, that all the land is passing over into the hands of non-working companies, bankers, rich men, while we, the vast majority of the people, are landless and in the power of those who do not work. You with your laws about landed property do not protect landed property, but take it away from those who work. You say that you ensure to each man the productions of his labour, whereas you do the very opposite : all people who produce costly articles are, thanks to your supposed protection, put in such a condition that they never can get the value of their labour, and that their whole life is in dependence on the non-working people and in their power."

Thus the people of the end of our century are beginning to understand matters and to talk. This awakening from the lethargy in which they were held by the governments is taking place in a rapidly increasing progression. Within the last five or six years the public opinion of the masses, not only in the cities, but also in the villages, not only in Europe, but also in Russia, has strikingly changed.

We are told that without the governments we shall

not have those cultural, educational, social establishments
which all need.

But why assume this ? Why think that non-govern-
mental people will not be able to arrange their lives for
themselves as well as they are arranged, not for themselves, but for others, by the governmental people ?

We see, on the contrary, that in the most varied circumstances of life, people in our time arrange their lives
for themselves incomparably better than they are arranged
for them by the men who govern them. People without
any interference from the government, and frequently in
spite of the government's interference, establish all kinds
of public enterprises, — labour unions, coöperative societies, railway companies, artéls, syndicates. If levies are
needed for public works, why need we think that free
people will not be able voluntarily and without violence
to collect the necessary means and to establish everything which is established with the taxes, if only these
institutions are useful for them ? Why must we think
that there cannot be any courts without violence ? The
judgment of men in whom the litigants have confidence
has always existed and always will exist, and does not
need violence. We have been so corrupted by a long
slavery that we cannot imagine a government without
violence. But that is not true. The Russian Communes,
when settling in distant regions, where our government
does not interfere with their life, arrange their own
levies, their management, their court, their police, and
always prosper, so long as governmental violence does not
interfere with their management. Even so there is no
reason for the assumption that people are unable by common agreement to distribute the use of the land among
themselves.

I have known of people, — the Ural Cossacks, — who
have lived without recognizing the ownership of land,
and the prosperity and order in the whole society have

been such as do not exist in the society in which the ownership of land is protected by violence. I know of Communes at the present time, which exist without recognizing the right of separate individuals to own land. The whole Russian people within my memory did not recognize the ownership of land. The protection given to the ownership of land by means of governmental violence not only fails to remove the struggle for the ownership of land, but, on the contrary, for the most part strengthens it and brings it about.

If landed property were not protected, and so made to rise in value, people would not crowd in one place, but would settle on free land, of which there is still so much on the globe. But now there is taking place an incessant struggle for the ownership of land, and this struggle is waged with those instruments which the government offers with its enactments about the ownership of land. In this struggle the victory is always obtained, not by those who work the land, but by those who take part in the governmental violence.

The same is true in relation to articles produced by labour. Articles which are actually produced by man's labour and which are necessary for life are always protected by custom, public opinion, and the sense of justice and reciprocity, and are in no need of protection by means of violence.

Tens of thousands of desyatínas of forest land belonging to one owner, while thousands of people near by have no fuel, must be protected by violence. The same protection is needed for plants and factories where several generations of workmen have been plundered. Still more must such protection be given to hundreds of thousands of puds of corn belonging to one owner who has been waiting for a famine, in order to sell it at a trebled price to the starving population. But not a man, even the most corrupt, unless he be a rich man or a government official, will take from an agriculturist who supports himself with his labour the crops which he has raised, or the cow which he has raised and which supplies the milk for his children, or the plough, the scythe, the spade, which he has made and used. Even if there should be found a man who would none the less take from another the articles produced by him and needed by him, that man would provoke such indignation against himself in all men who live under the same conditions that he would hardly find such an act advantageous for himself. But if that man is so immoral that he will none the less do so, he will do the same under the most stringent protection of property by means of violence. We are generally told: "Try to destroy the right to own land and articles of labour, and not one man, since he is not assured that they will not take from him what he has produced, will care to work." The very opposite ought to be said: the protection offered by means of violence to the right to hold illegal property, such as is offered at the present time, has, if not completely destroyed, at least considerably weakened in men the natural consciousness of justice in relation to the use of articles, that is, in relation to the natural and inborn right of property, without which humanity could not live, and which has always existed in society.

And so there is no foundation for the supposition that without organized violence men will not be able to arrange their lives.

Of course, it can be said that horses and oxen cannot live without the exercise of violence by rational beings — men — over them; but why cannot men live without violence being exerted over them, not by some higher beings, but by men themselves? Why must men submit to the violence of those men who at a given time are in power? What proves that these men are wiser than those men against whom the violence is exerted?

Their allowing themselves to exert violence against people proves that they are not only not wiser, but even less wise than those who submit to them.   The Chinese examinations for the posts of mandarins, as we know, do not secure the wisest and best men for the power.   Just as little is this secured by heredity, or by all the systems of rank promotions or of elections in the European states.   On the contrary, those who get into power are generally less conscientious and less moral men than others.

We are asked: "How can men live without governments, that is, without violence?"   We ought, on the contrary, to ask: "How can men, rational beings, live, recognizing violence, and not rational agreement, as the inner force of their lives?"

One or the other is true: either men are rational beings, or they are not.   If they are irrational beings, they are all irrational beings, and there is no reason why some should enjoy the right to exert violence, while others do not enjoy this right, and then the violence exerted by the government has no justification.   But if men are rational beings, their relations must be based on reason, and not on the violence of men who have accidentally seized the power, and therefore the violence of the government has again no justification.

14

The slavery of men is due to enactments, and enactments are established by the governments, and so the liberation of men from slavery is possible only through the abolition of the governments.

But how are the governments to be destroyed?

All the attempts at destroying the governments by means of violence have so far everywhere and always led to this, that in the place of the governments overthrown there have been established new, frequently more cruel governments than those which they superseded.

To say nothing of the attempts already made at destroying the governments by means of violence, the now imminent destruction of the violence of the capitalists, that is, the socialization of the implements of production and the new economic structure, must, according to the theory of the socialists, be produced through a new organized form of violence, and this must be retained. Thus the attempts at destroying violence with violence, which so far have not in the past led, and obviously will not in the future lead, men to their emancipation from violence, and consequently from slavery.

Nor can it be otherwise.

Violence is exerted by one class of men against another (outside of outbursts of vengeance and anger) for no other purpose than to compel people against their wish to do the will of other men. But the necessity of doing against one's wish the will of other men is slavery. And so, as long as there shall be any violence, intended for the purpose of compelling people to do the will of other men, there will be slavery.

All the attempts at abolishing slavery by means of violence are like the extinguishing of fire with fire, or the damming of water with water, or the filling of one ditch with dirt taken out from another ditch.

And so the means for the emancipation from slavery, if it exists at all, must consist, not in the establishment of a new form of violence, but in the destruction of what produces the possibility of governmental violence. But the possibility of governmental violence, as of any violence exerted by a small number of men against a large number, has always had this effect, that the small number is armed, while the majority is unarmed, or that the small number is better armed than the majority.

Thus have things been done in the case of every conquest: thus have nations been vanquished by the Greeks, the Romans, the knights, a Cortes, and thus are people now vanquished in Africa and Asia, and thus do all the governments in time of peace hold their subjects in subjection.

As in antiquity, even so now, one set of men rules another, only because some are armed, while the others are not.

In ancient times the warriors with their leaders fell upon defenceless inhabitants and vanquished and plundered them, and all of them, according to the part they took, their bravery, their cruelty, divided up the booty, and it was obvious to every warrior that the violence practised by him was advantageous for him. But now the armed men, who are for the most part taken from among the working men, go against defenceless people, strikers, rioters, or inhabitants of foreign countries, and vanquish and plunder them (that is, compel them to give up their labour), not for themselves, but for those who do not even take part in the subjugation.

The only difference between conquerors and governments is this, that the conquerors with their warriors attacked defenceless inhabitants and, in case of their insubmission, carried out their threats of tortures and murders, while the governments, in case of insubmission, do not themselves practise tortures and murder on the defenceless inhabitants, but cause this to be done by deceived and specially bestialized men, who are taken from among the very masses which they oppress. Thus the former violence was practised through personal efforts, — through the bravery, cruelty, and agility of the conquerors themselves, while the present violence is practised through deception.

Therefore, if, to be freed from the violence of armed men, it was formerly necessary to arm oneself and to offer armed violence against armed violence, now, when

the masses are not vanquished through direct violence,
but through deception, all that is needed for the destruction of the violence is the arraignment of the deception
which makes it possible for a small number of men to
exert violence against a larger number.

The deception through which this is accomplished consists in this, that the small number of ruling men, who
have received their power from their predecessors, as
established by the conquerors, say to the majority:
" There are many of you, you are stupid and uneducated,
and you are not able to govern yourselves, nor to arrange
your own public affairs, and so we take this care upon
ourselves: we will defend you against foreign enemies,
will establish and maintain domestic order among yourselves, will judge among you, will establish and guard the
public institutions for you, — the schools, roads of com-
munication, posts, — and will in general care for your
weal; for all that you shall fulfil the few demands which
we will make upon you, among them also this, that you
turn over into our control a small portion of your incomes
and that you yourselves enter the army, which is necessary
for your safety and for your government."

And the men of the majority agree to this, not because
they have weighed the advantages or the disadvantages
of these conditions (they never have a chance to do this),
but because they find themselves under these conditions
from the time of their birth. If doubts arise in these
men as to the necessity of all that, every man, thinking
of himself alone, is afraid to suffer in case of a refusal to
fulfil these conditions, and hopes to make use of these
conditions for his own advantage, and all men agree to
this, assuming that the transference of a small portion
of their possessions to the government, and their agreement to do military service, cannot injure their lives very
much. But the moment the money and the soldiers are
in the power of the governments, these, instead of fulfilling

the obligation taken upon themselves of defending their subjects against foreign enemies and establishing their prosperity, do everything they can to irritate the neighbouring nations and provoke wars, and not only fail to contribute to the domestic prosperity of their nations, but also ruin and corrupt them.

In *The Thousand and One Nights* there is a story about a traveller who, having been brought to an uninhabited island, finds an old man, with dried up legs, sitting on the ground, on the bank of a brook. The old man asks the traveller to take him on his shoulders and carry him across the brook. This the traveller agrees to do. But the moment the old man seats himself on his shoulders, he winds his legs tightly around the traveller's neck and does not let go of him. Having taken possession of the traveller, the old man orders him about as he pleases, plucks fruits from the trees, which he eats without giving anything to the one who carries him, and in every other way scorns the traveller.

The same is done to the nations which have given money and soldiers to the governments. With the money the governments buy guns and hire, or prepare through education, irresponsible, bestialized military chiefs. But the chiefs, by means of artful methods of stultification, worked out through the ages, which are called discipline, prepare a disciplined army out of the men who are taken into the army. This discipline consists in this, that the men who undergo the instruction and have followed it for a certain time are completely deprived of everything which is precious to a man, — of the chief human property — rational freedom, — and become submissive, machine-like implements of murder in the hands of their organized hieratic authorities.

There is good reason why the kings, emperors, and presidents esteem discipline so highly, fear so much the violation of it, and consider their most important business to be inspections, manœuvres, parades, ceremonial marches, and similar foolish things.   They know that all that maintains discipline, and on discipline alone is based, not only their power, but also their existence.   The disciplined army is the means with which they can through other people's hands commit the greatest malefactions, and the ability to do so subjugates the peoples to them.

In this disciplined army lies the essence of the deception, in consequence of which the governments of modern times dominate the nations.   When this unwilled implement of violence and murder is in the power of the government, the whole nation is in its power, and the government no longer lets go of it, and not only ruins it, but also scorns it, impressing it, by means of a pseudo religious and patriotic education, with loyalty and even veneration for the government, that is, for those very men who keep the nation in slavery and torment it.

Consequently the only means for the destruction of the governments is not violence, but the arraignment of this deception ; it is necessary for the people to understand that, in the first place, amidst the Christian world there is no need to defend the nations against one another, that all the hostilities between the nations are provoked only by the governments themselves, and the armies are needed only for a small number of ruling men, but are not needed by the nations, to which they are even extremely harmful, in that they serve as an implement for the enslavement of men ; in the second place, it is necessary for men to understand that that discipline which is so highly esteemed by the governments is the greatest crime a man can commit, — an obvious proof of the criminality of the aims of the governments.   Discipline is the destruction of reason and of liberty in man, and cannot have any other purpose than merely the preparation for the commission of such malefactions as not one man will commit in his normal condition.   For a defensive national war it is unnecessary, as has lately been proved by the Boer War. All that it is needed for, and for this chiefly, is, as determined by William II., to commit the greatest crimes,— fratricide and patricide.

In precisely the same manner acted the terrible old man who was sitting on the traveller's shoulders: he laughed at him, knowing that so long as he was sitting on his shoulders, the traveller was in his power.

It is this terrible deception, by means of which a small number of evil men, in the form of the governments, dominate the nations, and not only ruin them, but even commit the most injurious of all deeds, corrupting them for generations from their very childhood, which must be laid open, in order that the destruction of the governments and of the slavery resulting from them may be made possible.

The German writer, Eugen Schmitt, who edited in Budapest the newspaper *Ohne Staat,* printed in it an article, true and bold not only in expression, but also in thought, in which he said that the governments, in justifying their existence by saying that they provide for their subjects a certain amount of security, do not differ in this from a Calabrese bandit who imposes a tax upon all those who want to travel safely over the highways. Schmitt was tried for this, but the jury found him innocent.

We are so hypnotized by the governments that such a comparison seems to be an exaggeration, a paradox, a jest, whereas it is no paradox and no jest, — in fact, the comparison is incorrect, because the activity of all the governments is much more inhuman and, above all things, much more harmful than the activity of the Calabrese bandit. The bandit for the most part robs the rich, while the governments for the most part rob the poor, while they protect the rich, who help them in their crimes. The bandit, in doing what he does, risks his life, while the governments risk nothing and build all their deeds on lying and deceit. The bandit does not forcibly take anybody into his band, while the governments draft their soldiers generally by force. With the bandit all those who pay the tribute receive equal security, while in the state a man receives the more security, and even reward, the more he takes part in the organized deception. Most secure is the emperor, king, or president (he is always surrounded by a guard of protection), and he spends the greatest amount of money, which is collected from the subjects who are burdened with taxes; then, in proportion with their greater or lesser participation in the governmental crimes, come the commanders-in-chief, ministers, chiefs of police, governors, and so on, down to the policemen, who are least protected and who receive the least salary. But he who does not at all take part in the governmental crimes, refusing to serve, to pay taxes, to have anything to do with the court, is subjected to violence, as one is subjected to it by the robbers. The bandit does not intentionally corrupt people, while the governments for the attainment of their purposes corrupt whole generations of children and adults by false religious and patriotic doctrines. Above all things, not one, the most cruel bandit, no Sténka Rázin, no Cartouche, can in cruelty, heartlessness, and refinement of tortures compare, not only with the sovereigns famous for their cruelty, John the Terrible, Louis XI., the Elizabeths, and so forth, but even with the present constitutional and liberal governments, with their solitary cells, disciplinary battalions, pacifications of riots, and slaughters in wars.

We must bear ourselves toward the governments as toward the churches, — either with awe, or with disgust. So long as a man has not come to understand what the government is, just as he does not understand what the church is, he cannot help but look with awe upon these institutions. So long as he is guided by them, he must, for the sake of his egoism, imagine that what he is guided by is something original, great, and sacred; but the moment he has come to understand that what he is guided by is nothing original or sacred, and that it is only the deception of evil men who have used it, under the guise of guidance, for their personal purposes, he cannot help but immediately experience disgust for these men, which is the greater, the more important the side of life is in which he was guided.

It is this that men must feel in relation to the governments, if they have come to understand their meaning.

People must understand that their participation in the criminal activity of the governments, whether by giving up part of their labours, in the form of money, or by a direct participation in military service, is not an indifferent act, such as people generally take it to be, but, besides the harm done to him and to his brothers by this act, also a participation in the crimes which are incessantly committed by all the governments, and a preparation for new crimes, for which the governments are always ready, when they maintain a disciplined army.

The time for a relation of awe to the governments, in spite of the whole hypnotization which the governments employ for the maintenance of their position, is passing more and more. And it is time for men to understand that the governments are not only useless, but also injurious and in the highest degree immoral institutions, in which an honest and self-respecting man cannot and must not take part, and the advantages of which he cannot and must not enjoy.

As soon as men shall come to understand this, they will naturally stop taking part in those acts, that is, giving the governments soldiers and money. As soon as the majority of men shall stop doing that, the deception which enslaves men will destroy itself.

Only in this way can men be freed from slavery.

15

" But these are all general reflections; whether they be just or unjust, they are inapplicable to life," I hear the objections of people who are accustomed to their position and who do not consider it possible or desirable to change it.

" Tell me, what is actually to be done ? How is society to be built up ? " generally say the men of the well-to-do classes.

The men of the well-to-do classes are so much used to their rôle of slave-owners that, when the amelioration of the working men's condition is under discussion, they, feeling themselves in the position of the landed proprietors, immediately begin to discuss all kinds of projects for the management of their slaves, but it does not even occur to them that they have no right whatever to dispose of other men, and that, if they really mean to do good to men, the one thing they can and must do is to stop doing the evil which they are doing now. The evil which they are doing is very definite and clear. The evil which they are doing is not only this, that they are using the compulsory labour of slaves and do not wish to renounce this exploitation, but also this, that they are themselves taking part in the establishment and maintenance of this compulsory labour. It is this that they must stop doing.

But the working people are so corrupted by the compulsory slavery that to the majority of them it appears that, if their condition is bad, the fault is with their masters, who pay them too little and own the implements of production; it does not even occur to them that their bad condition is due to themselves alone, and that, if they actually desire the amelioration of their condition and of that of their brothers, and not each his own advantage, the chief thing they should do is to stop doing evil. But the evil which they do consists in this, that, wishing to improve their material condition by those very means by which they are brought into slavery, the working men, to be able to gratify those habits which they have acquired, sacrifice their human dignity and liberty and accept degrading, immoral positions, or work at producing useless and injurious articles; but chiefly in this, that they support the governments, take part in them with their taxes and direct service, and thus enslave themselves.

For men's condition to improve, both the men of the well-do-men classes and the labourers must understand that it is impossible to improve men's condition by preserving their own advantage, that the ministration to men is not without sacrifices, and that therefore, if people really want to improve the condition of their brothers, and not their own, they must be prepared, not only for the change of the whole structure of life to which they are used, and to the loss of those advantages which they have been enjoying, but also for a tense struggle, not with the governments, but with themselves and their families, — they must be prepared for persecutions for not fulfilling the demands of the government.

Consequently the answer to the question as to what should be done is very simple, and not only definite, but also in the highest degree and always and for every man practicable and easy of execution, though it is not such as is expected by those who, like the men of the well-to-do classes, are fully convinced that they are called, not to mend themselves (they are good as it is), but to teach others and provide for them, or who, like the working people, are convinced that it is not they who are to blame for their bad condition, but only the capitalists, and that this condition can be changed only by taking away from the capitalists what they enjoy, and by making it possible for all men to enjoy those pleasures of life which the capitalists alone enjoy at present. This answer is quite definite, practicable, and easy of execution, because it invites to activity the only person over whom each has a real, legal, and undoubted power, — oneself, — and consists in this, that, if a man — be he slave or slaveholder — really wishes to improve, not his condition alone, but the condition of all men, he must himself stop doing the evil which produces his slavery and the slavery of his brothers. And, in order not to do the evil which produces his wretchedness and the wretchedness of his brothers, he must, in the first place, neither voluntarily nor by compulsion take part in governmental activities, and so not take upon himself the calling of a soldier, or field-marshal, or minister, or collector of taxes, or deputy, or elder, or juror, or governor, or member of parliament, or in general any office which is connected with violence. So much for one thing. In the second place, such a man must not voluntarily pay any direct or indirect taxes to the government, and must equally not make use of any money which is collected as taxes, either in the form of a salary or in the form of pensions, or rewards, and so forth, nor make use of any governmental institutions which are supported from the taxes that are forcibly collected from the people. So much for the second thing. In the third place, a man who wishes to contribute, not to his own welfare alone, but to the amelioration of men's condition, must not turn to the governmental violence, either for the protection of the ownership of land or other objects, or for his own security or the security of his friends, but must own the land, as well as all other products of other people's or his own labour, only to the extent to which no demands of other people are brought forward in regard to these articles.

"But such an activity is impossible: to refuse every participation in governmental affairs means to renounce life," I shall be told. "A man who will refuse to do military service will be imprisoned; a man who will not pay his taxes will be subjected to penalties, and the taxes will be levied on his property; a man who will refuse to enter the service of the government, without having any other means of existence, will perish with his family from hunger; the same thing will happen to a man who will refuse the governmental protection of his property and person; and it is quite impossible not to use articles that are burdened with taxes and not to use the governmental institutions, since often it is articles of prime necessity that are taxed, and it is similarly impossible to get along without the governmental institutions, such as the postoffice, roads, and so forth.

It is quite true that it is hard for a man of our time to renounce every participation in governmental violence; but the fact that not every man is able so to arrange his life as not to be in some measure a participant in governmental violence does not by any means show that there is no possibility of freeing oneself more and more from it. Not every man will have the strength to refuse to do military service (but there are and will be such), but it is in the power of every man not of his own free will to enter military, police, judicial, or fiscal service, and it is possible for him to prefer a less paying private activity to the more profitable governmental service.

Not every man will have the strength to renounce his ownership of land (though there are some men who do so), but it is possible for every man, if he understands the criminality of such property, to contract its limits. Not every man will be able to renounce the possession of capital (there are men who do) and the use of articles protected by violence, but it is possible for every man, diminishing his needs, to make less and less use of articles which provoke the envy of other people. Not every person is able to give up a governmental salary (there are also those who prefer starving to a dishonest governmental position), but it is possible for every man to prefer a small salary to a larger one, if only the duties to be performed are less connected with violence. Not every person can renounce the use of the governmental schools (there are also those who do), but it is possible for every man to prefer a private school to one by the government. And so it is possible for every man less and less to use articles that are burdened with duties, and the institutions of the government.

Between the existing order of things, which is based on coarse violence, and the ideal of life, which consists in a communion of men that is based on rational consent as established by custom, there is an endless number of steps over which humanity has walked incessantly, and the approach to this ideal is accomplished only in proportion as men are freed from participation in violence, from using it, and from the habit of it. We do not know and we cannot foresee, much less prescribe, as the so-called learned men do, in what way is to come about this gradual weakening of the governments and the emancipation of men from them; we do not even know what forms human life will assume as it is gradually emancipated from governmental violence; but we know indubitably that the life of men, who, having come to understand the criminality and harmfulness of the government's activity, will try not to make use of it and not to take part in it, will be a very different one and more in agreement with legitimate life and with our conscience than is the present one, when the men themselves, taking part in the violence of the governments and making use of it, pretend to be struggling against it and try to destroy the old violence by a new form of it.

Above all else, the present structure of life is bad; all men agree to that. The cause of the bad condition and of the slavery lies in the violence of the governments. To destroy the governmental violence there exists but one means: people's refusal to take part in violence. Consequently, whether it is hard for people to refrain from par-

ticipation in governmental violence, or not, and whether
the beneficent results of such a refusal will appear soon,
or not, — such questions are superfluous, because there is
but this one means, and no other, for freeing men from
slavery.

But to what extent and when the substitution of
rational and free consent, sanctioned by custom, for violence will be realized in every society and in the whole
world, that will depend on the strength of the lucidity of
people's consciences and on the number of separate individuals who have attained to such a state of conscience.
Every one of us is an individual, and every one of us may
be a participant in the common movement of humanity
by a more or less clear consciousness or beneficent purpose, and he may be an opponent to this movement.
Every man has the choice, either to go against God's will,
by building on the sand the frail house of his perishable
deceptive life, or to join the eternal, undying movement
of the true life according to God's will.

But, maybe, I am mistaken, and it is necessary to make
quite different deductions from the history of humanity,
and humanity does not march from violence to emancipation, and, maybe, it is possible to prove that violence is
a necessary factor of progress, that the state with its violence is an indispensable form of life, and that men will
be worse off, if governments, property, and the protection
of security are done away with.

Let us admit that that is so and that all the preceding
arguments are wrong; but, besides the general considerations about the life of humanity, every man has also the
question of his personal life, and, in spite of all reflections
concerning the general laws of life, a man cannot do what
he recognizes not only as injurious, but also as bad.

" It is very likely that the reflection that the state is a
necessary form of the development of personality and that
governmental violence is indispensable for the good of

society may be deduced from history, and that these reflections are right," every sincere and honest man of our time will answer. " But murder is evil, — that I know more certainly than all reflections ; but, by demanding of me military service or money for the hire and arming of soldiers, or for the purchase of cannon and the armament of ironclads, you wish to make me a participant in murder, and I not only do not want that, but am not even able to do that. Even so I will not and cannot use the money which you have collected from the hungry under threat of murder, and I will not make use of the land and of the capital which you protect, because I know that you protect only by means of murder.

" I was able to do all that so long as I did not understand the whole criminality of these matters; but the moment I came to see it I was unable to stop seeing it, and I am no longer able to take part in these things.

" I know that we are all so bound up by violence that it is hard fully to vanquish it, but I will none the less do what I can in order not to take part in it, I will not be its accomplice, and I will try not to use what is acquired and protected by murder.

" I have one life, and why should I in this my brief life act contrary to the voice of my conscience and become a participant in your abominable deeds? I will not do so.

" What will come of all that? I do not know; but I think that nothing bad can happen from my acting as my conscience commands me to act."

Thus must every honest and sincere man of our time retort to all the arguments about the indispensableness of governments and violence, and to every demand or invitation to take part in it.

Thus the highest judge, from whom there is no appeal, — the voice of conscience, — confirms for every man what he is led to by general considerations.

EPILOGUE

"WHY, that is again the old sermon : on the one hand, about the destruction of the existing order without the substitution of another for it, and on the other, about non-acting," many will say, upon reading the above. "The governmental activity is not good, and likewise the activity of the landowner or enterprising man is not good ; similarly bad is the activity of the socialists and anarchistic revolutionaries, that is, every practical activity, and what is good is some kind of a moral, spiritual, indefinite activity, which reduces itself to absolute chaos and non-acting." Thus, I know, many serious and sincere men will think and say.

What to men appears most confounding, in the absence of violence, is the unprotected condition of property, and so the chance offered for every man to take with impunity from another what he needs or wants. People who are accustomed to the protection of property and the person by means of violence imagine that without this protection there will be a constant disorder, a constant struggle of all against all.

I will not repeat what I have said in another place about this, that the protection of property by means of violence does not diminish, but increases disorder. But even if we admit that with the absence of protection there may arise disorders, what are people to do who have come to understand the cause of those calamities from which they suffer ?

If we understand that we are sick from intoxication, we

72

cannot continue drinking and hope to improve our condition by drinking moderately, or continue drinking and take medicine which is prescribed to us by short-sighted physicians.

The same is true of the disease of society. If we have come to understand that one set of people does violence to other people, it is impossible to improve the condition of society by continuing to maintain the governmental violence which exists, or by introducing a new, the revolutionary, socialistic violence. That was possible so long as the fundamental cause of men's calamities was not clearly discernible. But as soon as it becomes indubitably clear that men suffer from violence which is exerted by one class of men over another, it is no longer possible to improve the condition of men by continuing the old and introducing the new kind of violence. Just as for an alcoholic patient there is but one means for his liberation, — abstinence from liquor, the cause of the disease, — so there is but one means for the liberation of men from the bad structure of society, and that is, abstinence from violence, — the cause of calamities, — from personal violence, from the propaganda of violence, from every justification of violence.

Not only is this the only means for freeing men from their wretchedness, but its application is also necessary, because it coincides with the moral law of every separate individual of our time. If a man of our time has come to understand that every protection of property and personality by means of violence is attained only by the threat of killing and by killing itself, he can no longer calmly use what is acquired through murder or the threat of killing, much less can he take part in murder or the threat of killing. Thus, what is demanded for the liberation of men from their calamities is also necessary for the gratification of the moral feeling of every individual. And so there can no longer be any doubt for every separate individual that both for the common good and for the fulfilment of the law of his life he must not take part in violence, must not justify it, must not make use of it.

WHAT IS RELIGION

And in What Does Its Essence Consist?

1902

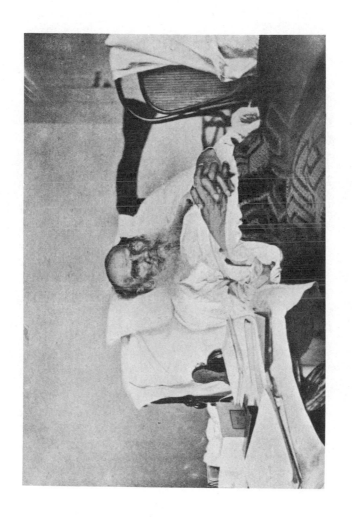

Portrait of Tolstóy during His Illness,1902

Photogravure from a Photograph

WHAT IS RELIGION?

———

In all human societies there always, at certain periods of their life, arrives a time when religion at first deflects from its fundamental meaning, then, deflecting more and more, loses its fundamental meaning and finally congeals in once for all established forms, and then its action upon the lives of men grows constantly less and less.

During such periods the cultured minority, not believing in the existing religious teaching, only pretends to be believing in it, as it finds this necessary in order to retain the popular masses in the established structure of life; but the popular masses, though through inertia abiding in the once established forms of religion, in their lives are no longer guided by the demands of religion, but only by the popular customs and state laws.

Thus it has been many times in various human societies, but there has never before happened what now is going on in our Christian society. It never happened before that the rich, ruling, and most cultured minority, which has the greatest influence upon the masses, should not believe in the existing religion, but should be convinced that in our time no religion is needed, and should impress upon the people who doubt in the truth of the professed religion, not some more rational and clearer religious doctrine than the existing one, but the fact that religion has in general outlived its time and is now not only a useless, but also a harmful organ of the life of societies, something like the blind gut in man's organism. Religion is studied by these men, not as something known to us through our inner experience, but as an external phenomenon, like a disease, to which some people are subject and which can be investigated only from its external symptoms.

Religion, according to the opinion of some of these men, originated in the spiritualization of all the phenomena of Nature (animism); according to others, in the conception of the possibility of establishing a relation with the deceased ancestors; according to others again, in the fear of the forces of Nature. And since, the learned men of our time continue to reason, science has proved that trees and stones cannot be vitalized, and the deceased ancestors no longer feel what the living are doing, and the phenomena of Nature are explained according to natural causes, there has also been destroyed the necessity of religion and of all those restrictions which, in consequence of religious beliefs, people have imposed upon themselves. According to the opinion of the learned there was a period of ignorance, — of religion. This period was long ago outlived by humanity, and only rare, atavistic signs of it are left. Then followed the metaphysical period, and that too has been outlived. But now we, the enlightened men, are living in the scientific period, in the period of positive science, which takes the place of religion and leads humanity to a high stage of development, such as it could never have reached by submitting to superstitious religious doctrines.

In the beginning of 1901 the famous French scholar, Berthelot, delivered a speech (*Revue de Paris*, Janvier, 1901) in which he informed his hearers that the time of religion was past, and that religion must now give way to science. I quote this speech, because it is the first which fell into my hands and because it was delivered in the capital of the cultured world by a well-recognized scholar ; but the same idea is constantly expressed everywhere, beginning with philosophic treatises and ending with newspaper feuilletons. M. Berthelot says in this speech that formerly there were two principles which moved humanity : force and religion. Now these movers have become superfluous, because science has taken their place. By science M. Berthelot, like all men who believe in science, apparently understands such science as embraces the whole field of human knowledge, harmoniously connected and distributed according to the degree of its importance, and is in possession of such methods that all the data acquired by it form an unquestionable truth. But since such a science does not exist in reality, while what is called science forms a conglomerate of accidental, disconnected bits of knowledge, which frequently are useless and not only do not represent an undoubted truth, but are filled through and through with the grossest delusions, which to-day are put forth as truths and to-morrow are overthrown, it is evident that there does not exist the very subject which, according to M. Berthelot's opinion, is to take the place of religion. Consequently the assertion of M. Berthelot and of the people who agree with him, that science will take the place of religion, is quite arbitrary, and is based on an ungrounded faith in the infallible science, which completely resembles the faith in the infallible church. Meanwhile, the people who call themselves and are called learned are absolutely convinced that such a science already exists, and that it must and can take the place of religion, and has even now overthrown it.

" Religion has outlived its usefulness, and it is a sign of ignorance to believe in anything but science. Science will arrange everything needed, and we should be guided in life by nothing but science," think and say both the

learned and the people of the crowd, who, though far
removed from science, believe in the learned and with
them assert that religion is an obsolete superstition, and
that in life we should be guided by science, that is, in
reality by nothing, since science, from its very aim, — to
study everything in existence, — is unable to give any
guidance in the life of man.

2

The learned men of our time have decided that religion is not necessary, that science will take its place, or
has already taken its place, and yet, as before so also now,
no human society, no rational man, has lived, or can live,
without religion (I say "rational man," because an irrational man, like an animal, can live without religion).
A rational man cannot live without religion, because it is
only religion that gives a rational man the necessary guidance as to what he should do, and what he should do first
and what next. A rational man cannot live without
religion, even because reason is the property of his nature.
Every animal is guided in its acts — except those toward
which it is driven by the direct necessity of gratifying
its wishes — by considerations about the nearest consequences of its acts. Having reflected upon these consequences by means of that power of cognition which it
possesses, the animal harmonizes its acts with these consequences and always without wavering acts in the self-
same manner, in correspondence with these considerations.
Thus, for example, a bee flies after the honey and brings it
into the hive, because in the winter it will need the food
collected for itself and for its young ones, and outside of
these considerations it does not know and cannot know
anything; even so acts a bird in weaving its nest and in
flying from north to south and back again. Even so acts
every animal in performing an act which does not result

from the direct, present necessity, but which is conditioned by considerations of expected consequences. But
it is not thus with man.

The difference between a man and an animal is this, that
the animal's faculties of cognition are limited by what
we call instinct, while man's fundamental faculty of
cognition is reason. The bee, in collecting the food, can
have no doubts as to whether it is good or bad to collect
it. But a man, in collecting the harvest or fruit, cannot
help but think as to whether he is destroying for the
future time the production of the corn or the fruit and
whether by his harvesting he is depriving his neighbours
of food. And he cannot help but think as to what will
become of his children whom he feeds, and many more
things. The most important questions of the conduct of
life cannot by a rational man be determined definitely
for the very abundance of consequences, which he cannot
help but see. Every rational man feels, if he does not
know, that in the most important questions of life he
must not be guided by his personal impulses, or by considerations as to the immediate consequences of his activity, because he sees too many various and frequently
contradictory consequences, that is, such as with equal
probability may be beneficent or injurious, both for him
and for other people. There is a legend as to how an
angel, who descended upon earth into the house of a God-
fearing family, killed the child in the cradle, and, when he
was asked why he did that, replied that the child would
have grown to be a great malefactor and would have caused
the family a misfortune. Not only the question as to
what human life is useful, useless, or harmful, but also
all the most important questions of life cannot be solved
by a rational man from a consideration of their nearest
relations and consequences. A rational man cannot be
satisfied with those considerations which guide the acts
of an animal. A man may consider himself as an animal

amidst animals who live in the present day, and he can consider himself as a member of his family and as a member of society, a nation, which lives by centuries, and he can and by all means must (since his reason irrepressibly draws him to it) consider himself as a part of the whole endless universe, which lives an infinite time. And thus a rational man has always been obliged in relation to the infinitely small phenomena of life which may influence his acts to make, and always has made, what in mathematics is called integration, that is, to establish, besides his relation to the nearest phenomena of life, his relation to the whole universe, infinite in time and space, by comprehending life as one whole. Such an establishment of man's relation to the whole, of which he feels himself to be a part and from which he deduces guidance in his actions, is what has been called religion. Therefore religion has always been and always must be a necessity and an irremovable condition of the life of a rational man and of rational humanity.

3

Thus has religion always been understood by men who are not deprived of the faculty of the higher, that is, the religious, consciousness, which distinguishes man from the animal. The oldest and most customary definition of religion, from which also comes the word " religion " itself (*religare*, to bind), consists in this, that religion is man's union with God. " *Les obligations de l'homme envers Dieu, voilà la religion*," says Vauvenargue. A similar meaning is ascribed to religion by Schleiermacher and Feuerbach, who recognize as the basis of religion man's consciousness of his dependence on God. " *La religion est une affaire entre chaque homme et Dieu* " (Beile). " *La religion est le résultat des besoins de l'âme et des effets de l'intelligence* " (B. Constant). " Religion is a certain method for man to realize his relation to the superhuman and mysterious forces on which he considers himself to be dependent" (Goblet d'Alviella). " Religion is the definition of human life by means of the connection between the human soul and that mysterious spirit whose government of the world and of himself is recognized by man and with whom he feels himself to be bound up" (A. Reville).

Thus the essence of religion has always been understood by men who are not deprived of the highest human quality to be the establishment by man of his relation to the infinite being or beings whose power he feels over himself. And this relation, no matter how it may differ for the different peoples and at different times, has always determined for men their destiny in the universe, from which naturally has resulted the guidance for their activity. A Jew understood his relation to the Infinite to be this, that he was a member of a nation chosen by God from among all the nations and so had to observe before God the covenant entered into with this nation by God. A Greek understood his relation to be this, that he, being related to the representatives of infinitude — the gods, must do what was pleasing to them. A Brahmin understood his relation to the infinite Brahma to be this, that he was a manifestation of this Brahma and must through a renunciation of life strive for a union with this supreme being. A Buddhist understands his relation to the Infinite to be this, that he, passing from one form of life to another, inevitably suffers, and that the sufferings are due to passions and desires, and that, therefore, he must strive for an annihilation of all passions and desires and for a transition into Nirvana. Every religion is the establishment of man's relation to the infinite existence to which he feels himself related and from which he deduces his rules of action. And so, if a religion does not establish man's relation to the Infinite, as, for example, is the case in idolatry and sorcery, it is not a religion, but only a degeneration of it. If a religion, though establishing man's relation to God, establishes it by means of assertions which are contrary to reason and contemporary knowledge, so that a man cannot believe in these assertions, this is again not religion, but only its semblance. If a religion does not bind up man's life with the infinite existence, this is again not a religion. Nor is that a religion which demands faith in propositions from which no definite direction for man's activity results.

True religion is man's relation to the infinite life about him, as established by him, a relation which is concordant with reason and human knowledge and binds his life up with this Infinity and governs his acts.

4

The learned men of our time, though nowhere and at no time men have lived without religion, say, like that physician against his will in Molière's comedy, who insisted that the liver was in the left side, " *Nous avons changé tout cela*," and that we can and must live without religion. But religion, as it has been, so it remains the chief mover, the heart of the life of human societies, and without it, as without the heart, there can be no rational life. There has always been a great variety of religions, because the expression of man's relation to the Infinite, to God or the gods, differs in time and according to the degree of the development of the various nations, but never has any society of men, from the time that men have been rational beings, been able to live without religion, and never has any lived without it.

It is true, there have been periods in the life of nations when the existing religion was so corrupted and so far removed from life that it no longer governed it. But this interruption in the action of religion upon the lives of men, which arrives for every religion at a certain time,

has been only temporary. Religion, like everything living, has the property of being born, developing, aging,
dying, again being born and always reborn in a more
perfect form than before. After a period of the highest
development of religion there always arrives a period of
its weakening and stagnation, after which generally follows a period of regeneration and of the establishment of a
more rational and lucid religious teaching than the former.
Such periods of development, stagnation, and regeneration
have existed in all religions : in the profound Brahmin
religion, in which, as soon as it began to age and petrify
in once established gross forms that deflected it from its
fundamental meaning, there appeared, on the one hand,
the regeneration of Brahminism, and, on the other, the
advanced teaching of Buddhism, which greatly promoted
humanity's conception of its relation to the Infinite. A
similar decadence happened in the Greek and the Roman
religions, and in a similar way, after the decadence
had reached the highest point, there appeared Christianity. The same happened with the ecclesiastic Christianity, which in Byzantium degenerated into idolatry
and polytheism, when, to counterbalance the corrupt
Christianity, there appeared, on the one hand, Paulician-
ism, and, on the other, in opposition to the doctrine about
the Trinity and the Holy Virgin, strict Mohammedanism,
with its fundamental dogma of the one God. The same
thing happened with Popish Christianity in the Middle
Ages, when it called the Reformation into life. Thus
the periods when religions weaken, as regards their effect
upon the majority of men, are an indispensable condition
of the life and the development of all religious teachings.
This is due to the fact that every religious teaching in
its true sense, no matter how gross it may be, always
establishes man's relation to the Infinite, which is the
same for all men. Every religion recognizes man as
equally insignificant in the presence of the Infinite, and

so every religion always includes the conception of the equality of all men before what it considers to be God, be it the lightning, the wind, a tree, an animal, a hero, a deceased or living king, as was the case in Rome. Thus the recognition of the equality of men is an inevitable, fundamental property of every religion. But since in reality there has nowhere and at no time existed any equality among men, the moment there appeared such a new religious teaching, which always includes the recognition of the equality of all men, those men for whom the inequality was advantageous immediately set out to conceal this fundamental property of the religious teaching, by distorting the religious teaching itself. This has been done wherever a new religious teaching has made its appearance. And this has generally happened unconsciously, merely in consequence of the fact that the men for whom the inequality was advantageous, the ruling men, the rich, in order to feel themselves right in the face of the newly accepted teaching, without changing their own condition, tried in every way to ascribe to the religious teaching a meaning with which the inequality would be possible. But the distorted religion, which made it possible for those who ruled others to consider themselves right, was naturally transmitted to the masses whom it impressed with the idea that their submission to the ruling people was a demand of the religion professed by them.

5

Every human activity is evoked by three impelling causes, by feeling, by reason, and by suggestion, by that property which the physicians call hypnosis. At times a man acts only under the influence of feeling, striving to obtain what he wishes; at other times he acts under the influence of reason alone, which points out to him what he ought to do; at other times again, and this most

frequently, man acts because he has suggested to himself
and has had suggested to him by others a certain action
and he unconsciously submits to this suggestion. Under
normal conditions of life all three factors take part in
man's activity. Feeling draws man toward a certain
action, reason verifies the conformity of this action with
what surrounds it, with the past and the assumed future,
and suggestion compels man, without feeling or thinking,
to commit acts that are evoked by feeling and approved
by reason. If there were no feeling, a man would not
undertake anything; if there were no reason, a man
would at once abandon himself to many contradictory
feelings, which would be harmful both to him and to
others; if there were no property of submitting to one's
own suggestion and to the suggestion of others, a man
would be obliged without cessation to experience the feeling which has impelled him to a certain course of actions,
and constantly to strain his reason for the verification of
the correctness of his feeling. For this reason all three
factors are necessary for the simplest human activity.
When a man walks from one place to another, this is due
to the fact that his feeling has impelled him to go from
one place to another, his reason has approved of this
intention and has prescribed the means of execution (in
the given case the walking along a certain path), and the
muscles of the body obey, and the man marches in
the direction prescribed. During the time that he is
walking his feeling and reason are set free for another
activity, which could not be, if there did not exist the
possibility of submitting to suggestion. This is what
takes place in all human activities as well as in the chief
activity, the religious. Feeling evokes the necessity of
establishing man's relation to God; reason defines this
relation; suggestion impels man to act in accordance
with this relation. This is true only so long as religion
is not subject to distortion. The moment this distortion

begins, suggestion becomes stronger and stronger, and the activity of feeling and reason grows weaker. The means of suggestion are always and everywhere the same. These means consist in making use of that condition of man when he is most receptive for suggestion (childhood, important events in life, — death, birth, marriage), and in affecting him through productions of art, — architecture, sculpture, painting, music, dramatic performances, — and in this condition of susceptibility, which resembles the one obtained over separate persons in a state of half-sleep, in suggesting to him what is desired by the suggesters.

This phenomenon may be observed in the case of all the ancient creeds: in the exalted teaching of the Brahmins, which degenerated into a coarse worship of numberless representations in various temples, with the accompaniment of singing and incense; in the ancient Jewish religion, which was preached by the prophets and which changed into the worship of God in a magnificent temple, with solemn songs and processions; in exalted Buddhism, which, with its monasteries and representations of Buddha, and its endless solemn rites, has changed into the mysterious Lamaism; in Taoism, with its sorcery and incantations.

In all religious teachings, when they are on the point of becoming corrupt, their guardians of the religious teachings have always employed every effort in bringing men into a condition of a weakened activity of reason, and in suggesting to them what they themselves want. What it has been necessary to suggest in all religions has been the same three propositions which serve as the foundation of all those distortions to which the aging religions have been subjected: in the first place, that there is a special kind of men who alone can be the mediators between man and God or the gods; in the second place, that miracles have taken place and that these prove and

confirm the authenticity of what the mediators between
man and God say ; and, in the third place, that there are
certain words, which are repeated by word of mouth or
are written down in books, and which express the invariable will of God or the gods, and so are sacred and infallible.   The moment these propositions are accepted under
the influence of the hypnosis, everything else which the
mediators between God and men may say is accepted as
the holy truth, and the chief aim of the distortion of religion is attained, that is, not only the concealment of the
law of the equality of men, but also the establishment
and confirmation of the highest inequality, the division
into castes, the separation into men and "goys," into
orthodox and infidel, into saints and sinners.   This very
thing has also happened in Christianity : there was recognized the absolute inequality of men among themselves,
who as regards the comprehensions of the teaching were
divided into clergy and laity, and as regards the social
position were divided into men who had the power and
those who must submit to them, — and this inequality
according to Paul's doctrine is recognized as established
by God himself.

6

The inequality of men, not only of the clergy and the
laity, but also of the rich and the poor, masters and
slaves, was established in the ecclesiastic Christian religion in just as definite and glaring a form as in the other
religions.   And yet, to judge from the data which we
have concerning the primitive condition of Christianity,
according to the teaching expressed in the gospels, it
seems, all the chief methods of distortion practised in the
other religions were foreseen, and a warning against them
is clearly expressed.   In relation to the class of the
priests it says directly that no man can be the teacher of
another (do not call yourselves fathers and teachers);

in relation to ascribing a sacred significance to books it says that what is important is the spirit, and not the letter, and that men must not believe in the traditions of men, and that the whole law and the prophets, that is, all the books which were regarded as sacred writings, reduce themselves only to this, that we should do to our neighbours as we wish that our neighbours should do to us. If nothing is said against miracles, and miracles are described in the Gospel as having been practised by Jesus, it is none the less to be seen from the whole spirit of the teaching that the truth of Jesus' teaching is not based on the miracles, but on the teaching itself. (" He who wants to know whether my teaching be true, let him do as I do.") Above all things, the equality of all men was proclaimed by Christianity, not as a deduction from men's relation to the Infinite, but as a fundamental teaching of the brotherhood of all men, since all men are recognized to be sons of God. For this reason, it would seem, it was impossible so to distort Christianity as to destroy the recognition of the equality of men among themselves.

But the human mind is inventive, and an entirely new means (" truc," as the French say) was thought out, maybe unconsciously or semiconsciously, for making the Gospel warning and the obvious proclamation of the equality of all men ineffective. This " truc" consists in ascribing an infallibility, not only to a certain letter, but also to a certain assembly of men, called the church, which has the right to transmit this infallibility to men chosen by them.

A short addition was invented for the Gospels, which was, that Christ, in ascending to heaven, transmitted to certain men the exclusive right, not only to teach men the divine truth (according to the letter of the Gospel verse He also transmitted the right to be immune against serpents, scorpions, and fire, though this right is generally not made use of), but also to make men saved or unsaved, and, above all else, to transmit this right to other men.   As soon as the concept of the church was firmly established, all the Gospel tenets which interfered with the distortion became inactive, because the church was superior to reason and to the Scriptures, which were considered to be sacred.   Reason was recognized to be the source of error, and the Gospel was not interpreted as was demanded by common sense, but as was wanted by those who composed the church.

Thus the previous three methods of the distortion of the religions, priesthood, miracles, and the infallibility of the Scriptures, were recognized and in full force in Christianity, as elsewhere.   The legitimacy of the existence of mediators between God and men was recognized, because the necessity and the legitimacy of the mediators was recognized by the church ; the reality of miracles was recognized, because the infallible church bore witness to it ; the Bible was recognized as being holy, because the church so recognized it.

Christianity was corrupted like all the other religions, but with this difference that, for the very reason that Christianity with peculiar clearness proclaimed the fundamental proposition about the equality of all men, as sons of God, it was necessary to make a particular effort to distort this teaching, in order to conceal its fundamental proposition.   This was done with the aid of the concept of the church, and it was done to an extent to which it was not carried in any other religious teaching.   Indeed, never has any religion preached propositions so discordant with reason and with the contemporary knowledge of men and so immoral, as those which are preached by the ecclesiastic Christianity.   To say nothing of all the insipidities of the Old Testament, such as the creation of light before the sun, the creation of the world six thousand years ago, the putting of all the animals in an ark, and of all kinds of immoral abominations, such as the slaying of children and of whole settlements by the command of God; to say nothing of that stupid sacrament, about which Voltaire said that there exist all kinds of stupid religious doctrines, but that there never existed one, in which the chief religious act consists in eating one's own God, — what can be more senseless than that the Mother of God is both a mother and a virgin, that the heaven opened and a voice was heard from it, that Christ flew to heaven and there sits somewhere on the right of the Father, or that God is one and three, not three gods, like Brahma, Vishnu, and Shiva, but one and at the same time three? And what can be more immoral than that terrible teaching according to which God, being evil and revengeful, punishes all men for Adam's sin, and for their salvation sends His son down upon earth, knowing in advance that the men will kill Him and will be cursed for that; and this, that the salvation of men from sin consists in being christened or in believing that all that actually happened thus and that the Son of God was killed by men for the salvation of men, and that those who do not believe this will be punished by Him with eternal torments? Thus, to say nothing of what is considered by some to be an addition to the chief dogmas of this religion, such as all the beliefs in all kinds of relics, the images of all kinds of Holy Virgins, the supplications directed to all kinds of saints, according to their specialties; to say nothing of the Protestants' doctrine about predetermination, — the universally recognized foundations of this religion, as established by the Nicene symbol, are so stupid and immoral, and are carried to such a contradiction to sound human feeling and reason, that people cannot believe in them. Men may with their lips repeat certain words, but they cannot believe in what makes no sense. It is possible to say with our lips, "I believe in this, that the world was created six thousand years ago," or to say, "I believe that Christ flew to heaven and

is sitting on the right of the Father, or that God is one
and at the same time three ; " but no one is able to believe
in all that, because these words make no sense. And so
the men of our world, who profess the distorted Christianity, in reality do not believe in anything. In this does
the peculiarity of our time consist.

7

The men of our time do not believe in anything, and
yet, according to that false definition of faith which they
take from the Epistle to the Hebrews, which is incorrectly ascribed to Paul, they imagine that they have a
faith. Faith, according to this definition, is the realization (ὑπόστασις) of things hoped for and the assurance
(ἔλεγχος) of things unseen. But, to say nothing of
this, that faith cannot be the realization of things hoped
for, since faith is a spiritual condition, while the realization of things hoped for is an external event, faith is as
little the assurance of things unseen, since this assurance,
as it says in the further elucidation, is based on trust in
the testimony of truth, whereas trust and faith are two
different concepts. Faith is not hope and not trust, but a
special spiritual condition. Faith is man's recognition of
his position in the world, such as obliges him to commit
certain acts. A man acts in accordance with his faith,
not because, as it says in the catechism, he believes in the
things unseen, but only because, having determined his
position in the world, he naturally acts in correspondence
with this position. Thus an agriculturist works the land
and a navigator navigates the seas, not because, as it says
in the catechism, either of them believes in the unseen,
or because he hopes to get a reward for his activity (this
hope exists, but it does not guide him), but because he
considers his activity to be his calling. Even so a religious man acts in a certain manner, not because he believes

in the invisible or expects a reward for his activity, but because, having come to understand his position in the world, he naturally acts in conformity with this position. If a man has determined his position in society by being a labourer, or an artisan, or an official, or a merchant, he considers it necessary to work, and he works as a labourer, an artisan, an official, or a merchant. Even so a man in general, having in one way or another defined his position in the world, inevitably and naturally acts in conformity with this definition (sometimes not even with this definition, but with a dim consciousness). Thus, for example, a man, having determined his position in the world by assuming that he is a member of God's chosen nation, who, to enjoy God's protection, must fulfil the demands of this God, will live in such a way as to fulfil these demands; while another man, having determined his position by assuming that he has been passing through various forms of existence and that his better or worse future will depend on his acts, will in his life be guided by this determination; and a third man, who has determined his position by assuming that he is a fortuitous combination of atoms, in which the fire has been temporarily kindled, and that this fire will be destroyed for ever, will act differently from the first two.

The conduct of these men will be quite different, because they have variously defined their positions, that is, because they believe differently. Faith is the same as religion, with this difference, that by the word " religion " we mean the phenomenon perceived externally, while by " faith " we mean the same phenomenon as experienced inwardly by man. Faith is man's cognized relation to the infinite world, from which results the direction of his activity. Consequently true faith is never irrational, or discordant with the existing knowledge, and its property cannot consist in supernaturalness and senselessness, as some think and as was expressed by a father of the church, " *Credo quia absurdum.*" On the contrary, the assertions of true faith, though they cannot be proved, not only never contain anything contrary to reason and discordant with men's knowledge, but always elucidate what in life without the propositions of faith presents itself as irrational and contradictory.

Thus, for example, an ancient Jew, who believed that there was a supreme, eternal, almighty being who created the world, the earth, the animals, and man, and so forth, and would protect his nation, if the nation would fulfil his law, did not believe in something irrational and discordant with his knowledge, but, on the contrary, this belief explained to him many otherwise inexplicable phenomena of life.

Similarly a Hindoo, who believes that our souls were in animals and that, according to our good or bad life, they will pass into higher or lower animals, by means of this faith explains to himself many phenomena which without it are inexplicable to him. The same is true of a man who regards life as an evil, and the aim of his life to be peace, which is attainable by the destruction of desires. He does not believe in something irrational, but, on the contrary, in what makes his world-conception more rational than it was without this faith. The same holds good in the case of a real Christian, who believes that God is the spiritual father of all men and that the highest good of man is attained when he recognizes his sonhood to God and the brotherhood of all men among themselves. All these beliefs, though incapable of proof, are not irrational in themselves, but, on the contrary, lend a more rational meaning to the phenomena of life, which, without these beliefs, seem irrational and contradictory. Besides, all these beliefs, in determining man's position in the world, inevitably demand certain acts to correspond to this position. Therefore, if a religious teaching asserts senseless propositions which explain nothing and only add to the confusion of the comprehension of life, this is not faith, but a distortion of it, such as has lost the chief properties of the true faith and not only does not demand anything of men, but even means to them a ministration. One of the chief distinctions between a true faith and its distortion is this, that with the distortion of faith a man demands of God that, in return for his sacrifices and prayers, God shall fulfil his wishes, shall serve man, but with the true faith a man feels that God demands of him, man, the fulfilment of His will, — that He demands that man shall serve God.

Not only do the men of our time not have this faith, but they do not even know what it is, and by faith they mean either the oral repetition of what is given out to them as the essence of faith, or the performance of rites which may help them to receive what they wish for, as they are taught to believe by the ecclesiastic Christianity.

8

The men of our time live without any faith. One part of mankind, the cultured, rich minority, having freed itself from the ecclesiastic suggestion, believes in nothing, because it considers every faith to be either foolish or a useful instrument for exerting power over the masses. But the vast majority of the poor and the uncultured, who, with the rare exceptions of men who actually believe, are under the influence of the hypnosis, think that they believe in what is suggested to them under the guise of faith, but that is not faith, because it does not explain to man his position in the world, and only confuses it more than ever. Of this position and mutual relation of the unbelieving, hypocritical minority and the hypnotized majority is the life of our world, which calls itself Christian, composed. And this life, both of the minority, which holds in its hands the means of the hypnotization, and of the hypnotized majority, is terrible, on account of the cruelty and immorality of the ruling men and of the crushed condition and stultification of the vast labouring masses. Never, at no time of the religious decline, has the neglect and oblivion of the chief property of every religion, especially the Christian, that of the equality of men, reached such a stage as in our day. The chief cause of the terrible present-day cruelty of man toward man is due, not only to the complete absence of religion, but also to the refined complexity of life, which conceals from men the consequences of their acts. No matter how cruel an Attila, a Dzhingis-Khan, and their men may have been, so long as they personally killed people, the process of killing must have been disagreeable to them, and still more dis agreeable the consequences of the killing, — the sobs of the relatives, the presence of the corpses. Thus the consequences of the cruelty moderated cruelty itself. But in our time we kill people through such a complicated system of transmission, and the consequences of our cruelty are so carefully removed and concealed from us, that there are no actions to restrain cruelty, and the cruelty of one set of men against another has been growing and growing, and has in our time reached limits never reached before.

I think that if in our time, not a Nero, who is by all men recognized as a malefactor, but the simplest kind of an enterprising man wanted to make a pond of human blood for the sick, the wealthy, to bathe in, by the prescription of learned physicians, he would be able without molestation to arrange this matter, provided he did so within decent, accepted forms, that is, provided he did not forcibly compel men to draw their blood, but placed them in such a condition that they could not live without doing so, and, besides, invited the clergy and the learned, the first — to sanctify the new pond, as they sanctify cannon, guns, prisons, gibbets, and the second — to discover the proof of the necessity and legality of such an establishment, just as they discovered the proof of the necessity of wars and of houses of prostitution. The fundamental principle of every religion — the equality of all men among themselves — has been so forgotten, abandoned, and choked up by all kinds of stupid dogmas in the professed religion, and in science this same inequality has, in the form of the struggle for existence and the survival of the fittest, been to such an extent recognized as a necessary condition of life, that the destruction of millions of human lives for the advantage of the minority of the ruling men is regarded as a most common and necessary phenomenon of life, and is constantly taking place.

The men of our time never get tired boasting of those brilliant, unusual, colossal results achieved by technical art in the nineteenth century.

Without any doubt there has never in history existed such material progress, that is, such a command of the forces of Nature, as has been achieved in the nineteenth century. But there is also no doubt concerning this, that there has never in history been an example of such an immoral life, free from all the forces which restrain the animal tendencies of man, as the one which our Christian humanity lives, growing more and more beastly all the time. The material progress achieved by the men of the nineteenth century is really great; but this progress has been bought by a neglect of the most elementary demands of morality, such as humanity never attained, not even in the time of Dzhingis-Khan, or Attila, or Nero.

Unquestionably it is all very nice to have ironclads, railways, printing, tunnels, phonographs, Röntgen rays, and so forth. All that is very nice, but not less nice, not to be compared with anything, as Ruskin said, are the human lives which now are mercilessly wasted by the million in order to acquire ironclads, railways, tunnels, which not only do not adorn life, but even distort it.

In reply to this we are generally told that they are now inventing and in time will have invented such appliances that men's lives will not be wasted as they are now, but that is not true. So long as men do not consider all men to be their brothers, and do not consider human lives to be the most sacred thing, a thing which cannot be violated, and the maintenance of which should be considered the first, most urgent duty, that is, if men will not act religiously toward one another, they will always waste each other's lives for their own personal advantages. No fool will consent to waste thousands, if he is able to attain the same end by spending one hundred with the addition of a few human lives which are in his power. In Chicago approximately the same number of men are killed every year by the railroads, and the owners of the roads systematically introduce no appliances by which people may not be killed, having figured out that the damages paid every year to the families of the injured are less than the interest on the sum necessary for such appliances.

It is very likely that the men who ruin human lives for their advantage will be put to shame by public opinion or will be compelled to introduce these appliances. But so long as men are irreligious and do their business before men and not before God, they will, though introducing life-saving appliances in one place, again use human lives in another business, as being the most profitable material for gains.

It is easy to conquer Nature and to make a lot of railways, steamships, museums, and so forth, if human lives are not spared. The Egyptian kings prided themselves on their pyramids, and we admire them, forgetting the millions of slaves' lives that were ruined in these structures. Even so we admire our exposition palaces, ironclads, cables, forgetting how we pay for all that. We could be proud of it all, only if it were all done without restraint by free men, and not by slaves.

Christian nations have conquered and subjugated the

American Indians, the Hindoos, the Africans, and now conquer and subjugate the Chinese, and are proud of this. But these conquests and subjugations are not due to the fact that the Christian nations are spiritually higher than the nations subjugated, but, on the contrary, to the fact that they are spiritually incomparably lower than they. To say nothing of the Hindoos and the Chinese, even the Zulus have certain religious, obligatory rules, which prescribe certain acts and forbid others; but our Christian nations have no such rules. Rome conquered the whole world at the precise time when it was free from all religion. The same thing, though in a much higher degree, is now taking place with the Christian nations. They are all in the same condition, without religion, and so, in spite of the inner discord, they are all united in one federative band of robbers, in which theft, pillage, debauchery, the murder of individual persons, and mass murder are not only committed without the slightest pricks of conscience, but also with the greatest self-satisfaction, as happened lately in China. Some believe in nothing and are proud of it; others pretend to be believing in what they, for the sake of their advantage, under the guise of faith, impress upon the people; and others again, the vast majority, all the masses, accept as faith that suggestion under which they are, and slavishly submit to everything which is demanded of them by the commanding and unbelieving suggesters.

These suggesters ask for the same thing that was asked for by all the Neros, who tried in some way to fill the void of their lives, — the gratification of their senseless, all-pervading luxury. Now luxury is obtained in no other way than by the enslavement of men; the moment there is enslavement, luxury is increased; and the increase of luxury invariably brings with it the intensification of enslavement, because it is only the hungry, the cold, the needy, who can work all their lives at something that

they do not need, but which is needed for the amusement
of their masters.

9

In the sixth chapter of Genesis there is a profound
passage, in which the writer of the Bible says that before
the flood God, seeing that the spirit which He had given
men to serve Him with had been used by them to serve
their own flesh, became so angered at them that He was
sorry for having created them and, before destroying men,
decided to shorten their lives to 120 years. It is precisely
the thing for which, according to the words of the Bible,
God grew angry and shortened their lives, that has now
happened with the men of our Christian world.

Reason is that force of men which determines their
relation to the world; and since the relation of all men
to the world is one and the same, the establishment of
this relation, that is, religion, unites men. But the union
of all men gives them the highest physical and spiritual
good accessible to them.

The perfect union, in the perfect, highest reason, and
so the perfect good, is an ideal toward which humanity is
striving; but every religion which gives the men of a
certain society the same answers to their questions as to
what the world is and what they, the men in this world,
are, unites men and so brings them nearer to the realization of the good. But when reason, abstracting itself from
its proper activity, — the establishment of its relation to
God and its activity in correspondence with this relation,
— is directed, not only upon the ministration of the flesh
and on an evil struggle with men and with other beings,
but also upon justifying this its bad life, which is contrary
to man's properties and destination, then there result
those terrible calamities from which the majority of men
suffer now, and that condition under which a return to a
rational and good life presents itself as almost impossible.

The pagans who are united among themselves by the grossest religious teaching are much nearer to the cognition of the truth than the so-called Christian nations of our time who live without any religion, and in the midst of whom the most advanced men are sure and impress upon others that there is no need of religion and that it is much better to live without any religion.

Among the pagans there may be found men who, having come to comprehend the lack of a correspondence between their faith and the ever increasing knowledge and demands of their reason, will work out or adopt a religious teaching which is more in accord with the spiritual condition of the people, and in which they will be joined by their compatriots and fellow believers.   But the men of our world, some of whom look upon religion as an instrument for ruling men, while others regard religion as a piece of foolishness, and others again, the vast majority of the people, being under the influence of a gross deception, think that they are in possession of the true religion, become impermeable for every forward movement and approximation to the truth.

Proud of their perfections, which are necessary for a physical life, and of their refined, barren reasoning, which has for its purpose to prove, not only their own righteousness, but also their superiority over all nations during all periods of history, they sink in their ignorance and depravity, fully convinced that they are standing upon such a height as has never before been reached by humanity, and that every forward step of theirs on the road of ignorance and depravity raises them to a greater height of enlightenment and progress.

10

It is proper for man to establish an agreement between his bodily — physical — and rational — spiritual

— activity. A man cannot be satisfied, so long as this agreement has not been established in one way or another. This agreement is established in two ways: one, when a man with his reason determines the necessity or desirability of a certain act or acts, and then acts in conformity with the decision of his reason, and the other, when a man commits acts under the influence of feeling, and then invents a mental explanation or justification for them.

The first way of harmonizing the acts with reason is characteristic of men who profess some religion and who, on the basis of its tenets, know what acts they should perform, and what not. The second way is characteristic chiefly of irreligious men, who have no common basis for the determination of the value of their acts, and who, therefore, always establish an agreement between their reason and their acts, not by a subordination of their acts to reason, but by this, that, having committed an act on the basis of a sentimental infatuation, they later employ reason for the purpose of justifying their acts.

A religious man, knowing what in his activity and in the activity of other men is good or bad, and why one thing is good and another bad, if he sees the contradiction between the demands of his reason and his acts or the acts of other men, uses all the efforts of his reason to find a means for the destruction of these contradictions, that is, for learning how in the best way to harmonize his acts with the demands of his reason. But an irreligious man, who has no guidance in the determination of the value of acts, independently of their agreeableness, in submitting to the whims of his feelings, which are most varied and frequently contradictory, involuntarily falls into contradictions; but in falling into these contradictions, he tries to solve or conceal them by more or less complex and clever, but always false, reflections. Therefore, while the reflections of the religious people are always

simple, not complicated, and true, the mental activity of
the irreligious people becomes particularly refined, complicated, and false.

I will take the simplest kind of an example. A man
is given to debauchery, that is, he is not chaste, is false
to his wife, or, without marrying, abandons himself to
debauchery. If he is a religious man, he knows that this
is bad, and the whole activity of his mind is directed to
finding means for freeing himself from the vice, — he
tries to have no communion with fornicators and harlots,
to do more work, to make his life as severe as possible, to
avoid looking upon women as an object of lust, and so
forth. All this is very simple and comprehensible for all
men. But if a depraved man is irreligious, he immediately invents all kinds of explanations as to why he loves
women so much. And here begin all kinds of most complex, cunning, refined reflections about the union of souls,
about beauty, about freedom in love, and so forth, which,
the more they spread, the more they confuse the matter
and conceal what is needed.

The same thing takes place for irreligious men in all
spheres of activity and thought. To conceal the inner
contradictions, complex, refined reflections are accumu-
lated, and these, filling the mind with all kind of bosh,
abstract people's attention from what is important and
essential, and make it possible for them to persist in the
lie in which the men of our time, without noticing it, live.

" Men loved darkness rather than light, because their
deeds were evil," it says in the Gospel. " For every one
that doeth evil hateth the light, neither cometh to the
light, lest his deeds should be reproved because they are
evil."

And so the men of our world, in consequence of the
absence of religion, having arranged for themselves a most
cruel, animal, immoral life, have also carried the complex,
refined, trifling activity of the mind, which conceals the

evil of this life, to such a degree of useless complication and intricacy that the majority of men have entirely lost the ability to see the difference between good and evil, between the lie and the truth.

For the men of our world there is not one question which they can approach directly and simply : all questions, — economic, internal and external governmental, political, diplomatic, scientific, — to say nothing of philosophic and religious questions, are with such artfulness put so incorrectly and are, therefore, swaddled in such a thick cloth of complex, unnecessary reflections, refined distortions of ideas and words, sophisms, and discussions, that all reflections about such questions circle in one place, without catching into anything, and, like wheels without the driving belt of transmission, lead to nothing but that one purpose for which they have arisen, — to concealing from oneself and from men that evil in which they live and which they do.

11

In all the spheres of the so-called science of our time there is the same feature, which invalidates all the efforts of men's minds that are directed upon the investigation of various spheres of knowledge. This feature consists in this, that all the investigations of the science of our time avoid the essential question to which an answer is demanded, and investigate side issues, the investigations of which lead to nothing and become the more entangled, the farther they are carried on. Nor can it be different with a science which chooses its subjects of investigation by chance, and not according to the demands of the religious world-conception, which determines what is to be studied and when, what first and what last. Thus, for example, in the now fashionable subject of sociology, or political economy, there would seem to be but one question : why do some people do nothing, while others work

for them ?   (If there is another question, which consists
in this, why people work separately, interfering with one
another, and not in common with all men, which would
be more advantageous, this question is included in the
first.   If there shall be no inequality, there will be no
struggle.)   There would seem to be but this one question,
but science does not even think of putting and answering
it, but introduces far-fetched considerations, in which it
deals in such a way that deductions from them can in no
case either solve the fundamental question or contribute
to its solution.   They begin with considerations as to
what has been and is, and this past and present are
viewed as something invariable, like the course of the
celestial luminaries, and they invent abstract ideas of
values, capital, profit, percentage, and there appears a
complex play of the minds of men quarrelling among
themselves, which has been lasting for a hundred years.
In reality the question can be solved easily and simply.

Its solution consists in this, that, since all men are
brothers and equal among themselves, everybody must
act toward others as he wishes that others should act
toward him, and, therefore, the whole matter is in the
destruction of the false religious law and the establishment of the new law.   But the advanced men of the
Christian world not only do not accept this solution, but,
on the contrary, try to conceal from men the possibility
of such a solution and for this purpose abandon themselves to that empty sophistry which they call science.

The same thing takes place in the juridical sphere.   It
would seem that the only essential question consists in
this, why there are men who allow themselves to offer
violence to other people, to rob, imprison, and execute
them, to send them to war, and many more things.   The
solution of the question is very simple, if we consider it
from the one relevant point of view, — the religious.
From the religious point of view a man cannot and must

not commit any acts of violence against his neighbour, and so, to solve the question, only one thing is needed, — to destroy all superstitions and sophisms which permit violence, and clearly to impress upon people the religious principles which exclude the possibility of violence.

The advanced people, however, not only fail to do so, but also use all the cunning of their mind for the purpose of concealing from men the possibility and the urgency of this solution. They write mountains of books about all kinds of laws, — civil, criminal, police, ecclesiastic, financial, and other laws, — and expound and discuss these themes, fully convinced that they are doing not only a useful, but also a very important work. But they do not even answer the question as to why men, being essentially equal, can some of them judge, coerce, rob, execute others, and do not even recognize its existence. According to their teaching it turns out that this violence is not exorted by men, but by something abstract called the state.

In a similar way the learned men of our time avoid and pass over in silence the essential questions and conceal the inner contradictions in all the spheres of knowledge. In the historical sciences there is one essential question : how have the working classes, that is, 999 thousandths of all humanity, lived ? To this question there is not even a semblance of an answer ; the question does not even exist, and mountains of books are written by the historians of one school as to how Louis XI. had a bellyache, what abominations were committed by Elizabeth of England and by John IV., who were the ministers, and what kind of verses and comedies were written by the literary men for the amusement of these kings and their paramours and ministers. But the historians of another school describe the locality in which the people lived, what they ate, what they traded in, what garments they wore, in general, what could not have had any influence upon the life of the people, but was the consequence of their religion, which by the historians of this category is recognized as the result of the food and the apparel used by the people.

However, the answer to the question as to how the working people used to live can be given only by recognizing religion as a necessary condition of the people's life, and so the answer is to be found in the study of those religions which were professed by the people, and which placed the people in the condition in which they were.

In the natural history sciences, it would seem, there was no particular necessity for dimming men's sound reason; but even here, thanks to the mental process applied by the science of our time, they lose themselves, instead of giving the most natural answers to the question as to what the world of living beings, plants, and animals is, and how it is subdivided, in an empty, obscure and absolutely useless prattle, which is chiefly directed against the Biblical history of the creation of the world, about how the organisms originated, which nobody needs to know and which nobody can know, because this origin, no matter how we may explain it, will always be lost for us in infinite time and space. And on these themes they have invented theories and retorts, and additions to theories, which form millions of books, and the unexpected deduction from which is this one, that the law of life to which man must submit is the struggle for existence.

The applied sciences, moreover, such as the technical sciences and medicine, on account of the absence of a guiding religious principle, involuntarily depart from their rational purpose, and receive false directions. Thus the whole of the technical sciences are not directed upon the alleviation of the people's labour, but upon improvements needed only by the wealthy classes, which still more separate the rich from the poor, the masters from the slaves.   If some advantages from these inventions and improvements, tiny bits of them, find their way among the popular masses, this is not so because they are intended for the masses, but only because by their property they cannot be withheld from the people.

The same is true of medical science, which in its false direction has reached a point where it is accessible only to the wealthy classes ; but the masses, from their manner of life and poverty and neglect of the chief questions of the improvement of their life of wretchedness, can make use of it to such an extent and under such conditions that this aid only shows more clearly the deviation of medical science from its purpose.

Most striking, however, is this deviation from the fundamental questions and their distortion in what in our time is called philosophy.   It would seem that there is one question which is subject to the solution of philosophy, and that is : What must I do ?   To this question there have been some kinds of answers in the philosophy of the Christian nations, though these were connected with the greatest unnecessary confusion of ideas : such answers were those by Spinoza, by Kant in his *Critique of Pure Reason*, by Schopenhauer, and especially by Rousseau.   But of late, since the time of Hegel, who recognized everything in existence as sensible, the question as to what we shall do has been put in the background, and philosophy directs all its attention to the investigation of what is, and to the subordination of this to a previously stated theory.   This is the first step down.   The second step that brings human thought even lower is the recognition of the struggle for existence as a fundamental law, only because this struggle may be observed in the case of animals and plants.   According to this theory it is assumed that the destruction of the weaker is a law that should not be interfered with.   Finally, we come to the third step, where the sophomoric attitudinizing of the half-witted Nietzsche, which does not even represent anything whole or coherent, — mere sketches of immoral, unfounded ideas, — is regarded by advanced men as the last word of philosophic science. In reply to the question as to what we shall do, we are told outright : we must live for our pleasure, without paying any attention to the lives of other men.

If any one should doubt the terrible intoxication and bestialization which has been reached by Christian humanity in our day, the unusual success of Nietzsche's writings, to say nothing of the late Boer and China crimes, which have been defended by the clergy and have been recognized as heroic exploits by the mighty of the world, may serve as an incontrovertible proof of it. We have before us the incoherent, most rankly sensational writings of a witty, but narrow-minded and abnormal German, who is obsessed by the mania of greatness. These writings, neither by talent nor by their thoroughness, can lay any claim to the public's attention. Such writings would not only not have attracted any attention in the days of Kant, Leibniz, or Hume, or even fifty years ago, but could not even have made their appearance then. In our time, however, all the so-called cultured humanity goes into ecstasies over Mr. Nietzsche's delirium, and discusses and elucidates it, and his works are printed in all languages and in an endless number of copies.

Turgénev said wittily that there are reverse commonplaces which are frequently used by untalented men who wish to attract attention. Everybody knows, for example, that water is wet, and suddenly a man says with a serious countenance that water is dry, — not ice, — but dry water, and such a seriously expressed assertion attracts attention.

Similarly the whole world knows that virtue consists in the suppression of the passions, in self-renunciation. This is not only known to Christianity, against which

Nietzsche pretends to fight, but is also an eternal supreme law arrived at by all humanity, in Brahmanism, in Buddhism, in Confucianism, in the ancient Persian religion. Suddenly there appears a man who announces that he has become convinced that self-renunciation, humility, meekness, love, — all these are vices that ruin humanity (he has in mind Christianity, forgetting all the other religions). Naturally such an assertion at first puzzles one. But after a little thought and after finding in the work no proofs of this strange proposition, every sensible man must reject such a book and marvel, seeing that there is nothing so foolish that in our time it cannot find a publisher. But with Nietzsche's books it is not so. The majority of so-called enlightened men seriously analyze the theory of the overhumanity, recognizing its author as a great philosopher, an heir of Descartes, Leibniz, and Kant.

This is all due to the fact that the majority of so-called enlightened men of our time hate the mention of virtue, of its chief foundation, — self-renunciation, love, — which embarrass and condemn their animal life, and rejoice when they meet with some even poorly, senselessly, incoherently expressed teaching of egoism, cruelty, and the assertion of their own happiness and greatness at the expense of other people's lives, a teaching which they live by.

12

Christ reproached the Pharisees and scribes for having taken the keys of the kingdom of God and for not entering themselves and not letting anybody else enter.

The same thing is being done nowadays by the learned scribes of our time : these men have seized the keys, not of the kingdom of heaven, but of enlightenment, and they do not enter themselves, and do not let others in. The priests, the clergy, have by means of all kinds of deceptions and hypnosis impressed upon people that Christianity is not a teaching which preaches the equality of all men and so destroys the whole present pagan structure of life, but that, on the contrary, it maintains this structure; prescribes that people be distinguished from one another like the stars; prescribes that it be accepted that every power is from God and must be obeyed without any discussion; and in general inculcates upon the oppressed the idea that their condition is from God and that they must bear it in humility and meekness, and must submit to those oppressors who not only may fail to be meek and humble, but must, correcting others, teach, punish, — as emperors, kings, popes, bishops, and all kinds of lay and spiritual powers, — and live in splendour and luxury, which their subjects are obliged to supply to them. But the ruling classes, thanks to this false teaching which they maintain by force, dominate the masses, whom they compel to serve their idleness, luxury, and vices. Meanwhile, the only men, the learned, who have freed themselves from the hypnosis, the men who alone could free the masses from oppression, and who say that they wish this, instead of doing what might attain this end, do the very opposite, imagining that they are thus serving the masses.

It would seem that from a mere superficial observation of what the men who keep the masses in subjection are interested in, these people might understand what the nations are moved by and what keeps them in a certain state, and should direct all their forces to this power; but, far from doing so, they consider this to be quite useless.

It is as though these men did not wish to see the truth and as though, in spite of their carefully, often even sincerely, doing for the masses the most varied things, they did not do the one thing necessary for them, so that their activity resembles the activity of a man who should try with the effort of his muscles to shift a train, whereas he needs but get on the tender and do what he constantly sees the engineer do, — move the lever which admits the steam to the cylinder. This steam is the religious world conception of men. They need only see with what zeal all the rulers defend this power, by means of which they rule over the nations, to understand to what they must direct their efforts, in order to free the masses from their enslavement.

What does the Turkish Sultan defend, and what does he cling to most? And why does the Russian Emperor, upon arriving in a city, make it his first business to visit the relics and images? And why, in spite of all his varnish of culture, does the German Emperor in all his speeches, in season and out of season, speak of God, of Christ, of the holiness of religion, of the oath, and so forth? Because they all know that their power is based on the army, and the army, the possibility of the existence of the army, only upon religion. And if rich people are particularly pious and pretend to be believers, attend church, and observe the Sabbath, they do so chiefly because their instinct of self-preservation tells them that with the religion which they profess is connected their exclusive advantageous position in society.

Frequently all these men do not know in what way their power is maintained by the religious deception, but they know from a feeling of self-preservation what the weak spot of their position is, and they first of all defend this spot. These men have always admitted and always will admit a socialistic, even a revolutionary propaganda, within certain limits; but they will never allow the religious foundations to be touched.

And so, if the advanced men of our time — the scholars, liberals, socialists, revolutionists, anarchists — cannot from history and from psychology understand what it is the nations are moved by, they could convince themselves by this objective experience that what moves them is not to be found in material conditions, but only in religion.

But, strange to say, the learned, the advanced men of our time, who very sensitively analyze and understand the conditions of the lives of the nations, do not see what blinds one by its very obviousness. If the men who do so leave the masses in their religious ignorance purposely, in order to maintain their advantageous position amidst a minority, this is a terrible, disgusting deception. Those who act like that are the very hypocrites whom more than any other, or even alone, Christ condemned, because no inhuman beings and scoundrels have introduced so much evil into the life of humanity as these men.

But if these men are sincere, the only explanation of this strange obfuscation is this, that, as the masses are under the influence of the false religion, so also the so-called enlightened men of our time are under the influence of the false science, which has decided that the chief nerve by which humanity has always lived is no longer of any use to it and may be supplanted by something else.

13

In this error or cunning of the scribes — the educated men of our world — does the peculiarity of our time consist, and in this is to be found the cause of that wretched condition in which Christian humanity lives, and of that bestialization in which it sinks more and more.

As a rule, the advanced, cultured men of our world assert that the false religious beliefs professed by the masses are not of any particular importance, and that it is not worth our while, nor even necessary, directly to struggle against them, as formerly did Hume, Voltaire, Rousseau, and others. Science, that is, all that scattered, incidental information which they disseminate among the masses, will, in their opinion, naturally attain this end, that is, a man, having learned how many millions of miles the earth is removed from the sun and what metals are to be found in the stars and the sun, will stop believing in the propositions of the church.

In this sincere or insincere assertion or assumption there is a great delusion or terrible cunning. From his earliest years, — an age most susceptible to suggestion, — when an educator cannot be careful enough about what is transmitted to the child, they inculcate upon him the stupid and immoral dogmas of the so-called Christian religion, which are not compatible with reason or with science. They teach the child the dogma of the Trinity, which is incomprehensible to a normal brain, the descent of one of these gods upon earth for the redemption of the human race, His resurrection and ascension to heaven; he is taught to expect the second coming and punishment with eternal torments for not believing in these dogmas; he is taught to pray concerning his needs, and many more things. And when these propositions, which are not in harmony with reason, nor with contemporary knowledge, nor with the human consciousness, are indelibly impressed upon the child's susceptible mind, he is left alone, to find his way as well as he can amidst the contradictions which result from the dogmas accepted by him and made his own as the undoubted truth. No one tells him how he could and should harmonize these contradictions. If the theologians attempt to harmonize these contradictions, these attempts only confuse the matter more than ever. By degrees a man gets used to the idea (and in this he is strongly supported by the theologians) that reason cannot be relied upon, and that, therefore, everything is possible in the world, and that in man there is nothing by means of which he can distinguish good from evil and the lie from the truth, and that in what is most important to him, — in his acts, — he must not be guided by his reason, but by what others tell him. Naturally a terrible distortion in a man's spiritual world must be produced by such an education, and this distortion is in maturer years main-

tained with all the means of suggestion, which is exercised
all the time against the masses with the aid of the
clergy.

But if a spiritually strong man with great labour and
effort succeeds in freeing himself from the hypnosis in
which he has been educated since his childhood and
maintained in his maturer years, that distortion of his
soul, through which he has been impressed with unbelief
in his own reason, cannot pass unnoticed, just as in the
physical world the poisoning of the organism with some
powerful venom cannot pass without leaving any trace.
Having freed himself from the hypnosis of the deception,
such a man, hating the lie from which he has just freed
himself, will naturally acquire that teaching of the advanced men according to which every religion is regarded
as one of the chief impediments in humanity's forward
movement on the path of progress. Having acquired
this teaching, such a man will become just as unprincipled a man as his teacher, a man who is guided in life
by nothing but his desires, and who, far from condemning
himself for this, considers himself for this very reason to
be on the highest accessible point of spiritual development.

Thus it will be with the men who are spiritually
strongest. Those who are less strong, though they may
awaken to doubt, will never fully free themselves from the
deception in which they are brought up, and, allying themselves with all existing kinds of finely spun, misty theories,
which are to justify the stupidity of the dogmas accepted
by them, and inventing others, will live in the sphere of
doubts, haziness, sophisms, and self-deception, and will
only contribute to the obfuscation of the masses and
will counteract their awakening.

But the majority of men, having no strength and no
chance to struggle against the suggestion exercised against
them, will live and die for generations, as they now live,

deprived of man's highest good, — the true religious concept of life, — and will always form nothing but a submissive tool for the classes that rule over them and deceive them.

It is this terrible deception that the advanced men say is not important and is not worth struggling against. The only explanation of such an assertion, if these who make it are sincere, is this, that they themselves are under the hypnosis of the false science; but if they are not sincere, the attack of the established beliefs is not advantageous and frequently is dangerous. In any case, in one way or another, the assertion that the profession of a false religion is harmless or at least not important, and that, therefore, it is possible to disseminate enlightenment without destroying the religious deception, is absolutely untrue.

The salvation of humanity from its calamities is only in its liberation from the hypnosis in which it is held by its priests as also from the one into which it is led by the learned. In order to pour something into a vessel it is necessary first to free it from what it contains. Just so it is necessary to free men from the deception in which they are held, in order that they may be able to accept the true religion, that is, a regular relation to the beginning of everything, to God, which would correspond to the development of humanity, and a guidance for their activity, as deduced from this relation.

14

"But is there a true religion? All the religions are infinitely varied, and we have no right to call any one of them true, simply because it more nearly fits in with our tastes," will say the men who consider the religions from their external forms as a certain kind of a disease, from which they feel themselves free, but from which the rest of the people are still suffering. But that is not true : the religions differ in their external forms, but they are all alike in their fundamental principles. It is these fundamental principles of all religions that form the true religion which alone in our time is proper for all men, and the adoption of which can alone save humanity from all its calamities.

Humanity has been living for a long time, and as it has traditionally worked out its practical acquisitions, so it could not help but work out those spiritual principles which form the foundations of its life, and the rules of conduct which result from them. The fact that the blinded men do not see them does not prove their non-existence. Such a religion of our time, common to all men, — not some one religion with all its peculiarities and distortions, but a religion which consists in those religious propositions which are identical in all the widely disseminated and well-known religions, as professed by more than nine-tenths of the human race, — does exist, and men have not yet become completely brutalized because the best men of all the nations, even though it be unconsciously, hold to this religion and profess it, and it is only the suggestion of the deception which with the aid of the priests and the learned is exercised against people that keeps them from accepting it consciously.

The tenets of this true religion are to such an extent proper to men that, as soon as they are communicated to men, they are accepted as something well known and natural. For us this true religion is Christianity, in those of its tenets in which it coincides, not with the external forms, but with the fundamental propositions of Brahmanism, Confucianism, Taoism, Judaism, Buddhism, and even Mohammedanism. Even so for those who profess Brahmanism, Confucianism, and so forth, the true religion will be the one whose fundamental propositions coincide with the fundamental propositions of all the other great religions. These propositions are very simple, comprehensible, and incomplex.

These propositions are that there is a God, the beginning of everything ; that in man there is a particle of this divine principle, which he is able by his life to increase or diminish in himself ; that for the increase of this principle a man must suppress his passions and increase his love in himself ; and that the practical means for doing this consists in acting toward others as we would that others should act toward us. All these propositions are common to Brahmanism, to Judaism, to Confucianism, to Taoism, to Buddhism, to Christianity, to Mohammedanism. (Though Buddhism does not give a definition of God, it none the less recognizes that with which man blends and into which he sinks, when he reaches Nirvana. Thus that with which man unites as he sinks into Nirvana is that principle which is recognized as God by Judaism, Christianity, and Mohammedanism.)

" But this is not religion," will be said by the men of our time, who are accustomed to accept what is supernatural, that is, senseless, as the chief symptom of religion. " This is anything you please, philosophy, ethics, and reflections, but not religion." Religion, according to their conception, must be absurd and incomprehensible (*credo quia absurdum*). And yet it is only out of these propositions or, rather, in consequence of their being preached as a religious teaching that by a long process of distortion have been worked out all those absurdities of miracles and supernatural events which are regarded as the fundamental symptoms of every religion. To assert that supernaturalness and absurdity form the fundamental properties of religion is the same as to assert, when one observes nothing but rotten apples, that the bitterness of decay and an injurious effect upon the stomach are the fundamental property of the apple.

Religion is the determination of man's relation to the

beginning of everything, and of man's destination, which follows from this proposition, and, following from this destination, of rules for his conduct. And the universal religion, the fundamental propositions of which are identical in all professions, fully satisfies these demands. It determines man's relation to God, as of the part to the whole, and from this relation deduces man's destination, which consists in the increase of the divine property in himself; now it is man's destination to deduce practical demands from the rule of doing unto others as we would that others would do unto us.

People frequently doubt, and at one time I myself doubted, whether such an abstract rule as this, that we should do unto others as we would that others should do unto us, could be as obligatory a rule and guide of acts as the simpler rules, — of fasting, prayer, communion, and so forth. But to this doubt an incontrovertible answer is given by the spiritual condition of, say, a Russian peasant, who would rather die than spit the Eucharist out on the manure pile, and yet is ready at the command of men to kill his brothers.

Why could not the demands which are deduced from the rule of not doing unto another what we should not wish another to do unto us — such as that we should not kill our brothers, should not curse, commit adultery, take vengeance, make use of our brother's want for the gratification of our lusts, and many others — be inculcated with the same force and become as obligatory and inviolable as is the belief in the sacredness of the Eucharist, the images, and so forth, to people whose faith is based more on trust than on any clear internal consciousness?

15

The truths of the religion of our time common to all men are so simple, so comprehensible, and so near to the heart of every man, that, it would seem, it would suffice for the parents, rulers, and instructors, in place of the obsolete and absurd doctrines about the Trinities, mothers of God, redemptions, Indras, Trimurtis, heaven-ascending Buddhas and Mohammeds, in which they frequently do not believe themselves, to inculcate upon the children and the adults the simple, clear truths of the religion which is common to all men, — the metaphysical essence of which consists in this, that in man there dwells the divine spirit, and the practical rule of which is this, that a man should act toward others as he wishes that others should act toward him, and the whole human life would change of its own accord. If only, as now children and adults are impressed with the faith that God sent His Son in order to redeem Adam's sins, and established His church, which must be obeyed, and the rules resulting from this, which are to pray at such a time and place, and to offer sacrifices, and at such a time to abstain from a certain kind of food and on certain days from work, it were inculcated upon men and asserted that God is spirit, whose manifestation lives in us and whose power we can increase by means of our lives! If this and everything which naturally results from these foundations were inculcated upon men, just as now they are impressed with useless stories about impossible events and with rules about meaningless rites resulting from these stories, there would, in place of a senseless war and disunion, and without the aid of diplomas, international laws, congresses of peace, political economists, and socialists of every description, very soon result a peaceful, concordant, happy life of humanity, guided by the one religion.

But nothing of the kind is taking place; not only is the deception of the false religion not destroyed and the true religion not preached, but men, on the contrary, more and more depart from the possibility of accepting the truth.

The chief reason why men do not do what is natural, necessary, and possible, consists in this, that the men of our time have become so accustomed, in consequence of a long irreligious life, to arranging and strengthening their existence by means of violence, bayonets, bullets, prisons, gibbets, that it seems to them that such a structure of life is normal, and even that there can be no other. Not only is this the belief of those to whom the present order is advantageous, but also those who suffer from it are so stupefied by the suggestion exerted against them that they consider violence the only means of order in human society. And yet it is this very arrangement and strengthening of human life by means of violence that more than anything else removes men from the comprehension of the causes of their suffering and so from the possibility of a true order.

What is taking place is very much what a bad and ill-intentioned physician does when he drives in a vicious eruption, not only deceiving the patient by this, but even aggravating the disease itself and making its cure impossible.

To the ruling men, who have enslaved the masses and who think and say, "*Après nous le deluge*," it seems very convenient by means of the army, the clergy, the soldiers, and the police, and by means of threatening bayonets, bullets, prisons, workhouses, gibbets, to compel the enslaved men to continue to live in their stultification and enslavement, and not to interfere with the rulers in their enjoyment of their position. And this the ruling people do, calling such an order of things good, though nothing so much interferes with the true social order as this. In reality such an order is not only not good, but is even an establishment of evil.

If the men of our societies, with the residue of those religious principles which none the less live in the masses, did not constantly see crimes committed by those men who have taken it upon themselves to watch over order and morality in the lives of men, — wars, executions, prisons, taxes, the sale of whiskey, and of opium, — they would never think of doing one-hundredth part of those evil deeds and deceits, and the violence and murder, which they now commit with the full assurance that these deeds are good and proper to men.

The law of human life is such that its improvement, both for the individual and the society of men, is possible only through an internal moral perfection. But all the attempts of men to improve their lives by external interactions by means of violence serve as a most efficient sermon and example of evil, and so not only fail to improve life, but, on the contrary, increase the evil, which grows more and more, like a snowball, and more and more removes men from the one possibility of the true improvement of their lives.

In proportion as the habit of violence and of crimes, which under the guise of law are committed by the guardians of the peace and of morality, becomes more and more frequent and more and more cruel, and is more and more justified by the suggestion of that lie which is given out as religion, men become more and more confirmed in the idea that the law of their life is not in love and in mutual service, but in struggle and mutual devouring.

And the more they become confirmed in this idea which debases them to the level of the animal, the more difficult it is for them to awaken from that hypnosis in which they are and to accept as the foundation of life the true religion of our time, which is common to all humanity.

A false circle is established: the absence of religion makes possible the animal life, which is based on violence; the animal life, which is based on violence, makes the liberation from the hypnosis and the acceptance of the true religion more and more impossible. For this reason men do not do what is natural, possible, and indispensable in our time, — they do not destroy the deception of the similitude of religion and do not accept and preach the true religion.

16

Is there a way out from this magic circle, and in what does it consist?

At first it appears that these men ought to be brought out of that circle by the governments which have taken it upon themselves to guide the life of the nations for their own good. Thus always thought the people who tried to substitute for the structure of life which is based on violence another structure of life, which is rational and based on mutual service and love. Thus also thought the Christian reformers, and the founders of various theories of European communism, and the famous Chinese reformer, Mi-ti, who proposed to the government, for the good of the nation, to teach the children in the schools non-military sciences and exercises, and not to give to adults rewards for military acts, but to teach children and adults rules of respect and love, and to offer rewards and encouragement for acts of love. Thus also have thought many Russian religious reformers from among the masses, many of whom I have known, beginning with Syutáev and ending with an old man who has five times petitioned the Tsar to command the false religion to be abolished and true Christianity to be preached.

It naturally seems to people that the governments, which justify their existence by their care for the public weal, ought, for the confirmation of this good, to wish to use that one means, which in no case can be injurious to the masses and which can be productive of only the most fruitful consequences. But the governments have never and nowhere taken this obligation upon themselves; they have, on the contrary, always and everywhere with the greatest zeal defended the existing false, obsolete creed, and have with all the means at their command persecuted those who have tried to give the masses the foundations of the true religion. In reality it cannot be otherwise : for the governments to show up the lie of the existing religion and to preach the true religion is the same as though a man should cut off the branch on which he is sitting.

But if the governments do not do that, it would seem that it ought to be done by those learned men who, having freed themselves from the deception of the false religion, wish, as they say, to serve the masses which have nurtured them. But these men, like the governments, do not do so, in the first place, because they consider it purposeless to subject themselves to the unpleasantness and dangers of persecutions from the governments by revealing the deception which is defended by the government and which, according to their conviction, will destroy itself ; in the second place, because, considering every religion an outlived delusion, they have nothing to offer to the masses in place of the deception if they should destroy it.

There are left those great masses of unlearned men, who are subject to the hypnosis of the ecclesiastic and governmental deception, and who, therefore, think that that semblance of religion which is suggested to them is the one true religion, and that there is and can be no other. These masses are subjected to a constant, intensified action of hypnosis ; generation after generation is born, lives, and dies in that stupefied condition in which it is held by the clergy and the government, and if men free themselves from it, they inevitably find their way into the school of the learned who deny religion, and their influence becomes as useless and harmful as the influence of their teachers.

Thus this is disadvantageous to some, and impossible to others.

17

There seems to be no way out.

Indeed, for irreligious people there is and there can be no way out from this condition : though the men who belong to the upper ruling classes may pretend to be interested in the weal of the popular masses, they will never seriously attempt to destroy that stultification and enslavement in which the masses live and which make it possible for the upper classes to rule them (nor can they do so, since they are guided by worldly considerations). Similarly the men who belong to the enslaved, who, too, are guided by worldly considerations, cannot wish to make their otherwise bad condition worse by a struggle with the upper classes as the result of revealing the false teaching and preaching the true.   Neither of them have any reason for doing so and, if they are wise people, will never try to do so.

But it is not so in the case of religious people, those religious people who, no matter how much society may be corrupted, with their own life preserve that holy fire of religion without which human life could not exist. There are times (our time is such) when these men are not to be seen, when they, despised and humbled by all, pass their lives ingloriously, as in our country, in exile, in prisons, in disciplinary battalions ; but they exist and through them the rational human life is maintained.   It is these religious people, no matter how few there are of them, who alone can and will break that magic circle in which all men are kept in fetters.   These men can do it, because all the inconveniences and dangers, which prevent a man of the world from going counter to the existing order of life, not only do not exist for a religious man, but even increase his zeal in his struggle with the lie and in his profession in words and deeds of what he considers to be the divine truth.   If he belongs to the ruling classes he not only will not wish to conceal the truth for the sake of the advantages of his position, but, on the contrary, despising these advantages, will use all the forces of his soul for the purpose of liberating himself from these advantages and preaching the truth, since in his life there will no longer be any other aim than that of serving God. But if he belongs to the enslaved, he, renouncing the desire to improve the conditions of his carnal life, which is common to men in his position, will similarly have no other aim than that of doing God's will, in arraigning the lie and professing the truth, and no suffering and no threats will be able to keep him from living in accordance with that one meaning which he recognizes in his life. Either will act as naturally as labours a worldly man who bears privations for the acquisition of wealth or for the purpose of pleasing the mighty of the world from whom he expects some advantage. Every religious man acts thus because a man's soul which is enlightened by religion no longer lives this life of the world alone, as it is lived by irreligious people, but the eternal, infinite life, for which sufferings and death in this life are as insignificant as are, for the labourer who ploughs the field, the calluses on his hands and the weariness of his limbs.

It is these men who will break the magic circle in which people are now held fettered. No matter how few such men there are, no matter how low their social position may be, no matter how feeble they may be in intellect or education, they will, as certainly as the fire consumes the dry steppe, inflame the whole world, all the hearts of men, which have dried up from a long irreligious life and which thirst for renovation.

Religion is not a faith, once for all established, in certain supernatural events which are supposed to have taken place in the past, or in the necessity of certain prayers and rites ; nor is it, as the learned think, a remainder of the superstitions of ancient ignorance, which in our time has no meaning and no application in life ; religion is an established relation, concordant with reason and modern knowledge, of man to everlasting life, to God, which alone moves humanity forward toward its predestined end.

"The human soul is God's lamp," says a wise Jewish proverb. Man is a weak, unfortunate animal so long as God's light does not shine in him. But when this light burns up (and it burns only in a soul that is enlightened by religion), man becomes the most powerful being of the universe. This cannot be otherwise, because then it is no longer his own force, but God's, that acts in him.

So this is what religion is and what its essence is.

February, 1902.

TO THE WORKING PEOPLE

1902

TO THE WORKING PEOPLE

" And ye shall know the truth, and the truth shall make you free " (John viii. 32).

I HAVE but little time left to live, and I should like before my death to tell you, working people, what I have been thinking about your oppressed condition and about those means which will help you to free yourselves from it.

Maybe something of what I have been thinking (and I have been thinking much about it) will do you some good.

I naturally turn to the Russian labourers, among whom I live and whom I know better than the labourers of any other country, but I hope that my remarks may not be useless to the labourers of other countries as well.

1

Every one who has eyes and a heart sees that you, working men, are obliged to pass your lives in want and in hard labour, which is useless to you, while other men, who do not work, enjoy all that you accomplish, — that you are the slaves of these men, and that this ought not to be.

But what should be done that this might not be ?

The first, simplest, and most natural means which from

131

olden times has presented itself to men is by force to take from those who live by your labour what they enjoy illegally. Thus since remote antiquity acted the slaves in Rome and the peasants in the Middle Ages in Germany and in France. Thus they have frequently acted in Russia, since the time of Sténka Rázin, of Pugachév. Thus even now Russian labourers at times act.

This means suggests itself to the injured working men before any other, and yet this means not only never attains its end, but always more certainly makes worse, rather than improves, the condition of the working men. It was possible anciently, when the power of the government was not yet so strong as it is now, to hope for the success of such uprisings ; but now, when in the hands of the government, which always protects those who do not work, are immense sums of money, and the railways, and the telegraphs, and the police, and the gendarmes, and the army, all such attempts end, as lately ended the uprisings in the Governments of Poltáva and of Khárkov, in the torture and execution of the rioters, and the power of the non-workers over the workers is only made more firm.

In trying to oppose violence to violence, you, working men, do what a man bound with ropes would do if, to free himself, he should tug at the ropes : he would only tighten the knots which fetter him. The same is true as regards your attempts by means of violence to take away what is withheld from you by means of violence.

2

It has now become obvious that the method of riots does not attain its purpose, and that it does not improve the condition of the working men, but rather makes it worse. And so of late, men who desire, or who at least say that they desire, the good of the working masses, have discovered a new means for the liberation of the working

Tolstóy and His Wife in the Crimea, March, 1903

Photogravure from a Photograph

men. This new means is based on the teaching that all
the working men, after being deprived of the land which
they formerly possessed, and after having become hired
labourers (which according to this teaching is to happen
as inevitably as the sunset at a given hour), will arrange
unions, societies, demonstrations, and will choose their
partisans for parliament, and thus will keep improving
their condition, and finally will appropriate to themselves
all the works and factories, in general all the implements
of labour, among them the land, and then will be absolutely free and prosperous. In spite of the fact that
this teaching, which proposes this means, is full of ob-
scurities, arbitrary propositions and contradictions and
simple absurdities, it has of late been disseminated more
and more widely.

This doctrine is accepted not only in those countries
where the majority of the population has for several generations fallen away from agricultural labour, but also
where the majority of working men have not yet thought
of abandoning the land.

It would seem that a doctrine which first of all demands the transition of the agricultural labourer from the
customary, healthy, and joyous conditions of varied agricultural labour to the unhealthy, sombre, and pernicious
conditions of monotonous, stultifying work, and from that
independence, which the village worker feels in satisfying
nearly all his needs, to the complete slavish dependence
of the factory workman on his master, ought to have no
success in countries where the labourers still live on the
land and support themselves by means of agricultural
labour. But the preaching of this modern doctrine, called
socialism, even in such countries as Russia, where ninety-
eight per cent. of the labouring population lives by means
of agricultural labour, is gladly accepted by those two
per cent. of working men who have fallen away from
agricultural labour.

This is due to the fact that, when he abandons the labour on the land, the working man involuntarily submits to those temptations which are connected with life in the city and in the factory. The justification of these temptations he finds only in the socialistic doctrine, which considers the increase of necessities a sign of man's improvement.

Such working men, who have filled themselves with fragments of the socialistic doctrine, preach it with particular fervour to their fellow working men, considering themselves, in consequence of this propaganda and in consequence of those needs which they have developed, to be advanced people who stand infinitely higher than a coarse peasant, a village worker. Fortunately, there are still very few such working men in Russia; the vast majority of Russian labourers, which consists of agriculturists, has never heard anything about the socialistic doctrine; if these labourers ever heard of it, they receive such a doctrine as entirely alien to them and not touching upon their real needs.

All those socialistic methods of unions, demonstrations, election of partisans for the parliaments, by means of which the factory hands try to lighten their condition as slaves, present no interest for free agricultural labourers.

If the agricultural labourers need anything, it is not a raise of wages, not a diminution of hours of work, not general funds, and so forth, but only one thing, — land, of which they have everywhere too little to be able to support themselves upon it with their families. But of this one necessary thing for the rural labourers nothing is said in the socialistic doctrine.

3

All sensible Russian labourers understand that land, free land, is the only means for the improvement of their condition and for their liberation from slavery.

This is what a Russian peasant, a Stundist, writes regarding it to a friend of his:

"If a revolution is to be started, while the land remains private property, then, of course, it is not worth while to start it. Thus, for example, our brothers who live abroad, in Roumania, tell us that there they have a constitution and parliaments, but that the land is nearly all of it in the hands of proprietors; so what use is this parliament to the masses? In the parliament, they say, there is taking place only a struggle of one party against another, but the masses are terribly enslaved and in servitude to the proprietors. The proprietors have huts upon their lands. Half of the land they generally lease to the peasants, as a rule only for one year. When a peasant has worked the land well, the proprietor himself sows in this plot the next year, and allots another piece of ground to the peasant. After these poor wretches have lived for a few years on the land of a proprietor, they still remain his debtors; the government takes their last possessions for taxes, — their horse, cow, wagon, plough, clothes, bed, utensils, — and sells them all at a low price. Then the poor wretch picks up his starving family and goes to another proprietor, who seems to him to be kinder. This one gives him oxen, a plough, seeds, and so forth. But, after he has lived here for some time, the same story is repeated. Then he goes to a third proprietor, and so forth. Then the proprietors who do their own sowing hire labourers during the harvest, but it is their custom to pay the wages at the end of the harvest, and but few of the proprietors ever pay their hands, — the majority hold back half the pay, if not all. And there is no way of getting justice. So there you have a constitution! There you have a parliament!

"The land is the first indispensable condition which the masses should strive after. The factories and works, it seems to me, will naturally pass over into the hands of the working men. When the peasants get land, they will work on it and live freely upon their labour. Then many will refuse to labour in the factories and works, consequently there will be less competition for the working men. Then the wages will rise, and they will be able to organize their circles and funds, and will be able themselves to compete with their masters; then the latter will not find it advantageous to have factories, and they will enter into agreements with the working men. Land is the chief object of the struggle. This ought to be explained to the working men. Even if they should obtain an increase in wages this would be only temporary, to allay their minds. Then again the conditions of life will change, if instead of one dissatisfied man ten others shall be waiting to take his place. How can they then ask for an increase of wages?"

Though the information given in the letter concerning the state of affairs in Roumania is not quite correct, and though in other countries these oppressions do not exist, the essence of the matter, which is, that the first condition for the improvement of the working men's condition is to be found in free land, is in this letter expressed with unusual clearness.

4

Land is the chief object of the struggle! so writes this unlearned peasant. But the learned socialists say that the chief object of the struggle is works, factories, and only lastly land. For the working men to get land they must, according to the doctrine of the socialists, first of all struggle against the capitalists for the possession of plants and factories, and only after they shall have taken possession of the plants and factories will they get possession of the land. Men need land, and they are told that for its possession they must first of all abandon it and then obtain it again by a complex process, as predicted by the socialistic prophets, together with unnecessary works and factories. This demand to get possession of works and factories, which are of no use to the agriculturists, in order to get possession of the land, reminds one of the methods used by certain usurers. You ask such a usurer for a thousand roubles in money, for you need only the money, but the usurer tells you: " I cannot give you just the one thousand roubles; take from me five thousand, four thousand of which will be in the form of a few tons of soap, of a few bolts of silk stuffs, and so forth, things which you do not need, and then I shall be able to give you the one thousand roubles in money which you need."

Even so the socialists, having quite irregularly decided that the land is just such an implement of labour as a plant or a factory, propose to the labourers who are suffering only from lack of land, that they go away from the land and busy themselves with taking possession of the factories which produce cannon, guns, soap, mirrors, ribbons, and all kinds of articles of luxury, and then only, after these labourers shall have learned quickly and rapidly to produce mirrors and ribbons, but shall have become unfit to work the land, take possession of the land also.

5

However strange it is to see a working man who has abandoned a life in the country amidst the freedom of the fields, meadows, and woods, and who ten years later, sometimes even after several generations, rejoices when he receives from his master a little house in the infected air with a twenty-foot garden in which he can plant a dozen cucumbers and two sunflowers, — such a joy is comprehensible.

The possibility of living on the land, of gaining one's sustenance from it by means of one's own labour, has always

been and always will be one of the chief conditions of a
happy and independent human life. This all men have
always known, and so all men have always striven and
never stop striving and always will strive, like a fish for
the water, at least for the semblance of such a life.

But the socialistic doctrine says that for the happiness
of men they do not need such a life amidst plants and
animals, with the possibility of satisfying nearly all their
daily wants by means of their own agricultural labour,
but a life in industrial centres with infected air, and with
increasing and ever increasing demands, the gratification
of which is possible only by means of senseless labour in
the factories. And the working men who are enmeshed
in the temptations of their factory lives believe this and
use all their efforts in a miserable struggle with the
capitalists for the sake of hours of labour and additional
pennies, imagining that they are doing some very important work, whereas the only important work, for which
those working men who have been torn away from the
land ought to use all their forces, should consist in finding
a means of returning to a life amidst Nature and to
agricultural labour. "But," say the socialists, "even
if it were true that a life amidst Nature is better than a
life in a factory, there are now so many factory workmen,
and these men have abandoned agricultural life so long
ago, that their return to life on the land is now impossible.
It is impossible because such a transition will without
any necessity diminish the productions of the manufacturing industries, which form the wealth of the country.
Besides, even if this were not so, there is not enough free
land for the settlement and sustenance of all factory
workmen."

It is not true that the working men's resettlement of
the land will diminish the wealth of the country, because
life on the land does not exclude the possibility of the
labourers' participation, for a part of their time, in manu-

facturing labour at home or even in factories. But if, in consequence of this resettlement, the manufacture of useless and injurious articles, which now are produced with great rapidity in the great manufacturing plants, shall be diminished, and the now usual overproduction of necessary articles shall come to an end, while the amount of corn, vegetables, fruit, domestic animals, shall be increased, this will in no way diminish the wealth of people, but will only increase it.

But that argument that there will not be enough land for the settlement and sustenance of all the working men in factories is untrue, because in the majority of countries, (to say nothing of Russia, where the land retained by the large landed proprietors would suffice for all the factory working men in Russia and in the whole of Europe), and even in such countries as England and Belgium, the land which belongs to the large landed proprietors would suffice for the sustenance of all working people, if only the cultivation of this land were to be carried to that stage of perfection which it can attain with the present perfection of the mechanical arts, or even to that degree of perfection to which it was carried thousands of years ago in China.

Let those who are interested in this question read Kropótkin's books, *La conquête du pain* and *Fields, Factories, and Workshops,* and the very good book published by the *Posrédnik,* Popóv's *The Corn Garden,* and they will see how many times the productiveness of agriculture may still be increased with intensive cultivation, how many times the present number of men may be fed from the same plot of ground. The improved methods of cultivation will certainly be introduced by the small proprietors, if only they shall not be compelled, as they now are, to give all their income to the large landowners, from whom they rent the land and who have no need to increase the productiveness of the land from which they without any care derive a great income.

They say that there will not be enough free land for all working people, and so it is not worth while to worry about the land which is kept from them by the landowners.

This reflection is as if an owner of a house were to say concerning a crowd standing in a storm and in the cold in front of an unoccupied house and asking him to be allowed to take shelter in it: "These people must not be let in, because anyway they cannot all of them be accommodated in it." Let in those who beg to be let in, and then we shall see, from the way they locate themselves, whether all can be accommodated, or only a part. And even if not all can be accommodated, why should not those be admitted who can find room?

The same is true of the land. Give the land which is kept back from the working men to those who ask for it, and then we shall see whether this land is sufficient or not.

Besides, the argument about the insufficiency of land for the working people, who now work in factories, is incorrect in its essence. If the factory population now feed on bread which they buy, there is no reason why, instead of buying the grain which is produced by others, they should not themselves work the land on which the grain is produced and on which they feed, no matter where this land may be, in India, Argentina, Australia, or Siberia.

Thus all the arguments about why the workmen in the factories should not and could not go back to the land have no foundation whatever; on the contrary, it is clear that such a change not only could not be injurious to the common welfare, but would even increase it and would certainly do away with those chronic famines in India, Russia, and other places which more obviously than anything else show the irregularity of the present distribution of land.

It is true, where the manufacturing industry is particularly developed, as in England, Belgium, and a few States in America, the life of the working people has to such an extent been corrupted that the return to the land presents itself as very difficult. But the difficulty of such a return of the working men to an agricultural life by no means excludes the possibility of realizing such a change. For it to take place it is necessary for the working people first of all to understand that this change is indispensable for their good, and that they should find means for its realization, instead of accepting (as the socialistic doctrine now teaches them) their factory slavery as their eternal, immutable condition, which can be alleviated, but never destroyed.

Thus even the working men who have left the land and live by factory labour do not need unions, societies, strikes, childish processions with flags on the first of May, and so forth, but only this, — the finding of means for freeing themselves from their factory slavery and for settling on the land, the chief impediment to which is found in the seizure of the land by the owners who do not work it. This they should ask and demand of their rulers. And, in demanding this, they will not be demanding something not their own, not belonging to them, but the restitution of their most unquestionable and inalienable right, which is inherent in every animal, to live on the land and get their sustenance from it, without asking anybody else's permission to do so.

It is for this that the deputies of the working men ought to struggle in the parliaments; this ought to be preached by the press which stands on the side of the working men; for this the working men in the factories must prepare themselves.

Thus it is in the case of the labourers who have left the land. But for labourers, like the majority of the Russian labourers, ninety-eight per cent. of whom still live on the land, the question consists only in this, how they may be able to improve their condition, without abandoning their land and surrendering themselves to the temptations of a factory life.

For this one thing is needed, — to turn over to the labourers the land which is now held by the large landowners.

Talk in Russia with any peasant you meet, who is working in town, ask why he is not faring well, and he will invariably answer one and the same thing: " I have no land, nothing to put my hands to."

And here, in Russia, where the whole nation raises an unabated cry on account of the insufficiency of land, men who think that they are serving the masses do not preach to them about means for returning to them the land which has been taken away from them, but about methods for struggling in the factories with the capitalists.

" But should *all* men live in the country and busy themselves with agriculture ? " will say people who are to such an extent accustomed to the unnatural life of the men of the present time that this presents itself to them as rather strange and impossible. But why should not *all* men live in the country and busy themselves with agriculture ? However, if people shall be found with such strange tastes as to prefer the factory slavery to the life in the country, nothing will keep them from doing so. The only point is that every man should have a chance to live in human fashion. When we say that it is desirable that every man should have a family, we do not say that every man should get married and have children, but only, that we do not approve of a structure of society in which a man cannot have the chance to do so.

6

Even during the time of serfdom, the peasants used to say to their masters, " We are yours, but the land is ours," that is, they recognized that, no matter how illegal and cruel the possession of one man by another was, the right of a man to own land without working it was even more illegal and cruel. It is true, of late a few of the Russian peasants, imitating the landowners, have begun to buy land and to deal in it, considering the ownership of it to be legal, no longer afraid that it will be taken from them. But thus act only a few frivolous peasants who are blinded by greed. The majority, all the real Russian agriculturists, believe firmly that the land cannot and must not be the property of those who do not work it, and that, although now the land is taken away from the workers by those who do not work it, the time will come when it shall be taken away from those who now own it and shall become, as it ought to be, a common possession. And the Russian peasants are quite right in believing that this is so and should be so. The time has come when the injustice, irrationality, and cruelty of the ownership of land by those who do not work it has become as obvious as fifty years ago were obvious the injustice, irrationality, and cruelty of the ownership of serfs. Either because the other methods of oppression have been destroyed, or because the number of people has increased, or because men have become more enlightened, all (both those who own land and those who are deprived of it) see clearly what they did not see before, that if a peasant who has worked all his life has not enough grain, because he has no ground' on which to sow it, if he has no milk for the children and for the old, because he has no pasture, if he has not a rod of timber with which to mend his rotten cabin and keep it warm, while the neighbouring landowner, who does no work, lives on an immense estate, feeding milk to his puppies, building arbours and stables with plate-glass windows, raising sheep and establishing forests and parks on tens of thousands of desyatínas of land, spending in food in a week what would keep a famished neighbouring village alive for a whole year, — such a structure of life should not exist. The injustice, irrationality, and cruelty of such a state of affairs now startles everybody, just as formerly men were startled by the injustice, irrationality, and cruelty of serfdom. And as soon as the injustice, irrationality, and cruelty of any structure become clear to men, this structure will in one way or another come to an end. Thus ended serfdom, and thus very soon landed property will come to an end.

7

Landed property must inevitably be destroyed, because the injustice, irrationality, and cruelty of this institution have become too obvious. The only question is how it will be abolished. Serfdom and slavery, not only in Russia, but also in all other countries, have been abolished by order of the governments. And it would seem that the ownership of land could be abolished by a similar order. But it is not likely that such an order can or will ever be promulgated by a government.

All governments are composed of men who live by other people's labour, and it is the ownership of land that more than anything else makes it possible to lead such a life. It is not the rulers and the large landed proprietors alone who will not permit the abolition of landed property : men who have nothing in common with the government or with the ownership of land, officials, artists, scholars, merchants, who serve the rich, feeling instinctively that their advantageous position is connected with the ownership of land, either always defend the ownership of land, or, attacking everything which is less important, never touch the question of the ownership of land.

A striking illustration of such a relation to the question

on the part of the men of the wealthy classes may be found in the change that has taken place in the views of the famous Herbert Spencer concerning the ownership of land. So long as Herbert Spencer was a young beginner, who had no ties with the rich and the rulers, he looked upon the question of the ownership of land as every man who is not tied by any preconceived notions must look upon it: he rejected it in the most radical manner and proved its injustice. But decades passed, Herbert Spencer from an unknown young man became a famous writer, who established relations with rulers and large landed proprietors, and he to such an extent modified his views upon the ownership of land that he tried to destroy all those editions in which he had so forcibly expressed the correct ideas about the illegality of landed property.

Thus the majority of well-to-do people feel instinctively, if not consciously, that their advantageous position depends on the ownership of the land. To this is due the fact that the parliaments in their pretended cares for the good of the masses propose, discuss, and adopt the most varied measures which are to improve the condition of the masses, but not the one which alone really improves the condition of the masses and is indispensable to them, — the abolition of the ownership of land.

Thus, to solve the question about the ownership of the land, it is necessary first of all to destroy the consciously concordant silence which has established itself in regard to this question. Thus it is in those countries where part of the power is in the parliaments. But in Russia, where the whole power is in the hands of the Tsar, the provision for the abolition of the ownership of land is still less possible. In Russia the power is only nominally in the hands of the Tsar; in reality it is in the hands of a few hundreds of fortuitous men, relatives and near friends of the Tsar, who compel him to do what pleases them.

Now all these men own immense tracts of land, and so they will never allow the Tsar, even if he should wish to do so, to free the land from the power of the landed proprietors. No matter how hard it was for the Tsar who liberated the peasants to compel his retainers to give up the right of serfdom, he was able to do so, because these retainers did not give up the land. But in giving up the land, the retainers and the relatives of the Tsar know that they lose their last chance of living as they have been accustomed to live.

Thus it is absolutely impossible to expect the emancipation of the land from the government in general, and in Russia from the Tsar.

It is impossible by means of violence to take away the land which is retained by the landed proprietors, because the strength has always been and will always be on the side of those who have already seized the power. It is quite senseless to wait for the emancipation of the land to be achieved in the manner proposed by the socialists, that is, to be prepared to give up the conditions of a good life for the very worst in expectation of the sweet by and by.

Every rational man sees that this method not only does not emancipate, but more and more makes the working men the slaves of their masters, and prepares them for slavery in the future in relation to those managers who will have charge of the new order. It is still more senseless to wait for the abolition of the ownership of land from a representative government or from the Tsar, as the Russian peasants have been waiting for it for the last two reigns, because all the retainers of the Tsar and the Tsar himself own immense tracts of land, and, though they pretend to be interested in the welfare of the peasants, never will give them the one thing which they need, — the land, — because they know that without the ownership of the land they will be deprived of their ad-

vantageous position as idle men who enjoy the labours of
the masses.

What, then, are the working men to do in order to free
themselves from the oppression in which they are?

8

At first it seems that there is nothing to be done, and
that the working men are so fettered that they have no
possibility whatever of freeing themselves. But that only
seems so. The working men need only ponder on the
causes of their enslavement, to see that, besides riots, besides socialism, and besides the vain hopes in the governments, and in Russia in the Tsar, they have a means for
freeing themselves, such as no one and nothing can interfere with and as always has been and even now is in their
hands.

Indeed, there is but one cause for the wretched condition of the working men, — it is this, that the landed proprietors own the land which the working men need. But
what is it that gives the proprietors the possibility of
owning this land?

In the first place, this, that in case the working men
attempt to make use of this land they send for troops,
which will disperse, beat, and kill those working men who
have seized the land, and will return it to the landowners. Now these troops are composed of you, the
working men. Thus you yourselves, the working men,
by becoming soldiers and obeying the military authorities,
make it possible for the landed proprietors to own their
land, which ought to belong to you. (That a Christian
cannot be a soldier, that is, that he cannot promise to kill
his like, and must refuse to use weapons, I have written
about many times, among others in a pamphlet, *The Soldiers' Memento*, where I tried to prove from the Gospel
why every Christian should do so.)

But, besides your making it possible, by your participation in the army, for the proprietors to own the land which belongs to all men, consequently also to you, you also give this possibility to the proprietors by working on the proprietors' lands and by renting them. You, the labourers, need only stop doing so, and the ownership of the land will not only become useless for the proprietors, but also impossible, and their land will become common property. No matter how much the landed proprietors may try to substitute machines for labourers, and instead of agriculture to introduce cattle-raising and forestry, they none the less cannot get along without labourers, and they will one after another and willy-nilly give up their lands.

Thus the means for freeing you, the working men, from your enslavement consists only in this, that, having come to understand that the ownership of land is a crime, you must not take part in it, either as soldiers, who take the land away from the workers, or as labourers on the lands of the proprietors, or as tenants on these lands.

9

" But the means of non-participation, both in the army and in the work on the lands of the proprietors, as also in the hiring of lands, would be effective," I shall be told, " only in case all the working people of the world struck and refused to take part in the crimes, to work on the estates of the proprietors, and to rent land, and this is not the case and never can be the case. Even if a part of the working men should agree to abstain from participating in the army and from working on the land of the proprietors and renting it, the other working people, frequently the working people of other nationalities, will not find such a restraint necessary, and the ownership of the land by the proprietors will not be impaired. Thus the working people who will refuse to take part in the ownership of the land will only be deprived of their advantages in vain, without alleviating the condition of all." This retort is quite just, if it is a question of a strike. But what I propose is not a strike. I do not propose a strike, but that the working people shall refuse to take part in the army, which exercises violence against their brothers, and in working on the lands of the proprietors, in renting them, not because this is unprofitable for the labourers and produces their enslavement, but because this participation is a bad thing, from which any good man must abstain, just as he must abstain, not only from every murder, theft, robbery, and so forth, but also from participation in these acts. That the participation in the lawlessness of the ownership of land and its support are bad things there can be no doubt, if the working men will only ponder on the whole meaning of this their participation in the ownership of the land by the non-workers. To support the proprietors' ownership of the land means to be the cause of the privations and sufferings of thousands of people, of old men and children, who are insufficiently fed, and who work above their strength, and who die before their time, only because they do not get the land which has been seized by the proprietors.

If such are the consequences of the ownership of land by the proprietors, — and it is obvious to any one that they are such, — it is also clear that participation in the ownership of land by the proprietors and in its maintenance is a bad thing from which every man must abstain. Hundreds of millions of men without any strike consider usury, debauchery, violence against the weak, theft, murder, and many other things to be evil, and abstain from these acts. The working men ought to do the same in respect to the ownership of land. They themselves see the whole lawlessness of such ownership and consider it a bad, cruel business. So why do they not only take part in it, but even support it ?

10

Thus I do not propose a strike, but a clear consciousness of the criminality, the sinfulness of the participation in the ownership of land, and, in consequence of this consciousness, the abstaining from such a participation. It is true, such an abstinence does not, like a strike, at once unite all interested people in one decision and so cannot give those results, defined in advance, which are obtained by a strike, if it is successful; but, on the other hand, such an abstinence produces a much more lasting and continuous union than the one produced by a strike. The artificial union of men which arises at a strike comes to an end the moment the aim of the strike is attained; but the union, from a concordant activity or from abstinence in consequence of an identical consciousness, not only never comes to an end, but constantly grows stronger, attracting an ever increasing number of men. Thus it can and must be in the case of the working men's abstaining from taking part in the ownership of land, not in consequence of a strike, but in consequence of the consciousness of the sinfulness of this participation. It is very likely that, when the working men shall understand the lawlessness of participation in the proprietors' ownership of land, not all of them, but only a small part, will abstain from working on the proprietors' lands and from renting them; but since they will not abstain in consequence of an agreement, which has a local and a temporary significance, but from the consciousness of what is right and wrong, which is always and for all men equally binding, it will be natural for the number of working men, who will be shown by word and by example, both the illegality of the ownership of land and those consequences which arise from this illegality, to be constantly increasing.

It is absolutely impossible to foresee what change in

the structure of society will actually be produced by the working men's recognition that participation in the ownership of land is bad, but there is no doubt that these changes will take place and that they will be the more significant, the more this consciousness shall be diffused. These changes may consist in this, that at least a part of the working men will refuse to work for the proprietors and to rent land from them, and the landowners, no longer finding the ownership of land to be profitable, will either enter into arrangements with the working men which will be advantageous for them, or else will entirely give up the ownership of land. It is also possible that the working men who are enlisted in the army, having come to comprehend the illegality of the ownership of land, will more and more frequently refuse to take part in acts of violence against their brothers, the agricultural labourers, and the government will be compelled to abandon the protection of the proprietors' landed property, and the land of the proprietors will become free.

Finally, it may be that the government, having come to see the inevitableness of the emancipation of the land, will find it necessary to forestall the victory of the working men by lending it the aspect of its own decree, and will by law abolish the ownership of land.

The changes which can and must take place in the ownership of land, in consequence of the working men's recognition of the illegality of participation in the ownership of land, may be very varied, and it is difficult to foresee of precisely what character they will be, but one thing is unquestionable, and that is, that not one sincere effort of a man to act in this matter in godly fashion or in accordance with his conscience will be lost.

" What can I alone do against all ? " people frequently say, when they are confronted with an act which is not countenanced by the majority. To these people it seems that for the success of a thing there must be *all*, or at least *many;* but there must be many only for a bad thing. For a good thing it is enough if there be one, because God is always with him who does a good thing. And with whom God is, sooner or later all men will be.

In any case, all the improvements in the condition of the working men will take place only because they will themselves act more in conformity with God's will, more according to their conscience, that is, more morally, than they have acted before.

11

Working men have tried to free themselves by means of violence, of riots, and they have not attained their end. They have tried to free themselves by socialistic methods through unions, strikes, demonstrations, elections to parliaments, but all this at best only for a time alleviates the convict labour of the slaves, and not only does not free them, but even confirms the slavery.

The working men have tried, each one separately, to free themselves by supporting the illegality of the ownership of land, which they themselves condemn, and if the condition of a few, and that, too, not always and but for a brief time, is improved by such a participation in an evil thing, the condition of all only gets worse from it. This is due to the fact that what permanently improves the condition of men (not of one man, but of a society of men) is the activity which is in conformity with the rule that we should do unto others as we wish that others should do unto us. But all the three means which so far have been employed by the working men have not been in conformity with the rule about doing unto others as we wish that others should do unto us.

The means of the riots, that is, of the employment of violence against men who consider the land which they have received as an inheritance or have purchased with their savings to be their property, is inconsistent with the rule about doing unto others as we wish that others should do unto us, because not one man who takes part in the riots would like to have taken from him what he considers to be his own, the more so, since such a seizure is generally accompanied by cruel acts of violence.

Not less inconsistent with the rule about doing unto others as we wish that others should do unto us is the whole socialistic activity. It is inconsistent with this rule, in the first place, because, by putting at its basis class strife, it provokes in the working men such hostile feelings toward the masters and the non-workers in general, as on the part of the masters can in no way be desirable for the working men. It is inconsistent with this rule for this reason, also, that in the strikes the working men are very frequently, for the success of their undertaking, brought to the necessity of using violence against those working men, of their own nation or foreigners, who wish to take their places.

Similarly inconsistent with the rule about doing unto others what we wish that others should do unto us, and even outright immoral, is the doctrine which promises to the working men the transference of all the implements of labour, of the factories and works, into their full possession. Every factory is the product of the labour, not only of many working men of the present, those who have built the factory and have prepared the material for its construction, and then of the men since its construction, but also of a vast number of mental and manual working men of former generations, without whose work no factory could exist. There is absolutely no possibility of figuring out the part of all men in the working of a factory, and so, according to the doctrine of the socialists themselves, every factory, like the land, is the common possession of the whole people, with this one difference, that the ownership of land can be abolished at once, without waiting for the socialization of all the implements of labour; but a factory can become the legal possession of the people only when the unrealizable fancy of the socialists shall be achieved, — the socialization of all, literally all, the implements of labour, — and not as is proposed by the majority of working socialists, when they shall have seized the factories of their masters and shall have made them their own. A master has no right whatever to own a factory, but just as little right have the working men to any factory whatever, so long as the unrealizable socialization of the implements of labour is not an accomplished fact.

For this reason I say that the doctrine which promises to the working men the seizure of those factories in which they work, previous to the socialization of all the implements of labour, as is generally proposed, is not only a doctrine which is contrary to the golden rule of doing unto others as we would that others should do unto us, but even downright immoral.

Similarly inconsistent with the rule about doing unto others as we would that others should do unto us is the working men's support of the ownership of land, be it by means of violence in the form of soldiers, or in the form of labourers or tenants on the land. Such a support of the ownership of land is inconsistent, because, if such acts for a time improve the condition of those persons who perform them, they certainly make the condition of other working men worse.

Thus all the means which have heretofore been used by the working men for the purpose of their liberation, such as direct violence and the socialistic activity, as well as the acts of separate individuals who for the sake of their advantage maintain the illegality of the ownership of land, have not attained their purpose, because they have all been inconsistent with the rule of morality about doing unto others as we would that others should do unto us.

What will free the working men from their slavery is

not even an activity, but the mere abstinence from sin,
because such abstinence is just and moral, that is, in
conformity with God's will.

12

" But want ! " I shall be told. No matter how convinced a man may be of the illegality of the ownership
of land, it is hard for him, if he is a soldier, to keep from
going whither he is sent, and from working for the
proprietors, if this work may give milk for his starving
children. Or how can a peasant abstain from renting the
proprietor's land, when he has but half a desyatína to
each soul and knows that ho cannot support his family
on the land which he owns ? It is true, this is very hard,
but the same difficulty is met with in refraining from any
bad thing. And yet men for the most part abstain from
anything bad. Here the abstinence is less difficult than
in the majority of bad acts, but the harm from the bad
act — the participation in the seizure of land — is more
obvious than in many bad acts from which people refrain.
I am not speaking of the refusal to participate in the army,
when the troops are sent out against the peasants. It is
true, for such a refusal it takes more than ordinary courage
and a readiness to sacrifice oneself, and so not everybody
is able to do so, but, on the other hand, the cases when
this refusal is to be applied are rarely met with. But it
takes much less effort and sacrifice not to work on the
proprietors' lands and not to rent them. If all working
men fully comprehended that working for the proprietors
and renting their lands are bad, there would be fewer and
fewer people ready to work on the proprietors' lands
and to rent them. Millions of people live without having
any need of the proprietors' lands, busying themselves at
home with some trade or attending to all kinds of industries away from home. Nor do those hundreds of thou-

sands and millions of peasants feel any need of the proprietors' lands, who, in spite of the whole difficulty of this matter, leave their old places and go to new places, where they get all the land they wish and where they for the most part do not suffer, but even grow rich, soon forgetting the want which drove them out. Even those peasants and good farmers live without working for the proprietors or renting their lands, who, though having but little land to till, live abstemiously and work their land well and so are not in need of any work for the proprietors or of renting their lands. Other thousands live without having any need of working on the proprietors' lands and of renting them, — the men who live a Christian life, that is, living, not each for himself, but aiding one another, as live in Russia many Christian Communes, of whom the Dukhobors are especially known to me.

There can be want only in a society of men who live according to the animal law of struggling against one another, but among Christian societies there ought to be, no want. As soon as men divide among themselves what they have, everybody always has what he needs, and much is still left. When the people who heard Christ's sermon grew faint with hunger, Christ, upon learning that some of them had provisions, commanded that all should sit down in a circle and that those who had the provisions should give them to their neighbours on one side, in order that the neighbours, having appeased their hunger, might hand them to those farther away. When the whole circle was made, all had their hunger appeased, and much was still left over.

Even so in the society of men who act similarly there can be no want, and such people do not need to work for the proprietors or rent their lands. Thus want cannot always be a sufficient reason for doing what is harmful to one's brothers.

If the working people now go and work for the proprietors and rent their lands, they do so only because not all of them have come to understand the sinfulness of their acts or the whole evil which they are doing to their brothers and to themselves by it. The more there shall be such men and the more clearly they shall understand the significance of their participation in the ownership of land, the more and more will the power of the non-workers over the workers destroy itself of its own accord.

13

The only sure, indubitable means for improving the condition of the working men, which, at the same time, is consistent with God's will, consists in the emancipation of the land from its seizure by the proprietors. This emancipation of the land is attained, not only through the working men's refusal to take part in the army, when the army is directed against the working people, but also by abstaining from working on the proprietors' lands and from renting them. But it is not enough for you, the working men, to know that for your good you need the liberation of the land from its seizure by the proprietors, and that this liberation is attained through your refraining from committing acts of violence against your brothers and from working on the lands of the proprietors and renting them; you must also know in advance how to manage the land when it shall be freed from seizure by the proprietors, how to distribute it among the workers.

The majority of you generally think that all that is necessary is to take the land away from the non-workers, and all will be well. But that is not so. It is easy to say: "Take the land away from the non-workers and give it to those who work it." But how is this to be done, without violating justice and without giving the rich again a chance to accumulate great extents of territory and thus again to rule over the workers? To leave it, as some of you think, to each individual worker or society to mow or plough wherever it be, as was done anciently and is even now done among the Cossacks, is possible only where there are few people and there is much land and the land is all of one quality. But where there are more people than the land can support, and the land is of varying quality, it is necessary to find a different means for the exploitation of the land. To divide the land according to the number of men? But if the land is divided up according to the number of men, it will also come into the hands of those who do not know how to work it, and these non-workers will let it or sell it to the rich purchasers, and there will again appear people who own large tracts of land and who do not till it. To prohibit the non-workers to sell or let the land? But then the land which belongs to a man who does not wish or is unable to work it will lie unused. Besides, in dividing the land up according to the number of men, how is it to be estimated according to its quality? There is black loam, fruitful land, and there is sandy, swampy, sterile land; there is land in the cities, which brings as much as one thousand and more roubles income from each desyatína, and there is land in the backwoods, which does not bring any income. How, then, is the land to be distributed in such a way that there may not again arise the ownership of land by those who do not work it, and that there may not be such as are improperly treated, that there may be no discussions, quarrels, civil wars? Men have for a long time been busy discussing and solving these questions. For the correct distribution of land among the workers many projects have been proposed.

To say nothing of the so-called communistic projects of the construction of society, in which the land is regarded a common possession and is worked by all men in common, I am acquainted also with the following projects: The project of the Englishman, William Ogilvie, who lived in the eighteenth century. Ogilvie says that, since every man, in being born into this world, in consequence of this has the full right to be there and to live by what it produces, this right cannot be limited by some people's regarding great tracts of land as their property. For this reason everybody has the free right to own such a plot of land as falls to his share. But if a person owns a greater extent of land than falls to his share, exploiting those plots to which the men who have a right to them make no claim, the owner should pay the government a tax for this possession.

Another Englishman, Thomas Spence, a few years later solved the land question by recognizing the land to be the property of parishes which could dispose of it as they pleased. In this way the private possession of separate individuals was completely abolished.

As a beautiful illustration of Spence's view concerning the ownership of land may serve the account of what happened with him in the year 1788 at Haydon Bridge, which he calls a "Sylvan Joke."

"While I was in the wood alone by myself a-gathering of nuts, the forester popped through the bushes upon me, and, asking me what I did there, I replied, 'Gathering nuts.'

"'Gathering nuts!' said he, 'and dare you say so?'

"'Yes,' said I, 'why not? Would you question a monkey or a squirrel about such a business? And am I to be treated as an inferior to one of these creatures, or have I a less right? But who are you,' continued I, 'that thus take it upon you to interrupt me?'

"'I'll let you know that,' said he, 'when I lay you fast for trespassing here.'

"'Indeed,' answered I, 'but how can I trespass here where no man ever planted or cultivated; for these nuts are the spontaneous gift of Nature, ordained alike for the sustenance of man and beast that choose to gather them, and, therefore, they are common.'

" ' I tell you,' said he, ' this wood is not common. It belongs to the Duke of Portland.'

" ' Oh ! My service to the Duke of Portland,' said I. ' Nature knows no more of him than of me. Therefore, as in Nature's storehouse, the rule is " first come first served," so the Duke of Portland must look sharp if he wants any nuts.' "

Spence, in conclusion, declared that if he were called upon to defend a country in which he durst not pluck a nut, he would throw down his musket, saying, " Let such as the Duke of Portland, who claim the country, fight for it ! "

The question was similarly solved by the famous author of *Age of Reason* and *Rights of Man*, Thomas Paine. The peculiarity of this solution consisted in this, that in recognizing the land to be a common possession, he proposed to abolish the right of the ownership of land by separate individuals in that the possession of land could not be passed by inheritance, and the land, which was private property, at the death of the owner became the possession of the nation.

It was Patrick Edward Dove, in our century, who was the next, after Thomas Paine, to write and think about this subject. Dove's theory consists in this, that the value of the land is due to two sources, — to the property of the land itself and to the work put into it. The value of the land due to the work which is put into it may be the possession of private individuals; but the value of the land which is due to its properties is the possession of the whole nation and so can never belong to separate individuals, as it is now supposed to be, but must be the common possession of the whole nation.[1]

[1] This information is taken by me from a beautiful English book by a modern writer, John Morrison Davidson, *Precursors of Henry George. — Author's Note.*

Such also is the project of the Japanese Land Reclaiming Society, the essence of which consists in this, that every man has the right to own as much land as is apportioned to him, on condition of paying for it an established tax, and so has the right to demand the allotment to him of his share of land by him who has more than the share allotted to each person. But the best, justest, and most applicable project, in my opinion, is the one by Henry George, which is called the Single Tax.

14

I personally consider Henry George's project the justest, most beneficent, and, above all, most easily applied of all the projects of which I know anything. This project may on a small scale be imagined as follows: let us imagine that in some locality the whole land belongs to two proprietors, one, very rich, who lives abroad, and the other, who is not well off and who lives and farms at home, and to a hundred peasants, who own small tracts. Besides, this locality is inhabited by a few dozen landless men, who serve and live in rented houses, — artisans, traders, officials. Let us assume that all the inhabitants of this locality, having come to the conclusion that the whole land is a common possession, have decided in conformity with this conviction to manage the land.

What shall they do?

It is impossible to take the land away from those who own it and to allow anybody to use the land he likes, since there will be several candidates to the same tract, and there will be endless dissensions. It is inconvenient for all to unite into one coöperative society and to plough, mow, and harvest in common, and then to divide up, because some have ploughs, horses, carts, while others do not have them, and, besides, some of the inhabitants do not know how to till the land, and have not the strength to do so. So, too, it is very difficult to divide the land according to the number of persons into such holdings as by their quality would be equal among themselves. If for this the whole land is divided up into small plots of various quality, so that each should get a plot of the best, and one of mediocre, and one of bad land, and one of field, and mowing, and woodland, there will be too many such tiny plots.

Besides, such a division is dangerous, because those who do not wish to work or who are in great need will for money turn over their land to the rich, and large landed proprietors will again come into existence.

And so the inhabitants of the locality decide to leave the land in the hands of those who now own it, but oblige each owner to pay into the common treasury an amount of money which represents the income which (according to the valuation of the land, not according to the labour put into it, but according to its quality and location) the owners derive from the land in use by them, and this money they decide to divide into equal parts. But since such a collection of money from all the owners of the land and its subsequent equal distribution among the inhabitants is troublesome, and since, besides, all the inhabitants pay out money for common needs, — schools, churches, fire departments, shepherds, mending of roads, and so forth, and such money for public purposes is always insufficient, the inhabitants of the locality decide, instead of collecting the income from the land and distributing it to all and again collecting a part of it for taxes, to collect and use the whole income from the land on common necessities. Having established themselves in this manner, the inhabitants of the locality demand from the proprietors a fixed payment for the land in their possession, as also from the peasants who own small holdings; but nothing is demanded from the few dozen men who do not own any land, they being permitted to use gratis all that which is supported from the income on the land.

This arrangement has the effect of making it unprofitable for the proprietor who does not live in the country, and who produces little on his land, under the land tax, to continue holding his land, and he gives it up. But the other proprietor, who is a good farmer, gives up only a part of his land, and retains only that part of it on which he can produce more than what is demanded of him for the land cultivated by him.

But those of the peasants who own small tracts, and who have many workers, but little land, as also some who have no land, but wish to support themselves by means of work on the land, take up the land which is given up by the proprietors. Thus, with such a solution, all the inhabitants of this locality find it possible to live on the land and to support themselves from it, and the whole land passes over into the hands or remains in the hands of those who like to till it and are able to produce much on it. But the public institutions of the inhabitants of the locality improve, since more money is obtained for public needs than before, and, above all else, all this transference of landed property takes place without any disputes, quarrels, interference, or violence, but by the voluntary abandonment of the land by those who do not know how to cultivate it profitably.

Such is Henry George's project in its application to the separate state or even to all humanity. This project is just and beneficent, and, above all, easily applied everywhere, in all societies, no matter what order of agriculture may be established there.

For this reason I personally consider this project to be the best of all those in existence. But this is my personal opinion, which may be faulty. But you, the working men, will, when the time shall come to attend to the land, discuss for yourselves these and all other projects, and will choose the one which you will consider the best, or you will yourselves discover a juster or more applicable one.   The reason I have explained these projects more in detail is, that you, working men, understanding on the one hand the whole injustice of the ownership of land, and, on the other, the whole difficulty and complexity of a just distribution of the land, may not fall into those errors of a thoughtless distribution of the land, which would make your condition, in consequence of the struggle for the land by separate individuals and of land seizures in the new order, worse than what it is at present.

15

I shall briefly repeat the essence of what I wanted to say to you.   The essence of what I wanted to say to you is this, that I advise you, the working men, in the first place, to understand clearly what it is you need, and not to labour to obtain what is absolutely unnecessary for you ; you need but this one thing, — free land, on which you may be able to live and support yourselves.

In the second place, I advise you to understand clearly in what way you may be able to obtain the land you need.   You can obtain the land, not through riots, from which God save you, not through demonstrations, nor strikes, nor socialistic deputies in parliaments, but only through non-participation in what you yourselves consider to be bad, that is, by not supporting the illegality of the ownership of land, either by means of violence exerted by the army, or by working on the proprietors' lands and renting them.

In the third place, I advise you to consider in advance how you will distribute the land when it becomes free.

For you to be able correctly to consider this, you must not think that the land which will be abandoned by the proprietors will become your property, but must understand that, for the use of the land to be regularly and without bias apportioned among all men, the right to own land, though it be but one square rod, should not be acknowledged in the case of any one. Only by recognizing the land as just such an article of common possession as the sun and air will you be able, without bias and justly, to establish the ownership of land among all men, according to any of the existing projects or according to some new project composed or chosen by you in common.

In the fourth place, and this is most important, I advise you, for the purpose of obtaining everything you need, to direct your forces, not to a struggle with the ruling classes by means of revolts, revolutions, or socialistic propaganda, but only to yourselves, to how you may live better.

People fare badly only because they themselves live badly. And there is no more injurious thought for people than that the causes of the wretchedness of their position is not in themselves, but in external conditions. A man or a society of men need but imagine that the evil experienced by them is due to external conditions and to direct their attention and efforts to the change of these external conditions, and the evil will be increased. But a man or a society of men need but sincerely direct their attention to themselves, and in themselves and their lives look for the causes of that evil from which they suffer, in order that these causes may be at once found and destroyed.

"Seek ye the kingdom of God and His righteousness, and all these things shall be added unto you." This is the fundamental law of human life. If you live badly, contrary to God's law, no efforts of yours will procure for you the well-being for which you are seeking. If you live well, morally well, in accordance with God's will and making no efforts for the attainment of this well-being, it will naturally establish itself among you, and at that in a way you have never thought of.

It seems so natural and simple to push against the door behind which is that which we need, and the more natural, since back of us stands a crowd that is pressing against us and jamming us against the door. However, the more stubbornly we press against the door behind which is that which we consider a good, the less hope there is to penetrate through it. The door opens toward us.

Thus, to obtain the good, a man must not trouble himself about the change of external conditions, but only about changing himself: he must stop doing what is evil, if he is doing it, and must begin to do good, if he is not doing it. All the doors which lead men to the true good open only outwardly.

We say, the working people are enslaved by the government, by the rich; but who are these men who form the government and the wealthy classes? Are they heroes, each of whom can vanquish tens and hundreds of working people? Or are there very many of them, while there are but few working men? Or are these men, the rulers and the wealthy, the only ones who know how to make everything necessary and to produce everything the people live by? Neither the one, nor the other, nor the third. These men are no heroes, but, on the contrary, weakened, helpless people, and not only are they not numerous, but they are even hundreds of times fewer than the working people. And everything which men live by is produced not by them, but by the working men, while they are both unable and unwilling to do anything, and only devour what the working men produce. Why, then, does this small band of feeble, idle men, who cannot and will not do anything, rule over millions of working men? There is but one answer to this: it is due to the fact that the working men are in their life guided by the same rules and laws by which their oppressors are guided. If the working men work and do not exploit the labours of the poor and the feeble to such an extent as do the non-working rulers and the wealthy, this is not due to the fact that they consider this bad, but because they cannot do it so well as the rulers and the rich, who are more agile and cunning than the rest. The rulers and the rich rule the working people only because the working people wish in precisely the same manner to rule their own fellows, the working men. For this same reason — the equal comprehension of life — the working men are unable successfully to rebel against their oppressors. No matter how hard it is for the working man to be oppressed by the rulers and the rich, he knows in his heart that he himself would act similarly toward his brothers, or that in a small way he is acting thus toward them. The working people have fettered themselves by their desire to enslave one another, and so it is easy for the shrewd people who have already got them in their power to enslave them. If the working people did not consist of enslavers exactly like the rulers and the rich, who are concerned only about exploiting their neighbour's want for the purpose of establishing their own well-being, but lived in a brotherly way, thinking of one another and mutually offering aid, no one would be able to enslave them. And so, to free themselves from the oppression in which they are held by the rulers and the rich, the working people have but one means, — to free themselves from those principles by which they are guided in their lives, that is, to stop serving mammon and begin serving God.

The pretended friends of the people tell you, and you yourselves — at least a few of you — say to yourselves, that the present order must be changed, that you must take possession of the implements of labour and of the land, and that you must overthrow the present government and establish a new one. And you believe this, and you hope and work for the attainment of these ends. But let us assume that you will attain what you wish, that you will overthrow the present government and will establish a new government, and that you will take possession of all the factories, works, and the land. Why do you assume that the people who will form the new government will be guided by new principles different from those by which the present men are guided? And if they shall be guided by the same principles, they will, like those of the present, not only retain, but also strengthen their power, and will for their advantage extract as much from their power as they can. Why do you assume that the people who will have charge of the factories, of the land (all men cannot manage all institutions), being people with just such views as the men of the present, will not find, as at present, means for seizing the lion share, leaving to the humble and meek only what is indispensable. I shall be told: "It will be so arranged that it will be impossible to do so." But see how well all was arranged by God Himself, or by Nature, — the ownership of the earth by all who are born and live upon it, — and yet people have been cunning enough to violate this divine arrangement. And so thousands of means for distorting the human order will always be discovered by those men who in their lives are guided by nothing but care for their personal well-being. No modifications of the external order will ever improve or ever can improve the condition of men. And so my fourth and most important advice to you, working men, consists in this, that, without condemning other people, your oppressors, you should direct your attention to yourselves and change your inner lives.

If you think that it is lawful and useful forcibly to take away and appropriate to yourselves what has been taken from you and is retained by force; or, if you think that, following the teaching of erring men, it is lawful and useful to take part in the struggle of the classes and to strive after the acquisition of the implements of labour created by others; if you think that, serving as soldiers, you are obliged to obey the authorities, who compel you to offer violence to your brothers and kill them, and not to obey God, who commands you not to do so; or if you think that, in maintaining the lawlessness of the ownership of land by your work on the lands of the proprietors and by renting them, you are not doing anything wrong, — your condition will become worse and worse, and you will for ever remain slaves.

But if you come to understand that for your true good you need only live a brotherly life according to God's law, doing unto others what you wish should be done to you, — then in the measure in which you will understand this and, understanding this, will execute it, will also that good be realized which you wish for, and your slavery be destroyed. "Ye shall know the truth, and the truth shall make you free."

Yásnaya Polyána, September, 1902.

RELIGION AND MORALITY

1894

RELIGION AND MORALITY [1]

ADD to vol. xix. p. 517, after the second paragraph

" To the word 'religion' three different meanings are generally ascribed.

" The first is this, that religion is a true revelation, given by God to men, and the divine worship which results therefrom. Such a meaning is ascribed to religion by men who believe in some one of the existing religions, and who, therefore, consider this religion to be the one true religion.

" The second meaning ascribed to religion is this, that religion is a code of certain superstitious propositions and the superstitious worship of God, which results from these propositions. Such a meaning is ascribed to religion by men who do not believe at all or who do not believe in the religion which they define.

" The third meaning ascribed to religion is this, that religion is a code of propositions and laws, invented by wise men, which are necessary for the coarse popular masses, both for their consolation and for the restraint of their passions and their control. Such a meaning is ascribed to religion by men who are indifferent to religion, but who consider it a useful tool of state.

---

[1] After this article, given in vol. xix. p. 517, had been printed, the translator succeeded in getting a copy of the Swiss edition, which contains all the passages rejected by the Russian censor. These are given below, and thus an exact idea may be gained of the manner in which the Russian censor deals with " objectionable " passages.

" According to the first definition, religion is an undoubted, incontrovertible truth, which it is desirable and even obligatory for the good of men to disseminate among them with every possible means.

" According to the second definition, religion is a collection of superstitions from which it is desirable and even obligatory for the good of humanity to free men with every possible means.

" According to the third definition, religion is a certain useful appliance, which, though it is not necessary for the men of higher development, is indispensable for their government, and which, therefore, it is necessary to maintain.

" The first definition resembles the one a man would make of music, by saying that music is that song which he knows well and likes and which it is desirable to impart to as many people as possible.

" The second is like the definition of music made by a man who does not understand and so does not like it, when he says that music is the production of sounds by means of the throat and mouth, or by means of the hands on a certain instrument, and that it is necessary as quickly as possible to teach people to give up this useless and even injurious occupation.

" The third is what a man would do to music, by saying that it is a useful thing for the teaching of dancing or for marching and that it ought for this reason to be kept up.

" The difference and the insufficiency of these definitions are due to this, that none of them cover the essence of music, but all of them define only its symptoms, according to the view-point of the defining person.   Even so it is with the definitions of religion.

" According to the first definition, religion is what the man who defines it rightfully believes in.

" According to the second definition, it is what, according to the observations of the definer, other people wrong-fully believe in.

"According to the third definition, it is what it is use-ful to make other people believe.

"In all three definitions what is defined is not the essence of religion, but men's faith in what they consider to be religion. With the first definition they substitute for the concept of religion the faith of him who defines religion; with the second definition, the faith of other people in what the others regard as religion; with the third definition, the faith of men in what is given out to them as religion.

"But what is faith? And why do people believe in what they do believe in? What is faith, and how did it arise?"

P. 522, l. 27, after "Romans" add: "our ecclesiastic-governmental religion, which was reduced to this stage by Augustine, though it is called by an improper name, — Christian."

P. 523. l. 1, after "Rome," add: "all the complex Jewish ritualism, which has for its aim the preser-vation of the covenant of the chosen nation with God, all the domestic and public church-Christian suppli-cations for the welfare of the state and the success of arms."

P. 523, l. 19, after this paragraph add:

"All the rites of the ancient religions which result from this comprehension of life, and all the modern external forms of communion by the Unitarians, Univer-salists, Quakers, Servian Nazarenes, Russian Dukhobors, and all so-called rationalistic sects, all their sermons, singing of psalms, talks, and books are religious manifes-tations of this relation of man to the world."

P. 525, l. 13, after "mediæval," add: "church-Christian."

P. 526, l. 16, after "society," add: "under the name of Christian."

Ib. l. 27, after "calling," add: "The church-Christian science has been an investigation of those conditions under which man's salvation is obtained."

P. 528. l. 9, after "Schopenhauer," add: "as was assumed by the most highly cultured bishops."

P. 529, l. 28, after "Renascence," add: "have recognized as the essence of Christianity its grossest distortion."

Ib. l. 30, after "social," add: "governmental."

P. 532, l. 11, after "social," add: "and governmental."

Ib. l. 14, after "but," add: "this domestic-governmental, that is."

P. 535, l. 13, after "another," add: "and not to leave the hazy region of metaphysics."

P. 538, l. 32, after "prove," add:
"Mr. Huxley in the innocence of his soul imagines that in the present English society, with its Ireland, popular poverty, senseless luxury of the rich, its opium and whiskey trade, its executions, its conquest and destruction of nations for commercial and political advantages, its latent corruption and hypocrisy of men, a man who does not violate the demands of the police is a moral man and that this man is guided by an ethical law, forgetting that the qualities which may be necessary to

preserve the society in which this member lives may be useful for the society itself, as the qualities of the members of a robber band are useful, as even in our society the qualities of hangmen, jailers, judges, soldiers, hypocritical priests, and so forth, are useful, but these qualities have nothing in common with morality."

Ib. l. 35, change " any external means " to " means of the gibbet and the axe."

P. 529, l. 2, after "morality," add: "On the contrary, every violation of the existing orders, not only such as was the violation by Christ and His disciples of the orders of the Roman province, but also such as is the violation of the present orders by a man who refuses to take part in a court, in military service, in the payment of taxes used for military preparations, will not only not be contrary to morality, but even will be a necessary condition of its manifestation."

Ib. l. 4, after "society," add: "And so the acts which violate the order of every society may be immoral."

P. 540, l. 13, after "forms," add: "There they kill with arrows and knives, and here with famine."

P. 541, l. 32, change "morality" to "humanity," and add:
"Indeed, it would be desirable to have a moral teaching without any admixture of superstitions, but the point is that the moral teaching is only the result of a certain established relation of man to the world or God. If the establishment of such a relation is expressed in forms which to us appear superstitious, we must, in order that this may not be so, try to express this relation more sensibly, clearly, and precisely, or even, having destroyed

the now inadequate, older relation of man to the world,
put in its place a higher, clearer, and more sensible
relation, but we must not by any means invent the so-
called worldly, irreligious morality, which is based on
sophisms or on nothing at all."

A FEW WORDS CONCERNING THE BOOK "WAR AND PEACE"

1868

A FEW WORDS CONCERNING THE BOOK "WAR AND PEACE"

IN printing the work on which I have spent five years of constant and exclusive labour, under the best conditions of life, I should like in the introduction to this work to expound my view upon it and thus to disperse the misunderstandings which may arise in the readers. I wish my readers would not see or seek in my book what I did not want or could not express, and would direct their attention to what I meant to convey, but (considering the conditions of the production) did not think it suitable to dwell on. Neither my time nor my skill permitted me to do in full what I had intended to do, and I will make use of the hospitality of this special periodical for the purpose of expounding, even though briefly and incompletely, the author's view of his production for those readers who may be interested in the matter.

1. What is *War and Peace?* It is not a novel, still less is it a poem, still less a historical chronicle. *War and Peace* is what the author wanted and could express in the form in which it is expressed. Such an announcement as to the author's neglect to attend to the conventional forms of an artistic prose production might appear

as a bit of self-confidence if it were intentional and if it had no precedent. The history of Russian literature since the time of Púshkin not only furnishes many examples of such a departure from the European form, but does not offer even a single contrary example. Beginning with Gógol's *Dead Souls* and ending with Dostoévski's *Dead House*, in the new period of Russian literature, there is not a single artistic prose production, which ever so little rises above mediocrity, that is completely arranged in the form of a novel, epic, or story.

2. The character of the time, as some readers said to me at the appearance of the first part in print, is not sufficiently defined in my work. To this rebuke I have the following answer to make: I know in what consists that character of the time which is not found in my novel,— the horrors of the serf right, the immuring of wives, the flogging of grown sons, Saltýchikha, and so forth; but this character of that time, as it lives in our imagination, I do not consider correct and did not wish to express. In studying letters, diaries, and traditions, I did not find all the horrors of this savagery to any greater extent than I find them at present or at any other time. In those days they also loved, envied, searched after the truth and virtue, were carried away by passion; there was also a complex, mental, and moral life; at times even more refined than at present in the upper class. If in our conception there has been formed an opinion of arbitrariness and brute force as regards that time, this is so only because in the traditions, memoirs, stories, and novels there have come down to us exaggerated cases of violence and brutality. To conclude that the prevailing character of that time was brutality is as incorrect as it would be for a man, who beyond a mountain sees nothing but the tops of trees, to conclude that in that locality there is nothing but trees. There is a character of that time (just as there is a character to every epoch), which

results from a greater alienation of the upper circle from
the other classes, from the ruling philosophy, from the
peculiarities of education, from the habit of using the
French language, and so forth. It is this character that
I tried to express as well as I could.

3. The use of the French language in a Russian production. Why in my work do not only Russians but also
Frenchmen speak partly Russian and partly French? The
reproach that persons speak and write French in a Russian
book is like the reproach a man would make, who, looking at a picture, sees black spots (shadows) on it, which
do not exist in reality. The artist is not to blame because
to some the shadow which is made by him on the face
of the picture appears as a black spot, which does not
exist in reality; the artist is to blame only if these
shadows are put on wrongly and coarsely. Busying myself with the epoch of the beginning of the present century, and representing Russian persons of a certain class
of society and Napoleon and the French, who took such
a direct part in the life of that time, I was involuntarily
carried away more than was necessary by the form of
expression of that French manner of thinking. And so,
without denying that the shadows put on by me are in
all likelihood incorrect and coarse, I wish only that those
to whom it will appear funny that Napoleon speaks now
Russian and now French should know that this only
seems so to them, because, like a man who is looking at
a portrait, they do not see the face with its lights and
shadows, but see a black spot under its nose.

4. The names of the acting persons, Bolkónski, Drubetskóy, Bilíbin, Kurágin, and so forth, remind one of
well-known Russian names. In confronting acting non-
historical persons, with other historical persons, I felt the
awkwardness for the ear of making Count Rostopchín
speak with Prince Prónski, with Stryélski, or with some
other princes and counts, of an invented double or single

family name. Bolkónski or Drubetskóy, although they
are neither Volkónski nor Trubetskóy, sound familiar and
natural in the Russian aristocratic circle. I was unable
to invent for all persons such names as would seem to
me to be false to the ear, such as Bezúkhi and Rostóv,
and I was not able to avoid this difficulty in any other
way than by taking at random names which were most
familiar to the Russian ear and changing a few letters in
them. I should be very sorry if the similarity between
the invented names and the real ones could give any
one the idea that I wanted to describe this or that actual
person; especially, since that literary activity which
consists in the description of actually existing persons has
nothing in common with the one I busied myself with.

M. D. Akhrosímov and Denísov are the only persons
to whom I involuntarily and without thinking gave
names that closely approach two extremely characteristic
and charming actual persons of the society of that time.
That was my mistake, which arose from the peculiar
intrinsic character of these two persons, but my mistake
in this respect is limited to the mere introduction of these
two persons. All the other persons are purely invented,
and have not even for me any definite prototypes in tradition or reality.

5. My divergence in the description of historical events
from the narrative of the historians. It is not accidental,
but inevitable. The historian and the artist, in describing
a historical epoch, have two entirely different subjects
before them. Just as the historian will be wrong if he
shall try to represent a historical person in all his entirety,
in all the complication of his relations to all the sides of
life, so also will the artist not fulfil his work, if he always
represents a person in his historical significance. Kutúzov did not always ride a white horse, with a field-glass
in his hand, pointing to the enemy. Rostopchín did not
always, with a torch in his hand, burn the Voronóvski

House (he even never did that), and Empress Márya Fédorovna did not always stand, clad in an ermine mantle, leaning with one hand on the code of laws; but it is as such that the popular imagination represents them to itself.

For the historian there are heroes, in the sense of people who contribute to some one purpose; but for the artist there cannot and must not be a hero, but must be a man, in the sense of this person's correspondence with all the sides of life.

The historian is at times obliged, by bending the truth, to subordinate all the actions of the historical person to the one idea which he has put into this person. The artist, on the contrary, in the very singleness of this idea finds an incompatibility with his problem and only tries to comprehend and show, not a certain actor, but a man.

In the description of the events themselves the distinction is still more sharp and essential.

The historian has to deal with the results of the event, the artist with the fact of the event. The historian, in describing a battle, says: " The left flank of such and such an army was moved toward such and such a village, defeated the enemy, but was compelled to retreat; then the cavalry which was sent to the attack overthrew," and so forth. The historian cannot speak otherwise. And yet these words have no meaning for the artist and do not even touch upon the event itself. Either from his own experience, or from letters, memoirs, and stories, the artist deduces his own conception about the course of the event, and frequently (as in the example of the battle) the deduction about the activity of such and such armies, which the historian permits himself to make, turns out to be the very opposite to the artist's deduction. The difference of the results obtained is also to be explained from those sources from which the two draw their information. For the historian (we continue the example of the battle) the chief source is found in the reports of the private commanders and of the commander-in-chief. The artist can draw nothing from such sources,—they tell him nothing, explain nothing to him. More than that: the artist turns away from them, as he finds in them a necessary lie, to say nothing of the fact that every battle is described by the two enemies in absolutely opposite ways. In every description of a battle there is a necessity of lying, which results from the demand for a description in a few words of the actions of thousands of men scattered over several versts and acting under the strongest moral incitement, under the influence of fear, shame, and death.

In the descriptions of battles they generally say that such and such armies directed their attack upon such and such a point, and then they were commanded to retreat, and so forth, as though assuming that that discipline which submits tens of thousands of men to the will of one man on the parade-grounds will have the same effect where life and death are in the scale. Everybody who has been in a war knows how untrue that is;[1] and yet, on this assumption are based the reports, and upon them the military descriptions. Make the round of the troops immediately after a battle, even on the next day, or the day after, before the reports are written out, and ask all the soldiers, the superior and inferior commanders, how the affair took place; you will be told what all these men experienced and saw, and you will form a majestic, complex, infinitely varied and heavy, indistinct impression,

---

[1] After my first part was printed with the description of the battle of Schöngraben, I was told of the words of Nikoláy Nikoláevich Muravév-Kárski concerning this description of the battle, — words which confirmed for me my conviction. Nikoláy Nikoláevich Muravév, the commander-in-chief, said that he had never read a more correct description of a battle, and that he had become convinced through his own experience that it is impossible during a battle to carry out the orders of the commander-in-chief. — *Author's Note.*

and from no one, least of all from the commander-in-chief, will you find out how the affair took place. But two, three days later they begin to bring in the reports, the talkers begin to tell how that happened which they did not see; finally a general report is made out, and from this report the general opinion of the army is formed. It is a relief for any one to exchange his own doubts and questions for this deceptive, but clear and always flattering representation. Question a man who has taken part in this battle a month or two later, and you will no longer feel in his story that raw vital material which there was before, for he is telling it now in accordance with the report. Thus I was told about the battle of Borodinó by many wide-awake, clever participants in the battle. They all told one and the same thing, in accordance with the incorrect description of Mikhaylóvski-Danilévski, Glínka, and others; even the details which they told, though the narrators were several versts distant from one another, were all the same.

After the loss of Sevastopol, the commander of artillery, Kryzhanóvski, sent me the reports of the officers of artillery from all the bastions, asking me to make up a report from these more than twenty separate reports. I am sorry I have not described these reports. This was the best example of that naïve, unavoidable, military lie from which descriptions are made up. I assume that many of my comrades who at that time made up those reports will, as they read these lines, laugh at the recollection of how they, by order of the authorities, wrote what they could not know. All those who have experienced a war know how capable Russians are of doing their work in a war and how little fit they are to describe it with the necessary boastful lie. Everybody knows that in our armies this duty of writing out the reports is for the most part attended to by men of foreign birth.

All this I say in order to show the inevitableness of

the lying in military descriptions, which serve as material
for the military historians, and, therefore, to show the
inevitableness of frequent disagreements between the artist
and the historian in the comprehension of historical events.
But besides the inevitableness of the untruth in the exposition of historical events, in the historians of the epoch
in which I was interested, I observed (no doubt in consequence of the habit of grouping events, of expressing them
briefly, and of complying with the tragic tone of the events)
a special form of soaring diction, in which the lie and the
distortion frequently pass, not only to the events, but even
to the comprehension of the meaning of the events. In
studying the two chief historical productions of this epoch,
Thiers and Mikhaylóvski-Danilévski, I frequently mar-
velled how such books could have been printed and read.
To say nothing of the fact that they treated the same events
in a most serious, significant tone, with references to mate-
rials, and yet were diametrically opposed to one another,
I came across such descriptions in these historians that I
did not know whether to laugh or weep, considering that
these two books are the only monuments of this epoch
and have millions of readers. I will adduce but one
example from the book by the famous historian Thiers.
After telling how Napoleon brought with him counterfeit
assignats, he says, " *Relevant l'emploi de ces moyens par un
acte de bienfaisance digne de lui et de l'armée française, il
fut distribuer des secours aux incendiés. Mais les vivres
étant trop précieux pour être donné longtemps à des étrangers, la plupart ennemis, Napoleon aima mieux leur fournir
de l'argent, et il leur fit distribuer des roubles papier.*"
This passage is striking in itself by its stupendous, I
shall not say immorality, but simply stupidity; but in the
whole book this is not so startling, because it fully cor-
responds to the general, soaring, solemn tone of the
discourse, which makes no direct sense.
Thus the problem of the artist and of the historian in

the description of events and persons in my book must not startle the reader.

But the artist must not forget that the representation of historical events, as formed among the people, is not based on fancy, but on historical documents, to the extent to which the historians have been able to group them; therefore, though the artist understands and represents these persons and events differently, he must, like the historian, be guided by historical material. Wherever historical persons in my novel speak and act, I have not invented, but have made use of material of which during my work a whole library has been formed, the books of which I do not find it necessary to cite here, but to which I can always refer.

6. Finally, the sixth and most important consideration for me refers to the small significance which, according to my ideas, is to be ascribed to so-called great men in the historical events.

In studying that epoch, so tragical, so rich in the grandeur of its events, and so near to us, in regard to which there live so many varied traditions, I arrived at the evident fact that the causes of the historical events, as they take place, are not accessible to our reason. To say (what to everybody seems very simple) that the causes of the events of the year 1812 consist in Napoleon's spirit of conquest and in the patriotic firmness of Emperor Aleksándr Pávlovich is as senseless as to say that the causes of the fall of the Roman Empire are these, that a certain barbarian led his nations to the west, and a certain Roman Emperor mismanaged the state, or that an immense hill which is being torn down fell because the last labourer struck it with his spade.

Such an event, where millions of people killed one another and in all killed half a million, cannot have for its cause the will of one man: just as one man could not have torn down the hill, so one man cannot cause five

hundred thousand men to die.   But what are the causes?
Some historians say that the cause was the French spirit
of conquest, the patriotism of Russia.   Others speak of
the democratic element which Napoleon's hosts carried
abroad and of the necessity for Russia of entering into an
alliance with Europe, and so forth.   But how did millions
of people begin to kill one another, — who told them to
do so?   It is possible to make an endless number of
retrospective conclusions as regards the causes of this
senseless event, and these conclusions are actually made;
but the great majority of these explanations and their
coincidence in one purpose only proves that there is an
endless number of these causes and that not one of them
may be called the cause.

Why have millions of people killed one another, when
it has been known ever since the creation of the world
that this is both physically and morally bad?

Because that has been inevitably necessary, because,
doing so, men have performed an elementary, zoological
law, the one performed by the bees, when they destroy
one another in the autumn, and the one according to
which the male animals destroy one another.   It is
impossible to give any other answer to this terrible
question.

This truth is not only apparent, but is so inherent in
every man that it would not be worth while to prove
it, if there did not exist another sentiment in man, which
convinces him that he is free at any moment, whenever
he is acting.

In viewing history from a common point of view, we
are unquestionably convinced of the Pre-eternal Law according to which events take place.   Looking at it from
the personal point of view, we are convinced of the
opposite.

A man who kills another, Napoleon who gives the
order to cross the Nyeman, you and I, petitioning about

a governmental appointment, raising and dropping our arms, are unquestionably convinced that every act of ours has for its base rational causes and our free will, and that it depended on us whether we should act in this manner or in that, and this conviction is to such a degree inherent in us and dear to every one of us that, in spite of the proofs of history and of the statistics of crimes (which convince us of the absence of freedom of the will in the acts of other men), we extend the consciousness of our freedom to all our acts.

The contradiction seems insoluble. In committing an act I am convinced that I commit it according to my will; but viewing this act in the sense of its participation in the general life of humanity (in its historical signifi- cance), I am convinced that this act was predetermined and inevitable. Where is the error?

The psychological observations concerning man's ability on the spur of the moment retrospectively to find a whole series of imagined free ratiocinations for an accomplished fact (this I intend to expound at a greater length in another place) confirm the assumption that man's con- sciousness of freedom, in the commission of a certain kind of acts, is erroneous. But the same psychological observations prove that there is another series of acts in which the consciousness of freedom is not retrospective, but sudden and unquestionable. No matter what the materialists may say, I am always able to commit an act or to keep from it, so long as the act refers to me alone. I have unquestionably by nothing but my will just raised and dropped my arm. I can at once stop writing. You can at once stop reading. Unquestionably I have by nothing but my own will and regardless of all obstacles just transferred myself mentally to America or to any de- sired mathematical question. I can, testing my freedom, raise and forcibly drop my hand in the air. I did so. But near me stands a child, and I raise my hand over him, and I want to drop it upon him with the same force. I cannot do so. A dog makes for this child, and I cannot help raising my hand against the dog. I am standing in the battle-line and I cannot help following the motions of the regiment. I cannot avoid in a battle making an attack with my regiment and running, when all men about me are running. When in the court-room I stand as a defender of a defendant, I cannot stop talking or knowing what I am going to say. I cannot help winking when a blow is directed against my eye. Thus there are two kinds of acts: some that depend on my will, others that do not depend on it. And the mistake which produces the contradiction is due only to this, that the consciousness of freedom (which legitimately accompanies every act that refers to my ego, up to the highest abstractions of my existence) is involuntarily transferred by me to my acts which are committed in conjunction with other men and which depend on the coincidence of other free wills with my own. It is very hard to determine the border between freedom and dependence, and the determination of this border forms the essential and only problem of psychology; but, observing the conditions of the manifestation of our greatest freedom and greatest dependence, it is impossible to avoid seeing that the more our activity is abstract and therefore the less it is connected with the activities of other men, the more it is free; and, on the other hand, the more our activity is connected with the activities of other men, the less free it is.

The most potent, indissoluble, heavy, and constant bond with other men is the so-called power exerted by one set of men against another, which in its true meaning is but the greatest dependence upon others.

Whether this is faulty or not, having become fully convinced of it in the course of my work, in describing the historical events of the years 1805, 1807, and es-

pecially 1812, in which this law of predetermination
appears boldly in relief,[1] I was unable to ascribe any
significance to the acts of those men to whom it seemed
that they guided the events, but who less than all the
other participants of the events introduced into it a free
human activity. The activity of these men was interesting to me only as an illustration of that law of predetermination which in my opinion guides history, and of that
psychological law which compels a man who commits a
most un-free act to find in his imagination a whole series
of retrospective ratiocinations, the purpose of which is to
prove his freedom to himself.

[1] It is worthy of note that nearly all those who have written about
the year '12, have seen in this event something peculiar and fatal. —
Author's Note.

VERSES

VERSES

I. [1]

As in the presence of the rose
   The onion vainly feels regret,
So I feel shame to meet in prose
   Your challenge, my beloved Fet.

And thus I'll answer you in rhyme, —
   My first attempt, — which makes me fret:
Decide yourself where? at what time?
   Be sure you come to see us, Fet.

What care I if the summer's wet
   Or dry, and I lose all my corn,
So long as I can walk with Fet,
   And talk with him from morn till morn?

We worry both our lives away, —
   The future sorrows may beget, —
Sufficient is unto the day
   The evil of it, comrade Fet.

---

[1] Only the first number is authentically Tolstóy's. It was written in 1872. The second is given on the authority of Behrs, Tolstóy's brother-in-law. It was supposed to have been written at Sevastopol. The third has been shown to have originated in conjunction with other officers. It is impossible to ascertain which of these lines were composed by Tolstóy himself.

II.

On September, day the eighth,
Fighting for our Tsar and faith,
 From the French we fled.

And so bravely we departed
That the wounded men who started
 In the steppe fell dead.

Ménshik, admiral the sane,
In the deep and briny main
 Scuttled every ship.

" Luck to you," so Ménshik said,
To Bakchisaráy he fled,
 " . . . take you all ! "

Saint Arnot, — he acted squarely, —
For he left the trenches early,
 Flanked us from behind.

He'd have taken us, no doubt,
Had our saint not helped us out
 On that fateful day.

And they stormed from land and sea
Sevastopol mightily
 With enormous guns.

And the clergy with devotion
Prayed to God to shake the ocean
 And to drown the French.

Up then sprang a mighty gale,
But the French lost not a sail
 On the stormy sea.

Grand dukes came to bluff the French,
But the enemy did not blench,
 Firing off their guns.

Sharpshooters we needed sadly,
But the Guard did want them badly, —
  Took them all from us.

We were waiting for a throng
Speedily to come along
  Down from Kishinév.

Dánenberg they told outright
To proceed with them and fight,
  Sparing not a man.

Sóymonov and Pávlov went
Up a steep and hard ascent,
  And they never met.

And Liprándi, who was told
That the French were getting bold,
  Did not lend a hand.

Some ten thousand were laid low,
So the Emperor did not show
  Any grace to us.

And the Grand Duke, he got mad,
" Ours have turned their backs," he said,
  " Are not worth a fig."

From this great and bloody scrape
Only two came out in shape, —
  Their two Highnesses.

With St. Georges decorated
They were taken to be fêted
  To St. Petersburg.

In the winter we rushed out, —
Soldiers fell in many a rout
  Near the gabions.

Reinforcements Ménshik needed ;
His request the Emperor heeded, —
  Sáken was despatched.

Ménshik, admiral the sly,
Wrote the Tsar a tart reply:
　　" Bátyushka our Tsar,

" Erofyéich is too dense,
And your babies have no sense,
　　They do me no good."

Ménshik's letter made him mad,
At the muster he looked sad,
　　And at once grew ill ;

Then the Tsar to heaven sped,
Where they wanted him, though dead, —
　　Wished him long ago.

And before the Tsar was gone,
He spoke firmly to his son:
　　" You be on your guard ! "

So the son to Ménshik wrote :
" I don't care for you a groat,
　　Damn you, admiral !

" I will soon despatch another, —
Gorchakóv, who did so bother
　　Formerly the Turks.

" He will get no mighty host:
He is glad if he can boast
　　Pants of crimson hue."

Even though they sent Khrulév,
Drive we could not from Kozlóv
　　Any of the Turks.

Work we shall unto the end,
Sevastopol to defend, —
　　Maybe they will run.

III.

On the fourth we sallied out,
Carried by the devils' rout,
　　Mounts to occupy.

Baron Vrévski was commanding
Gorchakóv, who then was standing
   At the mountain's foot:

"Prince, this mountain you must seize, —
No discussions, if you please,
   Or you'll be denounced."

All big guns with epaulette
Solemnly in councils met, —
   Even Chief Bekók.

And Commandant Chief Bekók
Tried to say something, — got stuck,
   Did not say a word.

Long they counselled what to do,
Which topographers all drew
   On a map of war.

This war map was nice and clean, —
How to get through the ravine
   They forgot to say.

Forward hastened princes, counts,
And topographers on mounts
   To the great redoubt.

Gorchakóv said: "Go, Liprándi!"
But Liprándi, "No, *attendez*,
   I don't want to go;

"For that job there is no need
Of a clever man; send Read, —
   I'll be looking on."

Read without a moment's doubt
To the bridge ran with a shout:
   "Rush it with 'hurrah!'"

Weimar wept and begged of Read
Not to rush; he did not heed:
   "No, I cannot stop."

Merrily we yelled "hurrah,"
The reserves remained away, —
    Some one was at fault.

Of whole regiments did arrive
But two companies alive
    At Fedyúkhin Heights.

Ushakóv the general, —
He was not afraid at all
    Waiting for a change.

And he could not wait much longer,
And his heart grew strong and stronger,
    And he crossed the rill.

And Byelávtsov shook the flag
Like a piece of dirty rag, —
    'Twas not nice at all.

Our army was not strong,
When the Frenchmen rushed along,
    And no succour came.

From the garrison, we thought,
A fresh column would be brought,
    And we gave the sign.

General Sáken had a scare,
He read prayer after prayer
    To the Holy Maid.

We were pressed and had to run
 .   .   .   .   .   .
    Whither we were led.

We did wait at Fot-Salá
For our bátyushka the Tsar, —
    He came on the first.

Everybody with emotion
Was expecting some promotion, —
    Did not get a thing.

LEV N. TOLSTÓY

An Analysis of His Life and Works by the
Translator

Portrait of Tolstóy

Photogravure from a Photograph taken in 1895

LEV N. TOLSTÓY

An Analysis of His Life and Works by the
Translator

I.

THERE is a well-known philological phenomenon by
which exactly opposite meanings may bo dorivod from
one and the same root, not by any *lucus a non lucendo*
method, but booauoe a slight shifting of an emphasis frequently leads to an inversion of the idea under consideration. It is by a similar process that Tolstóy's life and
works have been interpreted from diametrically opposite
sides. Some would make us believe that Tolstóy is a
modern saint, while others decry him as a mountebank
and hypocrite. If we are to believe one set of authors,
Tolstóy is a far-sighted statesman, a practical Christian, a
trenchant critic of the existing order of things, an educator of marvellous insight, an artist, and a profound art
critic ; while others prove to us persuasively that his
teachings are subversive of all order, that his Christianity
is the claptrap of the sectarian verbalist, that he is a
dreamer and does not know anything about the actual
state of affairs, that he is an indifferent teacher, that his
productions rarely rise above mediocrity, and that as an
art critic he is absolutely wrong. According to some
he belongs to the same category of writers as Dostoévski,

Turgénev, and the rest of the great Russian authors, while according to others he stands outside all literary circles and traditions.

This great diversity of opinions is by no means confined to foreign critics, for even in Russia Tolstóy is viewed variously, and what adds there to the confusion of him who would get an exact picture of the man is the strange fact that contrary conceptions are held by the same individuals. Thus the men of state, who see in him a harmless, impractical fanatic, none the less fear him as a tremendous power, to whose insidious activity they would ascribe much of the present agitation. So, too, the revolutionists and liberals, who stand at the opposite pole of political wisdom from the one pointed out by Tolstóy, and who differ widely from him in all practical questions, are quick to recognize him as a factor in the liberation of the country and have placed his name at the head of their constitutional programmes, as that of one who augurs the greatness of the new Russia.

Wherever the truth may be, it is obvious that only a nature of gigantic proportions could give rise to such varied valuations. But here we are again confronted with the question as to how much Tolstóy's peculiar genius is the outcropping of a soil rich in literary talent, such as Russia has been the home of since the forties of the nineteenth century, how much originality we should ascribe to the author's ideas, which show direct obligations to a large number of foreign writers, mainly American, and how much influence he is exerting, or likely to exert, in his own country and abroad. The answer is fraught with many difficulties, as so far little or no attention has been directed to this aspect of Tolstóy's activity, and these difficulties are still further enhanced for an American, because, in spite of the remarkable parallelism of the intellectual movements of the two countries in the last 150 years, literature has had such widely different functions in Russia that it is not always easy for an American correctly to appraise any given literary production or the whole literary activity of a Russian author.

That the Russian and the American intellectual life have many points in common must be apparent even to the casual observer. While Franklin developed an astounding energy in every imaginable field of human endeavour, Lomonósov wrote tragedies, poetry, and history, taught in the academy and lectured, established laboratories and investigated, simultaneously with Franklin, the electricity of the clouds. What Benjamin Rush and other men of his stamp did for the young American republic was, at the end of the reign of Catherine (who, by the way, gave a commission to the American naval hero, John Paul Jones), inaugurated by the zealous band of Masons, by men like Nóvikov, and Radíshchev's *Journey from St. Petersburg to Moscow* advocated reforms which Benjamin Rush helped to inaugurate in Pennsylvania, among them the abolition of slavery.

Alexander I.'s offer to mediate in the American war of 1812, which was contemporaneous with the French invasion of Russia, was not a mere whim of the emperor, but was based on his genuine interest in everything American, as is evidenced by his request to be given a draft of the American constitution, which Thomas Jefferson sent him, and by his great partiality to Americans visiting Russia, to one of whom, Poinset, he offered any commission he would be willing to accept. The interest of Russians in America, first shown by Radíshchev, who in his work refers to the United States, and evinced by Alexander, was quite apparent in the first quarter of the nineteenth century, when Polétika, a member of the famous literary society of the "Arzamas," of which Púshkin and other distinguished authors were members, passed a number of years in the United States and wrote one of the first books on America. This work, written originally in

French, but, as the author said, intended for his Russian fellow citizens, interested even people in America, where, in the year 1826, it was translated into English.

Again, the abolition movement in the United States ran parallel with the agitation for the emancipation of the serfs in Russia, and Harriet Beecher Stowe's *Uncle Tom's Cabin* finds its counterpart in Turgénev's and Grigoróvich's peasant stories; indeed, Grigoróvich was even called the Russian Beecher-Stowe. While the agitation for freeing the slaves culminated in America in the Civil War, the same agitation for the emancipation of the serfs ended in Russia simultaneously in their being set free.

We have so far traced the chronological parallelism in the intellectual movements in the two countries and have pointed out the great share that America has had in the literary life of Russia up to the sixties. But the divergencies, even up to that time, and certainly later, are more patent than the resemblances. Why, if Russia has kept in close contact with what has been going on in the United States and has drawn largely on its intellectual resources, has Russian literature developed so differently from American literature, and why has Russian political and social life not taken the same direction as in America? The elucidation of these questions will make it possible for us to find the proper setting for Tolstóy's activity, will clearly define his position in the Russian intellectual life, and will show us his indebtedness to American thought.

Revolt is the dominant note in a nation's forward movement toward a better future. Without revolt there can be no progress. A breaking away from established customs, beliefs, practices, is necessarily accompanied by a certain amount of violence. This opposition to stagnation may find its expression as revolt, reform, or protest, and in its acute stage rises to Revolution, Reformation, Protestantism, which mark the end of the old, and the beginning of the new, era. A revolution, the culmination of a long period of systematic protestations, is brought about in consequence of continued political action or by a thorough ferment of men's minds through literary means, or by both factors at the same time. Where political life has been able to evolve itself, the revolt partakes more of the nature of action; where that has not been the case, the revolt finds its expression chiefly through the written word.

Here precisely lies the difference between the evolution of liberty in the United States and in Russia. In America, with the inherited English political life, protests have even been made by political pamphlets, by means of the ephemeral press, by public meetings, — by resolutionizing, — and, in extreme cases, by an appeal to arms. Literature, that is, belles-lettres, with the probable exception of *Uncle Tom's Cabin*, has never entered into the arena of political struggle, and it would puzzle an American to hear one speak of a Democratic or a Republican literature. But countries like Russia have had neither the liberty to express their views collectively nor the historical training necessary for concerted action. Whatever progress has been made in Russia has invariably proceeded from a small, mentally energetic group of men who have reached out to larger and ever larger masses by means of the written word in its most attractive form, the belles-lettres, which alone could be accessible to the whole intellectual class of readers.

Thus we are led to formulate the lemma that literature stands in inverse proportion to the political life of a nation. The more vigorous the political action is, the more does literature fade as a factor of progress; the less developed a nation is politically, the more does literature come to the front as the all-absorbing subject of intellectual life. In America literature has ever been the mental sport of men of letters, and has served as a means of amusement or refinement for the leisure class. In

Russia it has, at least through the last three quarters of the nineteenth century, been the solemn occupation of men working for definite social and political purposes, and has served, not as a means for pleasantly passing the time, but as instruction, as the confession of the heart, as a species of national wisdom, as the forum of public opinion, for all those who read. While the chief purpose of literature in America has been to create laughter (witness the large number of humourists), Russian literature, with but rare exceptions, provokes tears, — tears of contrition, tears of despair, tears of emotion, but always tears.

When, toward the end of the eighteenth century, something like public opinion was beginning to formulate itself in Russia, it found its expression in satires, calling into life a whole series of satirical journals, and in comedies, which dealt with the same reverse sides of the national existence. At a time when in America the new wine of political freedom led to the practical realization of advanced ideas in the foundation of schools, in the upbuilding of states and cities, in the extension of commercial enterprises to most distant countries, Russia was concentrating all her efforts on the development of her literary resources. The reign of Alexander I., so famous for the gigantic struggle with the French intruder, is far more important as the period when all kinds of literary productions feverishly contended with one another for supremacy, when every foreign influence was brought to bear on the development of the national literature, when the pseudo-classic, the Romantic, the Sentimental schools existed side by side, when translations from the Greek, the Latin, the Italian, the German, the English, reached the highest possible linguistic perfection, — when the whole foundation was laid for a distinctly Russian literature.

But even then, when the youthful fervour of the

creative genius revelled in form rather than in contents, we clearly perceive the new mission that Russian belles-lettres were to have as a school of liberty for the people. As early as the end of Cathcrine's reign, Radíshchev, whose *Journey from St. Petersburg to Moscow* smacked too much of Franklin, as Catherine expressed it, and advocated reforms which were carried out in the emancipation of the serfs, suffered exile for his liberal views. Púshkin, who in his younger years fully comprehended his office of a poet to be that of a champion of liberty, was banished to the south of Russia. Rylyéev, whose ardent muse was devoted to patriotic songs, joined the Decembrist revolt and lost his life together with the other revolutionists.

The literary activity evolved in Russia during the reign of Nicholas I. differs even more widely from the literary activity of America for the same period. The poetry of the two countries, at least for the earlier part of the second quarter of the century, offers many parallels. Bryant, Whittier, Lowell, Longfellow, bear much resemblance to Púshin, Lérmontov, and the other poets of the period ; but very soon Russian poetry, though not discontinued, falls entirely into the background, overshadowed by the more powerful prose and put to rout by the incisive analysis of the Russian critics, while in America, where the cry against art for art's sake was not seriously considered, poetry, the same kind of poetry as before, and every kind of poetry, continues unabated to give its periodic crops. The revolt is voiced by Whitman alone, who thus is more akin to the Russian spirit. American prose, when, like Emerson's, it is not in a lighter vein, is accessible only to the choice spirits of refined society, and the social, political, religious revolts find their expression in the byways of literature, entirely escaping the attention of the public at large. The protest against the existing order leads to the formation of communities, such as the

Brook Farm, the Hopedale Community, the communities of the Perfectionists, or engages men, like William Lloyd Garrison, in a vigorous, untiring propaganda by public speeches and political pamphlets, or, as in the case of Parker, restricts the agitation to the narrower circle of the church. In Russia men like Ballou, Garrison, Parker would have become the shining lights of literature.

Meanwhile the Russian critics were applying aquafortis to the theory of art for art's sake, completely reducing the splendid poetry of the first third of the century to mere literary lees. The belles-lettres were put under tribute to the critics, who henceforth acted as appraisers and censors of every nascent genius. It was in the thirties that Russian youths first came in contact with German philosophy and that Schelling and Hegel dictated the terms on which all literary activity in Russia was to develop, and the authors hastened to apply these German ideas to their productions with much more zeal than was done in Germany itself. Russians have ever shown a readiness to adopt foreign ideas and make them much more thoroughly the basis of action than they are in the countries of their birth. Thus Sterne's sentimentalism, and Göthe's *Werther's Leiden* gave rise to Karamzín's *Poor Líza*, with the pilgrimage of hundreds of readers to Líza's Pond, the imaginary spot where the action of the story took place; Byron's romanticism found its perfervid advocates in Púshkin and Lérmontov, and gave rise to the ultra-romantic novels of Bestúzhev-Marlínski and the ultra-romantic love-affairs of the author himself. Moleschott and Büchner played havoc with the generation of men in the sixties, and Turgénev has given us a picture of such an ultra-materialism in Bazárov, the hero of his *Fathers and Sons*.

Several causes have brought about this unusual zeal for new ideas, chief among which are the absence of political, social, cultural traditions and the inherent rationalism of the Russian mind. Both causes preclude the principle of compromise, which has played such an important part in the evolution of Anglo-Saxon life. The clearly outlined class traditions and the readiness to accept ecclesiastic, political, and social fictions, which are common in English-speaking countries, make compromise a matter of necessity, for, to have one's idiosyncrasies respected, it is indispensable that those of one's neighbours be respected as well. This tendency to compromise, to consider expediency, rather than abstract truth and justice, leads the Anglo-Saxon to emphasize the practical side of life, to value an idea according to its immediate applicability.

For the Russian, compromise has no meaning. What nucleus of class tradition there may have existed previous to the reforms of Peter the Great was carried away by the introduction of distinctions of rank (the *chins*), which are granted only for service. This absence of a class tradition has remained permanent, because the successive generations of men of culture have been recruited from different centres and have been shifted from the higher nobility in the eighteenth century to the gentry in the first half of the nineteenth century, and since then to the men of various ranks, including the peasants since their emancipation. So constant and so complete has been the shifting of intellectualism that there have not existed any common points between fathers and sons, so that the very name of *Fathers and Sons* served Turgénev as the basis for what he intended to be the most characteristic Russian novel of the time. The bureaucracy, too, though forming a more compact body than any other class in the state, has always been recruited from all the different classes and has never been self-perpetuating. Thus neither social, nor cultural, nor political traditions have found any favourable soil in Russia, and the question of compromise has not been urgent.

Not only have the so-called "practical" considerations been inactive in Russian life, but there have also been positive incitements to the enthronement of reason, justice, and truth independently of their applicability and practical convenience. Even in the most remote past one is struck by the extremely rational sense of the Russians. The early chronicles startle one by their realistic narration, which is evidently based on actual participation in the events or on the reports of eye-witnesses. Nikítin's account of his journey to India could not have been written with greater straightforwardness at the present time, and stands in remarkable contrast to Marco Polo's story, which precedes Nikítin's by less than a century. The pilgrimage of Daniel the Palmer to Jerusalem is a remarkable document which baffles one by its modernness. Not less rational is the Russian peasant. It is only his ignorance, which is fostered by state and church, that keeps him down to a low level of life; the moment he frees himself from the incubus of state and church, he develops a remarkable mental activity, interprets the Gospel without reserve of thought or of action, and lives up to his convictions. By far the best part of the Russian peasant population is to be found among the dissenters, the Dukhobors, the Milkers, the Stundists, the Lashers, some of whom, by a wrong interpretation of Gospel tenets, carry their convictions to such excess that they commit self-mutilation and self-destruction. In the same way have the intellectuals of Russia unswervingly followed the dictates of their reason, independently of any consequences and making no concessions to the opinions of their antagonists.

Russia presents many examples of this uncompromising spirit: the ineradicable hostility between the bureaucracy and the intellectuals, the hopeless and useless Decembrist revolt, the mad daring of the Nihilists and Revolutionists, the wicked persecutions of the Greek Catholic Church, and the dogged passive opposition of the dissenting sects all bear witness to the unbending, indomitable mental attitude of the average Russian. With such material, it would seem, the liberal tendencies once expressed would inevitably lead in the end to victory, and all actions would be carried to their logical consequences. That would, indeed, be the case, if certain negative qualities in the Russian character, vacillation and aimlessness, did not constantly undo what is categorically dictated by reason.

Periodically there have appeared in Russia novels which centre about an individual intended as the personification of the average Russian. Such have been Púshkin's *Evgéni Onyégin*, Lérmontov's *The Hero of Our Time*, Herzen's *Who Is to Blame?* Gon<charóv's *Oblómov*, Turgénev's *Fathers and Sons*, Chernyshévski's *What Is to Be Done?* In all of these the heroes suffer from the fatal national vice, which leaves their activity unfinished and which puts to naught all their good endeavours by leading them to cheerless, hopeless resignation. The writer of these lines, like many other Russians, was probably more affected, during the formative period of his life, by Goncharóv's *Oblómov* than by any other book. He felt that Oblómov, with all his good intentions, but with his indolence, his vacillation, his aimlessness, was he himself; that he was certainly moving fast in the direction taken by the hero of the novel, and that there were no forces within him to save him from the pool of stagnation.

So long as this vacillation and fatalistic indolence was confined to the upper classes, as was the case in the beginning of the nineteenth century, the hero of the novel was an aristocratic Lovelace or a blasé Byronian who ascribed his despondency to a satiety with the artificial conditions of society. But in the thirties the educated young men, having come in contact with German philosophy, no longer lived the careless life of gentlemen :

they were anxious to tear themselves away from the slough of inactivity, they wanted to do something. Of this type are the heroes described in *Who Is to Blame?* and in *Oblómov*. Meanwhile a strong democratic sentiment was sweeping the whole country, and the "people," by which term the lower classes, preëminently the peasants, were meant, became the watchword for those who were endeavouring to find a useful activity for themselves.

The aristocratic feeling among the upper classes had never been very strong, as the previously mentioned bureaucratic régime of distinctions of rank seriously interfered with the consolidation of the nobility. The only permanent superior arbiter of thought and action was the class of the intellectuals, which kept shifting lower down in the social scale. The disintegration of the social classes, which was going on at a rapid rate, steadily removed the intellectuals, recruited from the upper social layers, from solidarity with their own nobility. It was evident to them that Russia was not to be found characteristically in the privileged minority, and yet these men must belong somewhere. They certainly could not ally themselves with Germany, from which country chiefly proceeded their new philosophical bias, since they not only differed from the Germans in language, but more especially in those foibles which, on the one hand, appeared to them as peculiarly Russian, and which, on the other, made them look with horror and contempt upon the precision and methodical ways of their German neighbours. Outside the amorphous nobility and the shifting class of the intellectuals were the vast, uncouth, unfathomed masses of the peasant. Here alone, if anywhere, was the pith of the Russian nation, the "people."

Those who, like Herzen, keenly felt their obligation to the West for their enlightenment, devoted themselves to the uplifting of the masses on a European basis.

Though recognizing the inherent qualities of the Russian peasant, these Westerners thought it necessary to raise them to a higher level, to Europeanize them. Others, the Slavophils, rejected all European admixture as foreign to the Russian spirit, and devoted all their interest to the masses, in so far as these differed from themselves and from the West. But the Slavophils made the grave mistake of regarding Greek Catholicism and autocracy as equally distinguishing features of Russia, and of ascribing the same potency to church and state that they ascribed to the people. Thus they inevitably led to retrogression, no matter how well-intentioned they may have been. However, the fact remains that the peasants, the "people," henceforth became the preoccupation of the intellectuals and the men of letters.

Tolstóy was born in 1828. His first literary production appeared in 1852. Thus his youth fell in a time when the ferment of men's minds was at its highest. The aristocratic circle to which he belonged no longer was the sole possessor of culture, for the men of the various ranks were meeting with those from the upper classes on the same intellectual level. Slavophils and Westerners were in the heyday of their democratic transports, vying with one another in giving expression to their love for the masses. Democracy, pervading all classes of society, was clamouring for the emancipation of the serfs. Men were anxious to do something, especially to improve the condition of the peasants, but their efforts were generally abortive, in consequence of the fatal national defects of vacillation and aimlessness. Revolt, intellectual revolt at least, was the dominant note of all literary endeavour, and literature absorbed the functions elsewhere assumed by political economy, philosophy, religion. Such was the soil from which the great genius of Russia was to sprout.

II.

MANY an attempt has been made to write a life of Tolstóy, but it cannot be said that a biography of the man has as yet been presented to the reader. The facts, sufficiently concrete for the first part of the author's life, pale by the time maturity is reached, and, as years proceed, entirely fade away. The intenser the internal life becomes, the less tangible is the relation of Tolstóy's thoughts to the incidents in his life, the less weight can we ascribe to the chronology of a brief three-score and ten. "The law of progress, of perfectibility, is written in the soul of each man, and is transferred to history only through error," says Tolstóy. Substitute man's material existence for history, and we get the reason why biography, the counterpart of history, must of necessity cover but a small part of the existence of one living intensely the spiritual life.

Even for the earlier days of his earthly career we get but few facts that are not, in one way or another, contained in the photographic records of his inner consciousness, which, chastened by reflection and but thinly disguised, are revealed to us in all his writings. What the author has chosen not to present to our gaze can hardly be of importance to us, since sincerity, one of the chief criterions applied by him in judging productions of art, is not only the keystone to his own thoughts and utterances, but has so thoroughly been applied by him, in his desire to tell the truth, the whole truth, and nothing but the truth, that we should in vain rummage through his soul for additional data or for any mental reservation.

218

Tolstóy is all in his writings, and if not one word more were heard from him or about his life, we should still have the whole man.

But such is human frailty that the saintly life of a man generally leads to the worship of his earthly relics, that we adorn our habitations with the images of those whose spirituality vivifies us, that we are more concerned about the carnal life of a teacher than about his teachership. We shall give our due to this natural desire, mustering such details as have become known, but will use this material chiefly in order to point out the correspondence between the author's life and his writings.

Tolstóy's ancestors on his father's side were distinguished boyárs, with rather shady political reputations, who had taken part in important affairs of state, and one of them, Peter Andréevich Tolstóy, was made a count by Peter the Great. Tolstóy's grandfather, Ilyá Andréevich, is depicted in *War and Peace* as the elder Rostóv. Tolstóy's father, Nikoláy Ilích, of whom we have a pen-sketch in *Childhood, Boyhood, and Youth*, served through the war of 1812 and, after having gambled away his fortune, married Márya Nikoláevna Volkónski, described as Princess Márya Bolkónski, in *War and Peace*. Four sons were born of the marriage, of whom Nikoláy was the eldest and Lev the youngest; there was also a daughter, Márya, who was one year younger than Lev.

Lev was born August 28 (old style), 1828. His mother died when he was but three years old, and his father, six years later. Tolstóy thinks he can recall some incidents from that early period. He has an impression that he was swaddled and that he wanted to free himself, that he felt the cruelty and the injustice of fate, that he was conscious of his own weakness and of the strength of others. This was the first and most powerful impression of his life. It was only when he was five years old that he came to see Nature. About the same time he was put in charge of the German tutor, Fédor Ivánovich Rössel, who had been instructing his elder brothers, without, however, being taken from the care of his "tall, plump, black-haired, kindly, tender, compassionate" aunt, T. A. Érgolski.

The family had just settled in Moscow, when the father died, and the children were taken back to Yásnaya Polyána, where they grew up under the guardianship of their father's sister, Countess A. I. Ósten-Sáken. In 1840, however, this aunt died, and the children were taken to Kazán, to the house of another aunt, P. I. Yúshkov, "a pure soul," who later on kept telling him that she wished nothing so much as that he should form a liaison with a married woman, become an adjutant to the emperor, and marry a very rich girl. Tolstóy was but ten years old when he became imbued with religious doubts, and soon after he read Voltaire. His home instruction was carried on under the supervision of a French tutor, Prosper St. Thomas, who remained with the family until after Tolstóy had passed his examination for the University of Kazán, the Philological Department of which he entered in the year 1843.

Tolstóy did not devote himself much to study at the university, which was partly due to the fact that the professors were not in the least interesting and that they were arbitrary in their judgment of the students' progress. He twice failed in subjects, only because the professor in question happened to be quarrelling with members of Tolstóy's family. After two years' desultory studying, Tolstóy left the university and returned to Yásnaya Polyána, which was his share of the inheritance. Here he devoted himself to the uplifting of the peasants, meeting with disastrous results, which are minutely described in *A Morning of a Landed Proprietor*. In 1848 he went to St. Petersburg, where he passed his candidate's examination at the university, but he very soon returned to Yásnaya

Polyána, bringing with him a dissipated German musician, Rudolph by name. With this Rudolph he devoted himself to music, especially to Beethoven.

For two years Tolstóy abandoned himself with his brother Sergyéy to dissipations of every kind, to gambling, to the chase, to music. Then his elder brother, Nikoláy, to whom he was most affectionately attached, returned from the Caucasus, where he served in the army. Nikoláy tried to persuade his brother to go back to the Caucasus with him, but Tolstóy withstood all his blandishments, until, having in 1851 lost very heavily at cards, he suddenly withdrew from his friends and from society, and buried himself in Pyatigórsk, in the Caucasus, passing most of his time in the company of an Old-believer, Uncle Epíshka (described as Eróshka in *The Cossacks*), a famous hunter. He here accidentally fell in with a great-uncle of his who was adjutant to Prince Baryatínski, and who persuaded him to enter the army of the Caucasus as a volunteer.

It was here, in the Caucasus, that Tolstóy wrote his first literary productions, *Childhood*, *Boyhood*, the first chapters of *Youth*, *A Morning of a Landed Proprietor*, and *The Incursion*, and sketched the plan for the *Cossacks*. On July 9, 1852, Tolstóy sent his sketch, *Childhood*, to Nekrásov, who was editing the *Contemporary*, and shortly after that it was published, although the author received no payment for it.

Such is briefly the chronological sequence of Tolstóy's external life from his birth to the end of his experience in the Caucasus. We shall now scrutinize the author's inward life, as depicted in his writings of that time.

The subtle influences that determine the career of a genius cannot be fathomed, but there are generally some separate factors which more than any others seem to determine the course which it is likely to take. In *Child-*

hood, Boyhood, and Youth we are told that Nikoláy Irténev, who is obviously no other than Tolstóy himself, was awkward and homely, and that these untoward qualities were coupled with an agonizing supersensitiveness. Persons who are so little endowed with graces by Nature are apt to keep their ego prominently before their eyes for the purpose of inflicting torments upon themselves. When, in addition, we have every reason to assume that Tolstóy came early under the spell of Rousseau, whom he quotes several times, apparently as his mentor, we can understand why he should have launched into literature with a Confession, which is but a species of self-castigation.

Of the three conditions for the infectiousness of art, Tolstóy values sincerity as the most important of all. The test which he would apply to any production of art fully justifies us in classing his first literary ventures as artistic productions : such is the frankness with which the child's, the boy's, the youth's foibles are laid bare, so true is the by no means faultless life of the father, so touching is the death of the mother, that, although we have difficulty in deciding whether it is Nikoláy Irténev or Dmítri Nekhlyúdov who really represents the author himself, although Tolstóy had barely a remembrance of his father and certainly did not have any personal knowledge of his mother, we are quite sure that he is describing actual incidents from his own life. This first production, which already contains in the embryo all the artistic qualities and all the personal defects of his later writings, is extremely important to the student of the author's life and works. It is the zero point on the thermometer of his literary and religious activity.

Childhood, Boyhood, and Youth, of which we shall speak collectively as one work, begins with the description of the tutor, Karl Ivánovich, the kindly, half-educated, methodical, excitable German, the very antithesis of the typical Russian. Here the author simply falls in with the general dislike of the German, which is not based on any race or national animosities, but only on the incompatibility of the Russian character with that of the neighbouring country, so many of whose citizens have, through their employment in various governmental and military positions, come in contact with the more mercurial and less precise Russians, whose sensibilities they somehow have managed to rouse. To no class of foreigners has Tolstóy devoted so much space as to the Germans, and there is hardly one among these, no matter how desirable their qualities must appear to any one else, that does not irritate him. Such are Lieutenant Rosenkranz, who "frequently spoke of his genealogy . . . and proved conclusively that he and his ancestors had been pure Russians;" and Staff-Captain Kraut, who, in spite of his admirable character, had something lacking as a man, and who, "like all Russian Germans, in strange contradistinction to the ideal German Germans, was in the highest degree practical;" and boastful Kraft, "who wants to be a comrade;" and the exemplary Officer Berg, who puts his marriage to Vyéra Rostóv on a strictly commercial basis; and General Pfuel, who is more concerned about the scientific exactness of the military operations than about their successful issues. Nor was this feeling confined to the Russian Germans, for at the same time Tolstóy did not approve of the German teachers, nor of German methods in general. When later, under the influence of the Sermon on the Mount, he embraced all men under the general term of "our neighbours," he still found individual Germans most unattractive, and deserted Schopenhauer, to whom he had clung for so long a time, declared Nietzsche a wicked corrupter of morals, saw in Wagner an arch adulterer of art, and declared William II. to be the most comical of all the sovereigns.

Tolstóy's religiousness is by no means the result of a

sudden conversion, as he himself thought and his critics would make us believe, but was inherent in his nature. Two incidents bear witness to his early religious trend, the experience with the saintly fool, and his confession. The saintly fool is a peculiar Russian institution. Hundreds of men and women who are half-witted, or at least supposed to be, leading a vagrant existence, without home, or property, or labour, but with an abundance of simple, half-superstitious faith, march from monastery to monastery, where there may be holy relics, and now and then pass their time at some estate, where they frequently are hospitably entertained by the religiously inclined. They seem to typify the simple of faith of whom the Gospel speaks. The admiration expressed for the simple, ardent faith of the saintly fool, " Your faith was so strong that you felt the nearness of God, your love was so great that words flowed of their own will from your lips, and you did not verify them by reason," is but the youthful prototype of the later " love of God." There is no difference in quality of belief, — there is only a difference of maturity. The same religious fervour is displayed in Nikoláy's preparation for the confession and the second confession, both of which are preceded by the composition of " Rules of Life," by which to be guided in his daily conduct. A confession is a purging of sins, and reacts powerfully upon the person confessing, by creating a spirit of contrition and meekness, — such is Tolstóy's earliest conception of this sacrament, and though in the case of Levín he had doubts about all the externals of the act, he none the less later, when he completely breaks away from ecclesiasticism, speaks in *Resurrection* with emotion of the effect of the confession on Katyúsha, and frequently, in his religious writings, in his diary, and in his letters, dwells upon the necessity of a confession of sins, not as a truce with God, but as a purging of one's own sins. *My Confession* is the logical sequel of that religiousness which was part of Tolstóy's life in his earliest youth, and which received an additional impetus through his adherence to Rousseau's theories.

Next to religiousness, the love of outdoor life, and of hunting especially, was Tolstóy's greatest passion, until his humaner views on the sanctity of all life put a stop to his favourite diversion. Accordingly, immediately after the chapter dealing with the saintly fool, we get the account of the chase. There are few episodes which Tolstóy describes so well as the hunt. Not only do we in such cases have very spirited stories of the sport itself and of the dogs, which he describes with the love of a hunter, but we also get some of the best descriptive passages, for which he is so famous. It is, after all, not so much the sport itself that attracted him so powerfully as the magnificence of Nature, which at the time that the chase is most favourable is at the height of its beauty. Even in his first experience he lost his game by becoming all-absorbed in the busy life of the ants and the flitting about of a yellow-winged butterfly. In the *Cossacks*, the hunting scenes give him an opportunity to describe the voluptuous woods of the Caucasus, where even the stinging of the innumerable mosquitoes becomes a pleasure, and it is during one of these hunting expeditions, while resting in the chase of the stag, that he arrives at the conclusion that the highest good is happiness, and that happiness is to be found in love, in self-sacrifice, — a theme which later is to form the basis of his relation to God. Whether inborn or fostered by Rousseau's theory, the love of Nature is his strongest passion after religion, and it is this love of Nature that soon was to take him away from the unnatural conditions of a city life and was to determine his future actions.

Reflections, however, crowded upon him at all important events of life, and of these there is none upon which he dwelt so constantly and so profoundly as upon death.

An intense desire for life and a fearlessness of death have always been characteristic of Tolstóy, and he has devoted even more pains to the depiction of scenes of death than to the portraiture of passion, and has produced three stories, *Three Deaths*, *The Death of Iván Ilích*, and *Master and Workman*, which deal exclusively with various aspects of death. In his *Childhood, Boyhood, and Youth* we have no less than three deaths, that of the mother, the grandmother, and Natálya Sávishna. The grandmother's death is merely mentioned to contrast it with the unrestrained merriment and the Homeric laugh of boyhood in the full bloom of life. On the mother's death Tolstóy lavishes all the affection which he always had in store for a mother, to him the highest ideal of a woman. All the tenderness, devotion, forgiveness, which a woman is capable of are crowded into the last letter written by the mother. With what minuteness all the conflicting circumstances and details are, with more than usual faithfulness, even on account of the acute pain produced by the near demise of the mother, brought before us to accentuate the grandeur and importance of the last moment! The closed door, weeping Mimi, the father walking on tiptoe, the meaningless face of fool Akím who formerly used to amuse him, the darkened windows, Natálya Sávishna knitting a stocking, *la belle Flamande*, the mingled odour of mint, eau de cologne, camomile, and Hoffmann's drops, — what a wealth of simple, yet heartrending circumstances of death! And, then, death itself! How attracted Nikoláy is to the pale face, with the black spot under the transparent skin, on one of her cheeks, and how, in the presence of the lifeless body, pleasant thoughts and dreams take him away from reality! Then the single moment of real grief, and Mimi's insincere tears, and the hypocrisy of the consolations, and the one real sorrow of Natálya Sávishna, and the terror evoked by her who was once a beloved creature! What a mass of finely observed facts, later in life to be leisurely worked out with even greater insistence on the grandeur of the final incident in the earthly life!

To die properly,— that is the great problem of life, as Tolstóy sees it. In *War and Peace*, Platón Karatáev's meek life and peaceful death have been commented upon by the critics as the earliest instance of Tolstóy's glorification of the Christian life; but that is not quite correct: the first instance had already been given in ι e life and death of Natálya Sávishna, who, after a life of unswerving devotion to her mistress, a month before her death herself prepared all her funeral clothes, transferred all the property in her charge to the new stewardess, and, after much suffering, which she bore with Christian patience, confessed her sins, begged everybody's forgiveness, and " executed the best and highest act of this life,— she died without regrets or fear." Under the overpowering influence of these two deaths, childhood finds itself promoted to a new stage of life, and with death the first production fittingly ends.

The fundamental questions concerning religiousness, love of Nature, death, which form the chief preoccupation of Tolstóy's maturer years, having been fully treated in *Childhood*, we get in *Boyhood* the more worldly aspects of life; but even here are foreshadowed his future social and educational ideas. Here we are told of the first time when Nikoláy became aware of the difference between the rich and the poor, and of the shame he felt for being rich; of the terrible effect punishment, inflicted maliciously, has upon the mind of a boy; of the nascent sexual feeling; and, above all else, of his tendency to philosophize, which, in later years, was to imbue him with the idea of suicide, and which at this earliest period nearly drove him insane. Even then he was wavering between the opposite extremes: the highest good consisted either in the ability to bear sufferings, or in enjoying the present and not caring for the future. He tried to penetrate

the impenetrable and to solve the mystery of eternity.
He tried to "take nothingness by surprise," and, in his
abstract reasoning, he "fell into the inextricable circle of
the analysis of his thoughts," arriving at a point when he
"was thinking of thinking that he was thinking, and
reason was lost in empty speculation."

In *Boyhood* we are introduced to a character who afterward is frequently used by Tolstóy as the literary representative of himself. This is Dmítri Nekhlyúdov. It is
also clear that even here Nekhlyúdov is intended for the
author himself. This doubling of Tolstóy occurs also in
War and Peace, where both Pierre and Andréy Bolkónski
are reflections of the author's own life. Tolstóy's whole
existence has passed in a severe struggle between two
diametrically opposed natures within himself: now the
intensely worldly man within him gains supremacy, and
his artistic temperament has full sway, and now it is his
spiritual self that tries to crush out the carnal man. It is
this struggle which divides all his larger productions into
the unconsciously artistic and the consciously didactic
parts. As his years advance the spiritual side becomes
more and more accentuated, though in unconscious moments his artistic, human side breaks forth with daz-
zling brilliancy, while in his younger years his human
side was more in evidence, and gave rise to a series of
artistic productions. But even in his earliest works this
struggle exists, and it is due to this that he consciously
or unconsciously splits himself up into two separate individuals. In *Boyhood* and *Youth* Dmítri Nekhlyúdov
represents the nascent spiritual, more ideal man versus
Nikoláy Irténev, the more human and material man.
Nekhlyúdov completes Irténev, as later the Bible was to
complete a life that was under the spell of Rousseau.
Under the influence of Nekhlyúdov, Irténev began ec-
statically to worship the ideal of virtue and dreamed of
destroying all human vices and misfortunes, and, above

all, of correcting himself and appropriating to himself all virtues.

With Nekhlyúdov's friendship ends the *Boyhood*, as, indeed, the experiences related in *Youth* belong more properly to the period intervening between Tólstoy's experience in the Caucasus and his settlement on his estate, when the greater part of the chapters were actually written down. Of the two short stories, *The Incursion* serves, as it were, as a sketch for his other military stories, which were to culminate in *Sevastopol*, while *A Morning of a Landed Proprietor* deals with an important incident in Tolstóy's life, when he for the first time withdrew to the country to live the life of a country squire and to devote all his energies to the cause of the peasants.

Here it is Nekhlyúdov through whom the author speaks. The story is very characteristic of Tolstóy's whole activity and is typical of Russian conditions. Tolstóy at the age of nineteen conceived the idea of acting as a benefactor to the peasants, and so he set out to bestow all kinds of benefactions on his villagers. This was the time when Russians began to take interest in the peasant. Turgénev had already written his *Memoirs of a Hunter*, and society was divided into two hostile camps: there were those who saw in the peasant all the Russian virtues in an inchoate state, and those who saw no salvation for the degraded, improvident, hopelessly dull villagers. Those who, like Turgénev, took the lowly agriculturist under their wing found it necessary to idealize him, while their opponents were just as busy detracting from him and representing him as devoid of progressive tendencies. Not so Tolstóy. That his ardour for his humble brothers was at least as strong as that of his literary friends is evidenced by the fact that, while they preached a common brotherhood, Tolstóy actually went among them, planned a distribution of his property to them, and later for a series of years gave himself unreservedly to instructing the peasant children. But with his usual sincerity, he was unable to see in the peasants the ideal painted by those who preached the emancipation, nor the unconditional wretchedness which alone the adversaries depicted. With absolute frankness he details his attempts at relieving the suffering villagers by offering them superior advantages, which they reject from indolence and a sense of conservatism.

With a sickening feeling that all the dreams of his life were absurd, he walked home, only to fall into new reveries, about a woman, whom, no matter how enticing, he had to discard for the far more soothing ideal, " that love and goodness were truth and happiness, and the only truth and possible happiness in the world," and again he returned to the thought expressed by him before, that " love, self-sacrifice, — these constitute the true happiness which is independent of accident." From first to last this remains the key-note of all his actions and thoughts, and temporary failures do not reduce his zeal, but only urge him on to new endeavours. And how often he has to return to the theme of pious desires to do good to the peasants, with the invariable inability to carry his intentions to a happy issue! Pierre, and Levín, and Nekhlyúdov in *Resurrection* all make these abortive attempts, which are quite in keeping with the dreamy, well-meant, but aimless tendencies of the Russian character. To this story, as to all the longer stories of Tolstóy, there is really no end, even as there is no end to any event in life. Rudely disappointed in one of his reveries, Nekhlyúdov only falls into another, dreaming of a free and easy life in the open, like that of Ilyúshka the driver, and exclaiming, " Why am I not Ilyúshka ? "

III.

THE first period of Tolstóy's life closes with his flight to the Caucasus, to escape from the promptings of his baser nature and from the annoying triteness of society. "Rules of life" and the finer perception of Nekhlyúdov did not help him to curb his uncontrollable passions. He revolted against himself, and, instead of carrying his spiritual ideal to its legitimate issue, to which he carried it later, he rushed headlong into the whirlpool of riotous living, and at least externally for a whole decade did not seem to differ from any of the easy-going, reckless members of the literary fraternity of the time. In the Caucasus he plunged into the life of the camp, with its adventures, drinking bouts, festivities, and occasional hunting expeditions. The military life seemed to agree with him, and when the war broke out in 1853 between Turkey and Russia, he hastened by the way of Yásnaya Polyána to Bukarest and to the Army of the Danube. He was present at the disaster at Silistria, and then proceeded over Jassy to the Crimea, where he joined the besieged army in Sevastopol. His place was in the most dangerous Fourth Bastion, and such was his recklessness that, amidst the boom of cannon, he calmly composed his *Sevastopol in December,* and later, *Sevastopol in May* and *The Cutting of the Forest.*

The effect of his sketches from Sevastopol was tremendous. Not only did he at once become known to the reading public, but even Nicholas I. commanded that "the life of this young man be guarded." In August of the year 1855 he led his battery in the fight at the

Chérnaya, and after the capitulation of Sevastopol he was sent as a courier to St. Petersburg to carry there the general report, which he himself had been ordered to compose. Upon arriving in the capital he stopped at the house of Turgénev. The poet Fet, who after that became an intimate friend of Tolstóy, met him there, and this is what he tells of his first meeting with him.

"The next morning, as Zakhár opened the vestibule for me, I observed in the corner a short sword with an Anna ribbon.

"'Whose short sword is this?' I asked, walking toward the door of the drawing-room.

"'This way, if you please,' Zakhár said, half-aloud, pointing to the corridor on the left. 'This is the short sword of Count Tolstóy, who is sleeping in our drawing-room. Iván Sergyéevich is drinking tea in the study.'

"During the half-hour which I passed by with Turgénev we spoke in a subdued voice, for fear of waking the sleeping count.

"'He has been acting like this all the time,' Turgénev said, with a smile. 'He has come back from the battery at Sevastopol, has stopped at my rooms, and is painting the town red: carousals, gipsies, and cards the whole night long; and then, at two o'clock he falls asleep and sleeps as one dead. I have tried to hold him back, but I have given it up.'"

In spite of the respect shown to Tolstóy by Turgénev, who esteemed highly his *Childhood* and *Boyhood*, there were always frictions between the two. Any false note in a man's expressions, any deviation from absolute sincerity, was sure to provoke Tolstóy, and with his uncompromising spirit he would not let slip any opportunity to give vent to his irritation. It was only a short time after the above incident that a number of bachelor literati were gathered at the house of Nekrásov. Some political question was being discussed, and Turgénev almost choked with anger at Tolstóy's reserved, but none the less stinging, rebukes.

" ' I cannot admit,' said Tolstóy, 'that what you say is your conviction. I stand with a dagger or a sword at the door, saying, "So long as I live no one shall enter here." What a fine conviction! What you are trying to do is to conceal from one another the essence of your thoughts, and that you call a conviction.'

" ' What makes you come here?' Turgénev said, choking, and in a voice which passed into a falsetto (this was always the case with him in a dispute). 'This is not your camp! Go to Countess B-y B-y!'

" ' Why need I ask you where I am to go? And idle talk will not by my going be changed into convictions.' "

Upon another occasion Turgénev, beside himself with excitement, strutted through three rooms in Nekrásov's quarters, exclaiming, " I cannot stand this! I have bronchitis!"

" Bronchitis," Tolstóy grumbled, at his back, " is an imaginary disease. Bronchitis is a metal!"

Turgénev continued to strut through the three rooms, with his hands in his pockets, while Tolstóy lay on a morocco sofa in the middle room. To avert a catastrophe, Grigoróvich, who was present, went up to Tolstóy and said, " Dear Tolstóy, do not feel so agitated! You do not know how he respects and loves you!"

" I will not permit him to spite me," Tolstóy replied, with dilated nostrils. " He is purposely walking past me and wagging his democratic haunches!"

Outwardly Tolstóy at that time completely surrendered himself to the life of a society dandy. He wore a padded overcoat with a gray beaver collar, and his long, dark blond hair fell from underneath a natty hat, which he wore dashingly poised on one side, and in his hand he carried a fashionable cane, whenever he went out for a walk.

At that time the young society people considered it the right thing to busy themselves with gymnastic exercises, especially with jumping over a wooden horse. If a man wanted to see Tolstóy at about two o'clock, he needed only to go to the gymnasium on the Great Dmítrovka, where Tolstóy, dressed in tights, used to try to jump over the horse without touching a wool-stuffed leathern cone, placed on its back. In the evening he generally donned his dress suit and white tie, and attended evening parties and balls.

This was in the year 1857. During the same year he made his first journey abroad, stopping for a short time in Germany, and visiting Paris and Switzerland, where his stay at the Schweizerhof in Lucerne gave him the material for his sketch *Lucerne*. At the end of summer he was back at Yásnaya Polyána, and this is what his brother Nikoláy says of his life at that time : " Lev is seriously trying to become acquainted with country life and the management of the estate, with which he, like all of us, has so far been only superficially acquainted. I have my misgivings about the results : Lev wants to grasp everything at once, not omitting anything, not even gymnastics. For this purpose he has had a bar put up in front of his study window. Of course, if we put aside the prejudices, against which he is struggling so much, he is right : gymnastics does not interfere with the management of the estate ; but the village elder looks somewhat differently upon the matter : ' I come to the master for an order,' says he, ' and he, hanging with one leg on a pole, head downwards, and wearing his red blouse, keeps swaying to and fro ; his hair is flowing in the wind, his face is flushed with blood, and I stand and listen to his commands and marvel at what he is doing.' Lev has fallen in love with the way labourer Yufán spreads his arms while ploughing. And so Yufán has become for him an emblem of peasant strength, something like Mikúla Selyanínovich. He himself now spreads his arms, follows the plough, and Yufanizes."

Literature at that time gave him pleasure, and he enjoyed equally Turgénev's prose and Fet's poetry. "Turgénev has gone to Winzig," he wrote to his friend Fet, "to stay there until August and cure his bladder. The devil take him! I am getting tired of loving him. He will not cure his bladder, but will cause us a loss. And now, good-bye, dear friend; if there is no poem by the time I come to see you, I will squeeze it out of you."

Yet already agriculture was beginning to interest him even more than literature, and the two were sometimes strangely intertwined. This is what he wrote to Fet:

"DARLING UNCLE FET: — Upon my word 'darling,' and I love you terribly, just terribly. That is all. It is stupid and a disgrace to write stories. To write verses . . . Do write them. But it is very agreeable to love a good man. And maybe, contrary to my will and consciousness, it is not I, but a story which is sitting within me and has not yet come to maturity, that is making me love you. At times it so seems to me. Do as you please, but 'twixt manure and hen-bane something drives me to go and compose. It is lucky I do not allow myself, and will not allow myself, to write as yet. I thank you with all my heart for your trouble about the veterinary, and so forth. I have found one in Túla, and will begin the cure at once. What will come of it, I do not know. The devil take them all, anyway. Druzhínin begs me, as a friend, to write a story. Really, I want to write one. I will write one just to beat the band. The Shah of Persia is smoking tobacco, and I love you. That's what. Jests aside, how about your Hafiz? Twist and turn as I may, the acme of wisdom and firmness for me is only to enjoy somebody else's poetry, and not to let my own out among people in a monstrous habiliment, and to sit down myself and eat my daily bread. However, at times I want so much to be a great man, and I feel so provoked because that has not yet come to pass! I sometimes even hasten to get up or finish my dinner, in order to begin. I cannot tell all so-called foolish things, but it is pleasant to tell at least one to such an uncle as you are, who live by nothing but so-called foolish things. Send me one most wholesome poem by Hafiz, translated by you, to *me faire venir l'eau à la bouche,* and I will send you a sample of wheat. I am dreadfully sick of the chase. The weather is fine, but I do not go out by myself."

At the end of 1857 Tolstóy had made a short visit to Paris, and, except for a few intervals at Moscow, ever after passed his time at Yásnaya Polyána. Farming operations were more and more absorbing his attention. He tried to persuade Fet to purchase an estate near his own, and in a characteristic letter to him early in the year 1860 he began by giving a detailed account of the possible profits from a farm which he wanted Fet to buy. Then he passed over to a criticism of Turgénev's latest productions, more than ever finding fault with the literary banalities of "splenetic and dyspeptic" Turgénev; then he criticized Ostróvski's *Storm,* though he predicted a success for it. "Lovers of antiques, to whom I, too, belong, are not interfered with in their desire seriously to read poems and stories and seriously to talk about them. Now is a different time. It is not for us to study, but to teach Marfútka and Taráska a little of what we know." The letter ends with a request for Fet to see a German bookseller and order some new books for him, among them also popular books on medicine and the veterinary art, and to get for him six Starbuck ploughs, and to find out what the price of clover and Timothy seed was, since he had some for sale.

In June of the same year he wrote to Fet that he felt quite despondent, because the estate, as it was being managed, pressed heavily upon him, and because the sickness of his brother, from whom he had not yet heard, worried him very much. This brother, Nikoláy, was worshipped by Lev, and Nikoláy in his turn worshipped him. Nikoláy was in every way an admirable man and was beloved by all those with whom he came in contact; but during his military service in the Caucasus he had acquired a taste for liquor, and this, combined with a weak constitution, soon began to tell on him, and when a famous doctor, whom he consulted, observed an advanced stage of consumption in him, he sent him to Soden. Lev Tolstóy, in addition to these cares, felt also out of sorts, because his " bachelor life, that is, the absence of a wife and the feeling that it was getting late," weighed heavily upon him. In the same letter he advised Fet in the purchase of an estate not to be anxious to get too much land, telling him that through his bitter experience he had come to the conclusion that sixty or seventy desyatínas of four-field land was about as much as a man could handle. Later in life he decided that even this immensely reduced area of land was entirely too great to be cultivated by one man.

Toward the end of the month Lev started abroad, for the purpose of finally joining his brother. He went by water to Stettin, remained a few days in Berlin, where he visited some lectures at the university and became greatly interested in a working men's society, in which all kinds of questions were freely discussed by the working men, stopped a day in Leipsic, to visit the schools, which were supposed to be the best in Germany, in Dresden called on Berthold Auerbach, from whose peasant stories he had received so much inspiration, and on July 20th reached Kissingen. Here he fell in with Julius Fröbel, the nephew of Friedrich Fröbel and himself an educator, and in his company he passed much of his time, discussing general questions of education. The news that came from Soden was not encouraging: Nikoláy was failing rapidly, and toward the end of August Lev went to Soden, to take his brother to Frankfurt, and thence to the south, in the hope of prolonging Nikoláy's life. In Hyères he died in Lev's arms. This is what Lev wrote to Fet on October 17th:

"It seems to me that you already know what has happened: on September 20th, he died, literally in my arms. Nothing in my life has made such an impression upon me. He was right when he said that there is nothing worse than death. And when you come to think of this, that it is after all the end of everything, there is nothing worse than life. Why worry and try, if from what was Nikoláy Nikoláevich Tolstóy nothing is left for him? He did not say that he felt the approach of death, but I know that he watched its every step and knew for certain what was still ahead. A few minutes before his death he dozed off, and suddenly he awoke and in terror whispered: 'What is this?' He had seen it, — his absorption into nothingness. And if he did not find anything to hold on to, what shall I find? Still less. Certainly neither I nor any one else will up to the last moment struggle with it as he did. Two or three days before that I said to him, 'Some conveniences ought to be put in your room.' 'No,' he said, 'I am feeble, but not so feeble as you think, — I'll fight on.'

"Until the very last moment he did not give in, and did everything himself, tried to keep himself busy, wrote, asked me about my writings, advised me. But it seemed to me that he was not doing all that from an inner impulse, but from principle. One thing, — Nature, — that remained until the end. The day before he went to his chamber, and there from weakness fell upon his bed, near an open window. When I came, he said, with tears in his eyes, ' How I have been enjoying myself for a whole hour!' — From earth was he taken, and to the earth he will return. One thing is left, the dim hope that there, in Nature, part of which you become in the earth, something will be left and found. All those who knew and saw his last moments say, 'How remarkably calmly and softly he died;' but I know that it was extremely painfully, because not one sensation has escaped me. A thousand times I said to myself, ' Let the dead bury the dead,' but the strength which is in us must be used in some way. It is impossible to persuade a stone to fall upwards, instead of downwards, whither it is attracted. It is impossible to laugh at a jest which has grown stale. It is impossible to eat when you do not feel like eating. What is the use of anything, if to-morrow shall begin the torments of death with all the abomination of the lie, the self-deception, and will end in nothing, in a naught for ourselves. A funny thing. Be useful, be virtuous and happy so long as you are alive, people say to one another; but you, and happiness, and virtue, and usefulness consist in truth. And the truth which I have brought away in thirty-two years is this, that the condition in which we are placed is terrible. ' Take life as it is; you have placed yourself in this position.' Indeed! I take life as it is. As soon as man shall have reached the highest degree of development, he will see clearly that everything is confusion and deception, and that the truth, which he none the less loves more than anything else, is terrible. When you see it well and clearly, you will come to your senses and you will say in terror, as my brother said, ' What is this?' But, of course, so long as there is any desire to know and speak the truth, you try to know and speak. This is all that is left to me from the moral world, above which I cannot rise. This alone will I do, but only not in the form of your art. Art is a lie, and I can no longer love a beautiful lie — I will pass the winter here, for the reason that it makes no difference where one lives."

It was the death of the mother and of Natálya Sávishna that closed up the period of Irténev's boyhood, and served as the turning-point for a new stage of life. So, too, the death of Nikoláy served Tolstóy as a turning-point in his frivolous society life. In his *Confession* he tells us how during this decade he committed every crime in the calendar, and yet was regarded by all as a comparatively moral man. At that time he wrote through vanity and tried to conceal the better promptings in himself. When he returned from the war, he was accepted by the literary men as their own, was flattered by them, and was furnished with a theory to justify the looseness of his morals. " Faith in the meaning of poetry and in progress in life was a creed, and I was one of its priests." Soon, however, he lost this faith and, observing the priests more closely, came to the conclusion that the literary men actually stood lower than his former riotous companions. He did not lose faith in his own worth, and continued to teach, not knowing what. His sojourn in Europe, where he associated with prominent scholars, confirmed him in his faith in perfection, in progress. An execution, which he witnessed in Paris, and the death of his brother Nikoláy, shook his faith in the infallibility of progress. Such is Tolstóy's retrospective view on the state of his mind for the period preceding his settlement in Yásnaya Polyána and his marriage.

Though in the main this confession represents the author's feelings during that time, the more than twenty years that had elapsed since the decade of transition, coupled with a strong religious self-chastisement, materially modified the current sentiments of the author. For these we must go, not to his *Confession*, but to his own writings covering that period. Of these stories, about one-half deal with military experiences and were written down almost simultaneously with the occurrences described in them; but *The Cossacks*, though conceived in 1852, was finished in 1861, and thus, to some extent, reflects later experiences. Both the military sketches and the other stories show that as regards workmanship he really came under the sway of the literary clique. Few of the later productions show such exquisite balancing, such delicacy of language, such rhythmical motion as, for example, *Sevastopol*, *The Cossacks*, *The Snow-storm*, *Lucerne*, *Three Deaths*, and, though in Tolstóy it is never possible to detect any direct obligations and imitations, on account of the originality and power of his own genius, Tolstóy was to some extent affected by Turgénev's manner when he wrote *Three Deaths*, and *Albert* belongs to the same class of stories as those by Hoffmann or by Poe.

Outside of this purely technical influence we fail to observe any correspondence between the author's external conduct and his inward life, that is, while his spiritual existence proceeded on the same lines as laid down in his first productions and clearly represented an evolution toward his later world-conception, his outward ways, his dandyism, his belief in progress, his faith in literature and in his own mission, were never more than skin-deep and never formed a part of his real self.

Sevastopol in December, with its realistic description of the apparently peaceful, though busy city, the horrors of the hospital, the simple courage of the soldiers, is not intended as a glorification of carnage, but as an object-lesson in the inhumanity of war. In *Sevastopol in December*, the playing of the regimental music, the thoughts of love, the hope of advancement expressed by Staff-Captain Mikháylov, introduce us to more peaceful scenes than we are soon to hear of; and again the author tells us of the "vanity on the brink of the grave" and declares that "the literature of our age is only an endless story of snobs and vanity." This is surely in direct contrast with the aristocratic mannerism which he then seemed to assume and of which he has been accused even in his old age. He delights in contrasting the soldiers' courage with the pusillanimity of the officers, and puts to shame Prince Gáltsin's suspicions by the simple recital of the wounded soldier who was taking to the ambulance a more seriously wounded comrade. The officers are either in deadly fear of being killed, as was the case with Mikháylov, or they are downright cowards, like Praskú-khin, or braggarts, like Pest. The motives of those who take part in war are low and contemptible: "every one of them is a Napoleon in miniature, a monster in minia-ture, and forthwith ready to start a battle, to kill a hundred people, merely to get an additional star, or one-third additional pay." In sharp contrast with the officers, the soldiers, both the Russian and the French, amicably converse and exchange jests during the truce. Can any one doubt that Tolstóy's abhorrence of war, though he himself was then taking part in it, was then as sincere and complete as at any subsequent time, when one reads the closing lines where he invokes men in the name of Christianity to stop killing one another? *Sevastopol in August*, which, with its sad story of the brothers Kozel-tsóv, the detailed account of the life in the bastions, the depressing narration of the evacuation of the city, is more complete than the previous two sketches, only heightens the horror and tragedy of war.

In *The Cutting of the Forest* we again have the two contrasting divisions, the soldiers and the officers. For the first we get a minute classification, such as Tolstóy becomes more and more addicted to, of the various kinds of soldiers that are found in the Russian army. Of these, "the commonest type is a gentle, sympathetic type, which unites the best Christian virtues, meekness, piety, pa-tience, and submission to the will of God." Is not that an elaboration of the character of Natálya Sávishna, and a generalization of Platón Karatáev in *War and Peace*? With what love and artlessness the author depicts the "busily submissive Velenchúk," and the "sagacious commander," Maksímov, and the joker Chíkin, and simple-hearted Antónov, whose artless exclamation, as the ball fell within a short distance from his legs, put to shame the officers' endeavours to appear cool and unconcerned! And again it is the soldier Velenchúk, whose "last minutes were as clear and tranquil as all his life."

The types of the officers, however, are again far from attractive: we have honest Bolkhóv, who is ready to acknowledge his inability to take part in war, — his cowardice, — but who stays in the army, in order to gain a decoration and a majorship, the prerequisites of one returning from the service in the Caucasus; and Trosénko, who has served so long in the Caucasus that he has no other family than his military company, and no other home than his camp; and lying Kraft, — "a German who wants to be a good comrade." How much more charming is the final scene, when the soldiers were assembled at the camp-fire and after the tattoo the harmonious chorus of male voices amid the deep hush of the night said the Lord's Prayer; and the foot-soldier told of his experience at Dargí; and Zhdánov, without the slightest idea of boasting, explained the necessity of his reënlisting in the army, in order not to interfere with his brothers, from whom he had not heard for many years; and Antónov sang a melancholy song, causing tears to appear on Zhdánov's face.

A Moscow Acquaintance at the Front is merely an incident in the military life of the Caucasus, which gives the author an opportunity to describe a profligate, fawning, dissipated scion of Moscow aristocracy. If there is any truth in the statement that Tolstóy then displayed a certain snobbery, it is evident that this aristocratic peculiarity was not directed against those who stood far below him in the social scale, but against those whom he designated as aristocrats and whom he never could bear. At the same time he was conscious of his own failings, of his inability to control his passions, especially the passion for gambling, and this weakness apparently affected him to the extent of making him familiar with the thought of suicide. This state of his mind he transferred to Prince Nekhlyúdov in the *Memoirs of a Marker*. Nekhlyúdov thought with regret of the days when his childlike, genuine feelings had discovered the right path and had been kindled to a gentle heat by the objectless power of love; but he lacked strength to extricate himself from the slough into which he was sinking, and he was assailed by the thoughts of suicide. All that agrees completely with what, to judge from his other productions of about that time, must have been Tolstóy's mental condition.

In *Albert* the author has depicted the dissipated musician, Rudolph, whom he had brought with him from Moscow. In spite of Albert's insuperable passion for liquor, his ingratitude, his childishness, Delésov, who is no other than Tolstóy, has only pity for him, for, " What business have I to mend others, when I ought to be thankful to God if I were able to get myself straightened out ? " Tolstóy's faith in human nature and sympathy even for a criminal is nowhere expressed with greater emphasis than in *Polikúshka*, where the thief Polikúshka is entrusted with a sum of money, the loss of which causes him to commit suicide. The admirable sketch, *The Snow-storm*, is the only one of that period which is entirely devoid of any didactic purpose. It relates an experience in the Territory of the Don Cossacks, when the author lost his way in a blinding snow-storm. The intermingling of a dream with reality and the remarkable psychological analysis of the dream itself are themes to which he frequently returns in his later works. The incident of the snow-storm itself was afterward used by him as a background in *Master and Workman.*

The *Two Hussars* and *Lucerne* form a group by themselves, in that they deal with the reverse sides of modern civilization. In the *Two Hussars* there are contrasted the riotous, swearing, reckless, but at the same time generous, chivalrous, whole-hearted military men of the older generation, and the refined, talented, decent, but mean, hard-hearted, and unprincipled men of the middle of the nineteenth century. The elder Túrbin is given to drunkenness, beats his servant, passes his evenings with gipsy maids, but at the same time he robs the gambler of the money, in order to give it to the poor officer from whom he has won it, and who otherwise would have blown out his brains, and acts gallantly toward the fair widow, whom he kisses, before she has opened her eyes from her sleep, to see who the intruder is. The younger Túrbin, on the contrary, is a model officer, but he unscrupulously wins the money from the same simple, unsuspecting widow and, while he enjoys her hospitality, tries to seduce her daughter. Tolstóy could much more readily put up with outward coarseness than with insincere unconscionable refinement. That was the very characteristic that he observed in the case of the cultured Englishmen, the guests of the Schweizerhof in Lucerne, who did not give as much as a penny to a poor itinerant Tyrolese singer, and even laughed at him, though they had been willing to listen to his singing. It roused Tolstóy to the highest pitch of indignation against that sham which is called civilization. Tolstóy is not easily deceived by words: civilization, freedom, equality, mean nothing to him, if people who profess these have "no heartfelt human feeling for a personal good act." He objects to civilization, because "the impeccable, blissful voice of the Universal Spirit is drowned by the boisterous, hasty development of civilization." Here we have the succinct expression of all his future creed, — his detestation for the hypocrisy of society, his critical attitude toward civilization and progress, his positing of religion as the foundation of morality. And again he turns away from the heartless crowd of refined people to the simple singer, sitting somewhere on a threshold and singing amid the soft, fragrant night, and "in his heart there is no reproach, no malice, no regret." And thus even the foreign Tyrolese swells the long catalogue of the simple of faith and poor in spirit who, like Natálya Sávishna, the soldier Zhdánov, Platón Karatáev, shall inherit the kingdom of God. So, too, in *Three Deaths*, the quiet death of Uncle Fédor, who in his last moments gives away his boots to driver Seréga and is anxious not to disturb any one, is sharply contrasted with the death of the peevish, recriminating society woman.

Youth, though dealing reminiscently with an earlier period, was finished in the same year as *Lucerne*, and so reflects both the earlier and later transitional stage of the author's life. The ardent desire to apply virtuous ideas to life, the strong religious feeling and the earnestness during the confession, the absurdity of the system of university examinations and the petty despotism of the professors, themes which he has touched upon before, here become the subjects of special discussions. Irténev's great friendship for the morally superior Nekhlyúdov is the old striving after greater perfection. In the classification of love into fair, self-sacrificing, and active, of which the latter most unselfish sentiment is placed higher than any other, we have the incipient concept of love, not as an exclusive sentiment for a certain individual, but as an all-absorbing feeling, which is in no way confined to any person. Tolstóy's early aversion to society is treated in a number of chapters, and from the manner in which he speaks of acquiring a habit of drinking and smoking, in order to appear as a grown person, he shows that his heart never was with any of the dissipations which, in the weakness of his character, he practised at the time. Nor did that external decency, known as *comme il faut*, ever seriously affect him. It lived in him at the time when he wrote of it as a reminiscence of a brief fatuous aberration. Even during his university career, Irténev had opportunities to become acquainted with men who did not belong to the *comme il faut* circle, whose genuine worth, in spite of their rough exterior, inspired him with respect, and he soon came to the conclusion that his acquaintance with Prince So-and-so, his pronunciation of French, his linen shirt, his manicured nails, were but trifles in comparison with their earnest and persistent endeavours.

Youth was never completed, and we have no autobiographical record for the years intervening between Tolstóy's university career and his sojourn in the Caucasus, except *A Morning of a Landed Proprietor*, analyzed above. Of the stories dealing with the Caucasus none equals the power of *The Cossacks* in portraying that storm-and-stress period, during which the author's mind wavered between the life of an artist and that of a sternly moralizing philosopher, between activity and indolence, when every effort in any direction caused him to tear himself away from the effort in order to regain his liberty, when he gave up " his service, farming, music, to which he thought at one time of devoting himself, and even love of women, in which he did not believe." Olénin, that is Tólstoy, turns his back on Moscow, in order to begin in the Caucasus a new life, in which there shall be none of those blunders, and no remorse, and in which he certainly will be happy. Everything combined to make *The Cossacks* the most perfect artistic work produced by Tolstóy : it was conceived during the time when he submitted most to the influence of a literary tradition, it is preëminently autobiographical and sincere, it deals with incidents in a country from which the halo of romanticism had not yet been entirely lifted, it gave the author occasion to revel in Rousseauan naturalism and primitive simplicity, and was brought to a conclusion at a time when his contempt for modern civilization had reached its highest point, from which it was never again to recede to a less vigorous arraignment.

Olénin, tired of the vapidity of society life and of his dissipation at the gaming-table, left Moscow for the Caucasus. Not until he reached the region where he found simple people, with whom he could make simple jokes, and saw the mountains in all their grandeur, did he feel at ease. The Cossacks charmed him : their naturalness was in marked contrast to the artificiality of the society he had left behind him. Their very vices were more acceptable to him than those practised among the so-called refined people. The thieving, drunkenness, lax sexual relations, which he found among the Cossacks, did not offend him, because all that was done frankly, without any of that concealment and simpering, which in more civilized centres make up a hypocritical system of outward decency. He could without hesitation form a sincere friendship with Eróshka, arch-thief, arch-hunter, and naturalistic philosopher. Eróshka lived on such intimate terms with Nature that he could tell the time of the night by the noise made by the birds, and knew what the wild sow was announcing to her young ones; he was compassionate, not only to men, but also to animals, and would not let even a moth burn her wings; he knew no distinction between Tartar, and Armenian, and Russian soldier, and Cossack; he loved, and drank, and stole, conscious of no sin; his philosophy did not extend beyond the grave, upon which the grass would grow out, to mark the end. This Eróshka is no other than Olénin-Tolstóy in the moment of his most acute revolt against society. Abstract the elemental vices of the Cossack surroundings, and what we get is the same unbounded love of Nature and intimacy with it, the same universal pity, the same brotherhood of man, the same correspondence of a man's outer acts with the dictates of his conscience, the same opposition to what "the chanters say," which characterizes Tolstóy's later activity.

Eróshka's philosophy is food for Olénin's thoughts: from Eróshka's statements he deduces the fact that "the desire for happiness is inborn in man; consequently it is legitimate." Happiness, he continued to reason, consists in love, in self-sacrifice, in living for others. And so we come back to the fundamental note of Tolstóy's philosophy. Olénin felt that "he could not live entirely Eróshka's life, because his happiness was of a different nature, — he was restrained by the thought that happiness consisted in self-renunciation." The doubling of Tolstóy as Eróshka and Olénin is the same as that in the case of Irténev and Nekhlyúdov, except that now it represents the more vigorous struggle of youth. Then Maryánka, the "majestic woman in her pristine beauty, as the first woman must have issued from the hands of the Creator," crossed his path, and he fell in love with her, and for a moment it seemed to him that the self-renunciation which had been uppermost in his mind was only a refuge against love. For a moment he wavered and was ready to cast his philosophy to the winds, but Maryánka rejected him, and the episode of a momentary weakness came to an end.

It has been remarked that Tolstóy never experienced that romantic sensation of love of which the novelists prate. That accusation is certainly just: the young women who fall in love are by him always represented as carried away by a momentary infatuation; they are unable for any length of time, in the absence of their fiancés, to devote their love to those to whom they are betrothed, and invariably bestow their hearts upon undeserving persons. However, he does not mean to represent them as fickle, but wants to point out the inferiority and inconstancy of the mere sexual instinct, which is not permanently directed upon one person, and substitutes for this uncertain sentiment called love the far more ennobling feeling of motherhood. So, too, the mere sexual love for a woman is by a man to be kept in abeyance for the greater love of woman as a mother. This conception is for the first time uttered with full force in *Domestic Happiness.* The plot of the story, is, of course, a novelistic reproduction of Tolstóy's own experience, not actual but potential, in that he later married a woman many years younger than himself. Sergyéy Mikháylych is the same Olénin-Tolstóy, who has tasted all the bitterness of what is called life, but Másha is after her marriage made to demand what she thinks to be the broader life of the city, and so the two repair to the capital and abroad, and Másha lives in a whirl of worldly pleasures, to come out chastened and return with Sergyéy Mikháylych to the country, to live in the bosom of Nature. To Másha's question why, if he had loved her, he had allowed her for so many years to live in a society of shams, he says: " All of us, but especially you women, must in person live through all the nonsense of life in order to return to life itself." A new life began for Másha, but " the old sentiment became a precious, irretrievable reminiscence, and a new feeling of love for the children, and for the father of the children, laid the foundation for another, an entirely different and happy life."

IV.

AFTER the death of his brother, Tolstóy passed another six months in the West. After visiting Italy he went by way of Marseilles to Paris, everywhere observing the common people and studying the conditions of popular education. From Paris he ran over to London, where he was fortunate enough to hear Lord Palmerston deliver a three-hour speech in the parliament. He went home by way of Brussels, where he made the acquaintance of Proudhon and the Polish historian Lelewel, stopped at Weimar, where he investigated the Fröbel kindergartens, once more called on Berthold Auerbach in Dresden, went to Berlin, where he met Diesterweg, and from there back to Russia. After a brief stay in St. Petersburg, he went on May 10th to Yásnaya Polyána, two days later petitioned the government to be permitted to open a school for the peasant children, and took an active part in the allotment of land to the newly emancipated peasantry, in the capacity of mediator of the peace, an office established by the government for the adjustment of the land question.

It was soon after his return to Yásnaya Polyána that a rupture took place between him and Turgénev. It happened under the following circumstances. Fet, following Tolstóy's advice, had bought the estate of Stepánovka, which was but a short distance away from Yásnaya Polyána. Turgénev and Tolstóy were invited to pass a few days with Fet. On the second morning of their visit, the company was assembled at the tea-table, and during the conversation which ensued, Fet's wife asked Turgénev whether he was satisfied with his English gov-

erness, to whom he had entrusted the education of his
daughter.   Turgénev showered praises on the governess,
and among other things said that she had with English
punctuality asked him to determine the precise sum
which he wished to put into the hands of his daughter
for charitable purposes.   Fet reports the subsequent
event as follows :

" ' Now,' said Turgénev, 'the governess wants my daughter to take poor people's old clothes and mend them for
the people.'

" ' And this you consider good ? ' asked Tolstóy.

" ' Of course.   This brings the benefactress into contact
with actual want.'

" ' But I think that a dressed-up miss who is holding
in her lap dirty and ill-smelling rags is only playing an
insincere, theatrical part.'

" ' I ask you not to say this ! ' Turgénev shouted, with
dilated nostrils.

" ' Why should I not say what I am convinced of ? '
replied Tolstóy.

" Before I had a chance to call out ' stop ' to Turgénev,
he, mad with anger, exclaimed : ' If so, I will make you
stop by insulting you.'   With these words he jumped up
from the table and, clutching his hair, walked excitedly
into the next room.   A second later he came back and
said, turning to my wife, ' For God's sake, pardon my
monstrous conduct, which I regret deeply.'   Thereupon
he went out again."

It was not merely Turgénev's sudden excitability that
had caused this sally, but also a rankling feeling that
Tolstóy was outgrowing him.   " Turgénev cannot make
his peace with the thought that Lev is growing and
getting away from his guardianship," is what Nikoláy
Tolstóy once said about Turgénev.   On the other hand,
Tolstóy's retort was entirely in keeping with his character : he could not bear anything that was false and in-

sincere, and he never let slip an opportunity of giving vent to his indignation. The strained relations between the two great authors lasted until the year 1878, when Tolstóy extended his hand of forgiveness to his elder friend, and the whole incident was forgotten.

For two years Tolstóy devoted himself exclusively to his village school, for which he employed four students of the university, and a German, Keller, whom he had met in Jena during his European journey. The manner in which he conducted his school is amply discussed in his pedagogical essays, and to this we shall return later. His pedagogical ideas he developed in the periodical *Yásnaya Polyána*, which he himself edited. Meanwhile his old weakness for the gaming-table came back to him, and heavy losses thus incurred caused him to borrow one thousand roubles of the editor of the *Russian Messenger* as an advance payment for the *Cossacks*, which was not yet quite finished.

During his visits to Moscow he was a frequent visitor at Doctor Behrs's, whose three daughters seemed to have equal attraction for him. Doctor Behrs was a German of the Baltic provinces who had married the daughter of Islénev, a neighbour of the Tolstóys. For this Mrs. Behrs, who was but a year older than Tolstóy, Tolstóy had had a considerable affection when they both were little children, and now he transferred his attention to the younger generation of the Behrs. When the family removed for the summer to the suburban estate of Pokróvskoe, he frequently passed whole days there. During the summer of 1862 he took two of his best peasant pupils with him to Samára, going there from Nízhni-Nóvgorod by boat, to undergo a kumys cure. He was barely back home, when the family of the Behrs, on their way to the not very distant estate of the Islénevs, stopped for a few days at Yásnaya Polyána. They had just reached their own destination, when Tolstóy arrived on the scene.

Here he proposed to Sofíya, the second daughter, in precisely the same manner in which Levín made his proposal to Kitty. The engagement was kept secret for a time, and on September 23d they were married. On October 9th he wrote to Fet: "I have been married these two weeks, and I am happy, and a new, an entirely new man."

For the winter the newly married pair went to Moscow, stopping at Hotel Chevrier, formerly Chevalier. In the spring they were back in the country. The *Cossacks* and *Polikúshka*, which then appeared, evoked a mass of very favourable criticism, and Turgénev, in spite of his personal difference with Tolstóy, went into transports over them. In reply to a notice of these productions by Fet, Tolstóy wrote: "*Polikúshka* is the prattling on any chance subject by a man who 'indeed wields the pen,' and the *Cossacks* is 'juicy,' though poor stuff. Now I am writing the story of a piebald gelding; I shall have it printed by autumn, I think. However, how can I write now? Now even the invisible efforts are visible, and, besides, I am up to my ears in Yufanizing. Sónya is with me. We have no superintendent; we have only assistants in our agricultural labour and building operations, and she runs the office and the cash-box. I have bees, and sheep, and a new orchard, and a distillery. Everything goes well, though, of course, poorly in comparison with the ideal. What do you think of the Polish affairs? Things are bad! Shall we not be obliged to take the sword down from the rusty nail?" In reply to Fet's jest about Tolstóy's wife, who was so many years younger than her husband, Tolstóy again wrote to him in May: " My wife is not playing with dolls at all. Do not insult her. She is a serious helpmate of mine, and that, too, while she is carrying a burden, which she hopes to be relieved of in the beginning of July. What will come later? We are Yufanizing a bit. I have made an

Countess Tolstóy (née Sófiya Behrs)

Photogravure from a Photograph

important discovery, which I hasten to inform you of. Clerks and superintendents and elders are only a nuisance on an estate. Try to chase away all the managers and to sleep until ten o'clock, and things will certainly not go worse. I have made this experiment, and I am well satisfied with it."

Shortly afterward Fet visited the Tolstóys, and this is his account of the meeting: " I had just turned in between the towers, down the birch avenue, when I came upon Lev Nikoláevich, who was directing the drawing out of a seine along the whole length of a pond, and who was apparently taking every precaution to prevent the escape of the crucians, which concealed themselves in the ooze and rushed past the wings of the seine, without paying any attention to the furious snapping of the ropes and even axles.

" ' Oh, how glad I am ! ' he exclaimed, obviously dividing his attention between me and the crucians, ' Just a minute ! Iván ! Iván ! Pull the left wing in more sharply ! Sónya, have you seen Afanási Afanásevich ? '

" But this remark was apparently belated, for the countess, all dressed in white, had run up to me in the avenue, and continuing to run as fast, with an enormous bunch of household keys in her belt, and without paying any attention to her extremely advanced condition, had gone on in the direction of the pond, jumping over the slats of a low fence.

" ' What are you doing, countess ? ' I exclaimed in terror. ' How careless you are ! '

" ' Never mind,' she answered, with a pleasant smile, ' I am used to it.'

" ' Sónya, tell Nésterka to bring a bag from the storehouse, and let us go home.'

" The countess immediately separated an immense key from her belt and handed it to a boy, who started on a run to carry out the demand.

" ' Here,' said the count, ' you see a complete application

of our method: she keeps the keys and carries on all household operations by means of boys.'

" At the animated dinner there appeared the crucians which had been caught in our presence. Everybody seemed to be equally at ease and happy. This evening could justly be called full of hopes. It was worth seeing with what pride and bright hope the eyes of the good aunt Tatyána Aleksándrovna watched the dear nephew and his wife and, turning to me, spoke clearly, ' You see, of course, things cannot be different with *mon cher Léon.*'

" As to the young countess, the life of one in her condition, who jumps over fences, cannot help but be illumined with joyous hopes. The count himself, who had passed all his life in the search of novelty, during this period apparently entered into an unknown world, in the powerful future of which he believed with all the infatuation of an artist. I myself, carried away by the general tone of unbounded happiness, did not on that evening feel the stone of Sisyphus which was weighing heavily upon me."

In 1863 the rehabilitation of many exiles who had been sent to Siberia after the December revolt of 1825 revived the interest in that incident, and Tolstóy, too, began to busy himself with collecting material for a novel, *The Decembrists,* which, however, he never finished. During his research, he was taken back to the period preceding the revolt, and thus there ripened in him the desire to treat the great War of 1812. The subject grew upon him as he proceeded. He began with depicting the period preceding even the year of the French invasion under the name of *The Year 1805.* In the beginning of 1865 he wrote to Fet: " Do you know what a surprising thing I have to tell you about myself ? When my horse threw me, and I broke my arm, and I awoke from my swoon, I said to myself ' I am a litterateur.' And I am a litterateur, only a lonely litterateur, and all in the dark. In a few days will appear the first half of the first part of *The Year 1805*. Please give me your detailed opinion about it. I value your opinion and that of another man, whom I dislike in proportion as I am getting big, — Turgénev. He will understand it. What I have printed heretofore I consider only a trial of the pen; though I like what I am having printed now better than anything written by me before, it seems to me to be weak, as an introduction must be. What will be later, I tremble to think. Write me what they say in the various places where you are acquainted, and, above all, how it affects the crowd. No doubt it will pass unnoticed. I expect and wish that; if only they will not call me names, for scolding upsets me."

In May he wrote: "I am writing now and then, and I am satisfied with my work. The snipes still attract me, and every evening I shoot at them, that is, past them. My farming is going well, that is, it does not bother me much, — I have everything I ask from it. So much about myself. To your request to say something about the Yásnaya Polyána school I answer in the negative. Though your arguments are just, the periodicals have forgotten about it, and I do not want to bring it up, not because I have renounced anything I have said about it, but, on the contrary, because I do not cease thinking of it, and, if God grants me life, I hope from all that to make a book, with the conclusion at which I have arrived after three years of impassioned preoccupation with this matter. . . . Our agricultural affairs are now like the business of a shareholder who has shares that have lost their value and are not taken on Exchange. Of late I have been satisfied with my affairs, but the general course of things, that is, the imminent famine calamity of the masses, torments me more and more with every day. It is so strange, and even bad and terrible: at our table we have pink radishes, yellow butter, tinted soft bread on a clean table-cloth, the trees are green in the orchard, our young women wear muslin dresses and enjoy the heat and the shade, and there that evil demon Hunger is doing his work, covering the fields with orache, opening cracks in the parched earth, blistering the callus-covered heels of the peasant men and women, and splitting the horses' hoofs."

War and Peace proceeded slowly, the chief obstacle being the double problem set to himself by Tolstóy, of developing the historical plot by the side of the action of the characters. The parts as they appeared were received by the literary men in Russia with mingled feelings of delight and disappointment. His reputation became firmly established. Eugene Schuyler, who visited Tolstóy in 1868, tells of the excellent library which the author had in his possession and which dealt with Napoleon and his time. He not only investigated historical documents for his novel, but even went down to the battle-field at Borodinó, in order to get the local colouring. At the same time he was interested in philosophy and was carried away by Schopenhauer. "Do you know what happened to me this summer?" he wrote to Fet. "A continuous transport before Schopenhauer, and a series of spiritual pleasures which I never experienced before. I have ordered all his works and I have been reading them (I have also read Kant through). I am sure, not one student has during his course studied and learned so much as have I during the present summer. I do not know whether I shall ever change my mind, but now I am certain that Schopenhauer is one of the most genial of men. You said that he had just written something or other on philosophical questions. Just something or other? Why, this is a whole world in an incredibly clear and beautiful reflection. I have begun translating him. Won't you, too, take hold of the translation? We could get him out together. As I read him I marvel how it is his name could have remained unknown for so long a time. There is but one explanation, the one which he frequently repeats, that besides idiots there is hardly any one in the world."

Shortly afterward he announces that he is reading a great deal of Shakespeare, Göthe, Púshkin, Gógol, and Molière, and that he has given up reading periodicals and newspapers, to his great advantage. The drama for a while absorbed all his attention. "This whole winter I have been busying myself with the drama in general, and as always happens with people who up to their fortieth year have not thought of a certain subject and have formed no idea about it, and suddenly with a clearness which comes with forty years direct their attention upon a fresh subject, it seems to me that I see in it much that is new. The whole winter I have been enjoying myself by lying down, falling asleep, playing bézique, walking on snow-shoes, skating, and for the most part lying in bed (sick), when the characters of a drama or comedy begin to act. And they act very well. . . . I should also like to read Sophocles and Euripedes." In December of 1870 Tolstóy had proceeded sufficiently in the study of Greek to materialize his wish: "I am studying Greek from morning until night. I am not writing anything, because I am studying. To judge from the information which has reached me, your hide, offered as a parchment for my diploma of Greek, is in danger: incredible and unusual, — but I have read through Xenophon, and now I read him at random. But for Homer there is need of a dictionary and of some exertion. I am impatiently waiting to show this trick to somebody; but how happy I am that God has sent this madness on me. In the first place, I am enjoying myself; in the second place, I have convinced myself that of everything truly beautiful and simply beautiful produced by the human word I did not know anything before, just as all pretend to know it, but do not understand it; in the third, I am sure, I do not and will not write any wordy bosh. *Peccavi*, but upon my word, I never shall again. For the Lord's sake, explain to me why nobody knows Æsop's fables, nor even charming Xenophon, to say nothing of Plato, of Homer, who are still ahead for me. As much as I can judge even now, Homer has only been defiled by our translations, which are taken from the German model. A trite, but involuntary comparison: boiled and distilled water and water from a spring, which affects the teeth, with the sparkle and the sun and even the motes, which only make it purer. All these Vosses and Zhukóvskis sing in a syrupy, guttural, and fawning voice. But that devil sings, and shouts from a full breast, and it has never occurred to him that any one may hear him. You may triumph: without the knowledge of Greek there is no culture. But what knowledge? How is it to be acquired? What is it good for? For all that I have arguments which are as clear as day."

Tolstóy's health had never been very good, and his predisposition to consumption — he had lost two brothers by that disease — had once before caused him to go to Samára for the purpose of undergoing a kumys cure. He had continued this cure at home, manufacturing his own kumys, a malodorous ferment, which he kept close to his study. In June of 1871 his wife insisted upon his going once more to Samára, as his health was again failing. While living among the Bashkirs, whose simplicity and naturalness he admired greatly, he read Herodotus, and imagined that in the Bashkirs he recognized those very Scythians of whom the Greek author spoke. The virgin newness of the country attracted him, and he thought seriously of purchasing an estate there. After his return to Yásnaya Polyána he once more opened a peasant school, in which he himself and his wife and children acted as teachers. As early as 1868, when Eugene

Tolstóy's Daughters Tatyána and Márya
Luóvna

Photogravure from a Photograph

Schuyler visited him, he had been working on the composition of primers, as the existing ones seemed to him to be written in a poor language and to be beyond the children. At his request, Schuyler provided for him a number of American school-books, which aided him materially in his undertaking. These primers, four in number, containing original short stories, among them the *Prisoner of the Caucasus*, and a mass of translations and adaptations, he finished soon after he had again opened school. He put his whole soul into this matter, as he himself said, adding, changing, and correcting for a long time. Such is the simplicity and straightforwardness of the diction in the stories contained in these primers, that they even now form the best parts of Russian primers for the public schools.

At the same time he began to write *Anna Karénin*, " a work which is near to my heart," as he wrote at the time. Turgénev, who heard of Tolstóy's new literary work, hoped that there would not be any philosophy in it. Tolstóy's life was fully occupied with his work on his great novel, teaching school, and instructing his children in Greek and mathematics, attending to his agricultural labours, and now and then going out with an axe to fell trees or with a scythe to mow with the peasants. After eleven years of married life, death for the first time visited Tolstóy's home : he lost two children in rapid succession, and a little later his aunt passed away. Samára was visited several summers, the wide steppes and their inhabitants having an ever increasing attraction for him. " These two months I have not soiled my hands with ink or my heart with thoughts. Now I am once more taking up tiresome, sickening *Anna Karénin* with the one desire as quickly as possible to make room for myself, — to find time for other occupations, anything but pedagogical, which I love, but wish to give up. They take up too much of my time. I want to talk to you about many,

many things, but I cannot write about them. One must live, as we did, in the healthy wilderness of Samára, see this struggle of the nomad life (of millions upon enormous extents of territory) with the primitive agricultural life, which is taking place under our very eyes, feel all the significance of this struggle, to become convinced that, if more than one, there are three rapidly running and loudly shouting destroyers of the social order, that this social order is the disease of a parasite of the living oak, that the oak is not concerned about the parasite, — that this is not smoke, but a shadow which is running away from the smoke. Why my fate has taken me there, I do not know; but I do know that I have heard speeches in the English parliament (this, you know, is considered to be very important), and I felt annoyed and tired; while there, though there are flies, dirt, Bashkir peasants, I with tense respect and awe look and listen, and feel that everything there is important."

A change was slowly taking place in Tolstóy. The expressions of the critics interested him less and less, and he failed to become enthusiastic over the French translation of his works made by Turgénev and Madame Viardot. Again it was death, not so much the death of his children, as his own, which he anticipated within a short time, that closed the third period of his activity, during which his great novels, *War and Peace* and *Anna Karénin*, were produced. On April 29, 1876, Tolstóy wrote to Fet:

" From one of your last letters, in which I overlooked the phrase, ' I wanted to call you to see me go away,' which you wrote in the midst of a discussion on the feeding of horses, and which I have only just now grasped, I have transferred myself into your condition, which is comprehensible and very near to me, and I feel sorry for you. Both according to Schopenhauer and our conscience, compassion and love are one and the same thing, — and I wanted to write to you. I thank you for your idea of calling me to see you pass away, when you thought that the end was near. I will do the same, when I get ready to go *there*, if I shall have enough strength to think. I would need no one so much at that moment as you and my brother. Before death the communion with men who in this life look beyond its confines is dear and joyous; and you and those rare, real men whom I have met on a close footing in life, in spite of their wholesome relation to life, always stand on the very brink and see life clearly, for the very reason that they look, now into Nirvana, into unlimitedness, into the unknown, now into sansara, and this looking into Nirvana strengthens their vision. But worldly people, no matter how much they may speak of God, are disagreeable to men of our calibre and must be painful in the time of death, because they do not see what we see, namely, that God, more indefinite, more distant, but higher and more indubitable, as it says in that article. You are ill and you think of death; but I am well, and I do not stop thinking of the same and preparing for it. Let us see who will be first. But suddenly, from various imperceptible data, it has become clear to me how deeply related your nature, your soul (especially in relation to death), is to me, so that I have suddenly come to appreciate our relations and have begun more than ever to hold them dear. Much of what I have been thinking I have tried to express in the last chapter of the April number of the *Russian Messenger* (in the seventh part of *Anna Karénin*)."

V.

TOLSTÓY had from his earliest youth been sensitive to every false note and sham in our so-called civilization, and had taken every occasion to point out its flaws. But it was only when he directed his attention to school matters, and thus turned away from the activity of the artistic litterateur, whose opposition to the existing order had been taken by his contemporaries as a mere freak of a genius, as a desire to introduce something new and startling, that he was confronted with the necessity of establishing his views on a philosophic basis and proving his arguments and paradoxes. He at once defined the programme of his periodical, *Yásnaya Polyána,* in a leading article, *On Popular Education,* and from this programme he has never departed, though he has extended it, so as to include many other than purely pedagogical principles.

"Popular education" was the watchword of all those who claimed to be liberal, and to question the panacea of popular education was tantamount to aligning oneself with obscurantism. But Tolstóy was not carried away by words. Popular education! Very well. But why are the masses always opposed to receiving what is recognized as a boon, and why has it to be made compulsory? So popular education, like the army, like government, like the state religion, which are many years afterward brought into the circle of his vision, is based on violence, and what is born of violence cannot be beneficial. The freedom of the school has been the desideratum of philosophers from Plato to Kant, but in enforcing individual ideas, the school has every time been made an instrument of compulsion, and has thus failed of its purpose. No wonder it creates scientific parrots, morally irresponsible boobies, living machines, and becomes, "not a shepherd for the flock, but a flock for the shepherd."

The real school is life, which is unhampered by any pedagogical sophistries, and for this reason the labouring classes learn their lessons in the theatre, the café chantant, the dram-shops, and prefer *The Three Musketeers* and *Monte Cristo* to books written in a scientific lingo. Tolstóy has frequently been proclaimed a visionary, and yet so many of his educational ideas have since his day been realized, at least in America, that there is no reasonable ground to assume that his other pedagogical principles, though untried, are unsound. The elective system of education, which is extending down and lower in the educational hierarchy, the extension of library and laboratory facilities, the wide use to which popular lectures are put, the correspondence schools, the university extension, — all have come since the day Tolstóy preached the absolute, not the historical, freedom of the school. That the safety of the state depends upon the education of its citizens is a trite saying in America, but that is a sentiment which Tolstóy would emphatically reject, because such education is compulsory and leads to slavish obedience. He wants for education a much wider scope, for "education, in its widest sense, including the bringing up, is that activity of man which has for its base the need of equality and the invariable law of educational progress." In other words, equality, the brotherhood of man, is the final and only aim of education, as it is of religion.

Passing to particular points in education, the author casts a flood of light upon subjects which, by the modern so-called science of pedagogy, are left as densely obscure as ever. He scathingly arraigns that pedagogy which still looks upon the lower school as a nursery for the higher institutions of learning, thus practising the most irksome violence against the whole mass of pupils, in order to send an insignificant minority to the higher schools. In *On the Teaching of the Rudiments* he demands that the pupils of the lowest schools be given a useful education, fitting them for life, without considering whether or no it fits them for the universities. Alas, our public schools still insist on cramming into the heads of the poor children the capital of Nepaul, and intricate problems on deferred payments, and the difference between the republican and the democratic parties, subjects utterly unadapted to tender years! The worst of it is, that the "child is asked to comprehend in precisely the same manner that the teacher comprehends it," whereas all methods of instructing the rudiments are equally bad and equally good. Then Tolstóy proceeds to analyze the absurd method of object-teaching and the torture known as reading by sounds, and points out that frequently the old method of giving special names to letters, without any obvious relation to their sounds, has produced just as good results as any of the new-fangled methods of pedagogy. The teacher must know all methods and apply them in accordance with the individual cases. Every method is only a step and, "as the business of teaching is an art, completeness and perfection are not obtainable, while development and perfectibility are endless." In this last sentence the error of modern pedagogy and the philosophy of the real pedagogy are admirably defined. It is because pedagogy deems itself to be a science and capable of perfection that it blunders so egregiously. If it recognized the striving toward an impossible absolute perfection as its goal, it would be less doctrinaire and more liberal. On the other hand, we have here a particular case of Tolstóy's later complete system of perfectionism, whether religious, moral, or social: it is a striving toward an absolute, finitely impossible perfection, not the possession of it, which would be death.

In a *Project of a General Plan for the Establishment of Popular Schools* Tolstóy gives a telling blow to the paternal system of the establishment of popular schools by the government. After pointing out the fact that Russia cannot develop educationally along the same lines as America, he scrutinizes the governmental *Project*, lays bare its glittering generalities, indicates the hopelessness of any reform coming from above, and finally launches into an illustration of the manner in which the peasants would execute the school law. He predicts that every provision of the *Project* would become a mere farce, that the peasants would see nothing in the establishment of the schools but a method for imposing a new tax upon them. More than forty years have passed since that prediction was made, and every word of it has proven true, — so intimate was his acquaintance with the peasant mind and his knowledge of the devious ways of the government.

In the essay *Education and Culture* Tolstóy further develops the idea that education is only a species of violence, and draws a distinction between culture, which is free, and education, which is "the tendency toward moral despotism raised to a principle." This condemnation covers all institutions of learning, including the universities which, since they are not entirely free, have no other basis than arbitrariness and do not widely differ from the monastic schools. The universities, a dislike for which he had expressed in *Youth*, and which, as the seat of pseudo-scientific learning, he later in life treated with even greater contempt, are to him no better than the female boarding-schools, inasmuch as they both alienate the students from the influences of home, widening the gap between the educated and the lower classes. This alienation begins in the gymnasium and even in the popular schools, and grows in proportion as the so-called higher learning is acquired. The contempt expressed by

Tolstóy in *Youth* for the professors of a Russian university is here formulated as due to the feeling of abhorrence for the dogma of the professor's infallibility. For the university lectures he has little love, since they admit of no discussion by the students and since it is frequently easier and more convenient to acquire knowledge through the medium of books. A real university is "a collection of men for the purpose of their mutual culture."

In summing up his argument, Tolstóy comes to the conclusion that public lectures, museums, are the best examples of schools without interference in education, while the universities are not. To make the university free, not only must the student be free to choose subjects of instruction for himself, but the teacher must be allowed to teach, not merely as he pleases, but also what he pleases. The definite appointment of a teacher to lecture on a certain small part of some subject is as injurious as any other kind of violence. Here again a comparison with what has been done since in the United States in the matter of emancipating education from the bonds of violence will show the far-sightedness of Tolstóy. Many of his suggestions have been realized in institutions of higher learning. The lecture is not, as in Germany and Russia, the only means for imparting knowledge. Every good teacher knows how to temper his dictum with that discussion which is the essence of good instruction. Unfortunately, however, some of the universities, in their desire to equal the German schools, are falling back into the sin of lecturing. The practical side of education and the articulation with the life of the family is to some extent fostered by the agricultural, technical, industrial schools, by the correspondence schools and the university extensions, the latter being a feeble representation of what Tolstóy regards as a real university. Where so many suggestions of the author have to some degree been realized in life, it is fair to assume that his other suggestions, though still untried, will prove equally fertile of results.

In pointing out the parallelism between the American methods and Tolstóy's theories, I do not by any means insist on their identity. There is, in spite of the great resemblance, a vast difference between them. Tolstóy's theories are the logical deductions of a central idea, non-interference in education, the abolition of violence, not only in pedagogy, but in life in general. All these deductions every time correspond to the demands of reason, and have little to do with practical issues. According to the Russian conception, the practical issues must be accommodated to the dictates of reason. In the American system, the practical necessities call for reforms, and these are made without any uniform principle, change with every new demand, and stand isolated. Though apparently the same results are achieved as those aimed at by the preaching of Tolstóy, the Anglo-Saxon method of practical issues lacks the philosophical stability of the non-compromising Russian philosophy, while, on the other hand, the extreme logical deductions of Tolstóy's theories frequently fail to gain adherents on account of their disregard of existing conditions. Ultimately, however, it is the Tolstóyan system which must prevail, if education is not signally to suffer defeat.

The Russian pedagogues, educated in the German methods, took exception to Tolstóy's advanced views, which to them could not appear otherwise than heretical, and to one of these Tolstóy felt himself constrained to answer in a special article, *Progress and the Definition of Education*. This is not only a clear presentation of the subject of free education, but also summarizes his opposition to so-called progress, an opposition from which he has never receded. What Markóv, his opponent, brought up against Tolstóy was the claptrap of pedagogical science, — the demands of the time, historical evolution, progress.

But our author is not to be stormed by high-sounding words: he wants a formula by which the demands of the time can be precisely determined, — none such exists; to him historical evolution is merely a justification of the present order of things; progress, — but is progress universal and beneficial? The Chinese have not had any progress in the European sense of the word, and the Europeans have tried to introduce progress there by means of powder and cannon-balls. The masses of the people, in Russia as well as elsewhere, have always been opposed to it. It is only the upper classes, who preach the fetish of progress, that are benefited by the invention of printing, by literature, by the telegraph, the railways, the steamboats, and not the peasants, who are in no need of all these advantages of progress.

Here we meet for the first time with Tolstóy's economic ideas, which are these, that the Russian peasants cannot be gauged by the laws which lie at the foundation of political economy in the West. To the Russian agriculturist wages are not the measure of well-being. For them well-being consists in the increase of the powers of the soil and other agricultural factors. None of these are advanced by so-called progress. At the same time, it is the masses that form the most important part of the people: in them there is more force than in generations of barons, bankers, and professors. The progress of civilization is one of the most violent evils, and the progress of well-being is for the most part opposed to the progress of civilization. It must be recalled that this was enunciated by Tolstóy long before E. Carpenter declared civilization to be a disease, and independently of and previous to Henry George's *Progress and Poverty* and books of a similar turn. There are few views, held by Tolstóy, that have not at one time or another been enunciated by some European writer, but none have so persistently taken up a stand against so-called civilization and progress as

Tolstóy, and none have with such unabating zeal and with such oneness of purpose hunted down everything which bears upon itself the impress of violence. Even the usual relation of the educator to the educated is repulsive to him, and he establishes a new principle of education, namely, that education is the activity of man which has for its base the need of equality and the invariable law of educational progress. Thus the final aim of education is to equalize the pupil with the teacher, and education, as regards the educator, comes to an end when the pupil has become equal with his teacher.

So convinced has Tolstóy always been that there is more strength and original genius in the peasant class than in other classes, that he set out to prove that even the peasant children could teach us how to compose themes. This thought he developed in an article entitled, *Are the Peasant Children to Learn to Write from Us ? Or, Are We to Learn from the Peasant Children ?* In trying to teach the peasant children how to write compositions, Tolstóy soon discovered, as he thought, that the children have better ideas of the entity of the story, far more correctly and naturally develop the plot, and express themselves in much better language, than do authors of the literary class. The history of the creation of a number of compositions is unfolded to us as it took place under Tolstóy's guidance, and with an enthusiasm of surprise is pointed out to us the marvellous superiority of the child mind over that of maturer years. It has been remarked that what the peasant children did was, under the suggestive influence of Tolstóy himself, to create in his own style, thus evoking his admiration and transport. But this accusation is hardly just. The critics have been misled by Tolstóy's Rousseauan attitude as regards the perfection of the natural man to assume that this bias, and not the actual facts, lies at the base of Tolstóy's utterances. Indeed, he himself says in this essay that

Rousseau's statement that "Man is born perfect," remains firm and true as a rock. Proceeding from this, he argues that man's perfection lies behind, and not in front of him, and that the child is nearer to the original harmony than is man. Education is not a development of the harmony, but its progressive arrest. If this proposition is correct, then it follows that a child must be more artistic than man, for beauty, truth, and goodness express only the harmony of relations.

Still, however logical the conclusion may be, the average person will deny the fact that the child is born perfect and that education ruins this harmony. If so, let us turn to Tolstóy's riper judgment as expressed in *What Is Art?* There he makes sincerity one of the most important criterions of an artistic production. Now, sincerity is certainly to a greater extent found in children than in grown people. What makes us doubt the possibility of child perfection is the fact that we are in the habit of considering the adulterated art, which looks upon form and expression as the only points worthy of note, as the only art to be inculcated upon the children. With Tolstóy, it is simplicity, naturalness, sincerity, that are the characteristics of real art, and these are possessed by children much more than by those who are corrupted by life. The main point, then, in teaching children to write is not to spoil them, not to distract their attention by remarks about the cleanliness of their copy-books, or about their penmanship, orthography, structure of sentences, and logic. In other words, the greater the freedom of the instruction, the better the results.

This Tolstóy tried to illustrate in his own case by describing in detail the work done in the school established by him (*The School at Yásnaya Polyána for the Months of November and December, 1862*). His experiments are summed up in the following statement: "I am convinced that the school ought not to interfere in that part of the

education which belongs to the family; that the school
has no right and ought not to reward and punish; that
the best police and administration of a school consist in
giving full liberty to the pupils to study and settle their
disputes as they know best." Of course, he did not always
carry out his own principles, as old habits proved too
strongly ingrained to be entirely cast aside. None the
less, what he attempted to do was to make the school
absolutely free. Of the many practical suggestions based
on the freedom of instruction, where the children are not
compelled to attend to their lessons or to preserve any
order, none is probably more significant than this, that in
the ordinary schools the teacher strives after the method
of instruction which makes the teaching and the management easiest for him, whereas the more convenient the
instruction is for the teacher, the more inconvenient it is
for the pupils, and only that instruction is correct which
satisfies the pupils. By this criterion the public schools
of America, in spite of their vaunted superiority, stand
condemned, and the frightful mediocrity and low stand-
ard of their pupils are at once explained. The American
teacher, if he is not of the machine-made, "Normal"
kind, will find a treasury of valuable information in the
pages of this article; but again there is danger in the application of this method of disorder, if, in Anglo-Saxon
fashion, it is not adapted as a whole, but only as a series
of practical suggestions.

Incidentally we get in this essay two views, one on
the Bible, the other on art, which deserve more than
a passing notice, as they indicate the early trend of his
mind in the direction of an intimate study and love of
Scripture and the early stage of his negative attitude
toward modern art, as expressed later in *What Is Art?*
Tolstóy found that there was no book which interested
his pupils so much as the Bible, and that there was no
production that united all the sides of human thought in

such a compressed poetical form as is to be found in the Bible. He wished to use the Bible as a model for all manuals and readers for children, and declared that an idiomatic translation of the Bible would be the best popular book and would be an epoch in the history of the Russian nation. As to art, Tolstóy even then recognized that the art of cultured society is all false, and that there is more real art in the popular chap-book illustrations, inasmuch as they evoke a moral sentiment, whereas the Venus de Milo rouses in the masses nothing but a legitimate loathing for the nakedness and shamelessness of the woman. Similarly he found more real music in the popular songs than in Beethoven's quartette, and said that both Beethoven and Púshkin "flatter our freaky irritability." For this reason, in teaching young people and the masses music, the knowledge of the common laws of music possessed by us, and not the false taste which is developed in us, is to be transmitted to them.

Though after 1863 Tolstóy did not directly interest himself in the peasant schools, his interest in the education of the masses remained unabated, and in 1872 he brought out a series of primers for the use of country schools. In these he attempted to tell stories and give scientific information, whether of his own composition or based on borrowing and imitation, with the least literary elaboration and in the simplest language possible, so as to be adapted to the mind of the children of the masses. Among these stories are contained *God Sees the Truth, but Does Not Tell at Once* and *The Prisoner of the Caucasus*, which he later, under the influence of a searching criticism of artistic productions, whether his own or of others, considered as among the few specimens of good art produced by him. Here again the reader may feel inclined to differ from the author's judgment, considering these stories for children as in no way comparable with *The Cossacks* or *The Death of Iván Ílich*. But it is the simplicity, straightforwardness, sincerity, and, in the case of *God Sees the Truth*, the religious sentiment, which alone, according to Tolstóy, determine the artistic value of a production, and as these two stories please an infinitely greater number of men than his other writings, which are accessible to but a few, Tolstóy's valuation of his own works is not a mere freak, as has been said, but is entirely in keeping with his philosophy, which has not materially changed in the last half-century.

In 1875 Tolstóy once more reverted to his pedagogical activity by writing an exhaustive criticism of existing methods of education (*On Popular Education*). He here reiterates all his previous theories, finds that in the current school systems the whole attention is directed toward teaching the pupil what he already knows, that the German method of instruction is not fit for Russian children, and that the mechanical side of instruction predominates over the mental. He is led once more to emphasize the fundamental principle that "the only criterion of pedagogy is freedom, the only method — experience." The remaining part of the essay is devoted to a criticism of the village schools in Russia and to an analysis of how freedom in education, carried to its farthest consequences, would work in raising the mental level of the peasant population.

VI.

THE period during which Tolstóy produced his two great novels, *War and Peace* and *Anna Karénin,* was one of the tensest struggle for him. His opposition to civilization, progress, the false in art, the historical method, and his faith in the original harmony of man, the superiority of the untutored masses to the cultured classes, the freedom, not only of instruction, but also of all activities of life, tentatively striven after from his earliest youth, were now firmly established and attested by his experience with his peasants and their children. His spiritual life was permanently removed from the sphere of social forms, without as yet culminating in an abstract uniform creed. On the other hand, his happy domestic life, his pedagogical and agricultural labours, the demands of his impassioned nature, held him vise-like in the toils of the present, submerging the spiritual man in the carnal. His convictions removed him to a distant future and eliminated him from the companionship of men. His life, rooted in the present, drew him nearer to a more vigorous past, in which men were not yet affected by harrowing doubts. The two moods constantly intruded upon one another, philosophy poisoning the pure enjoyment of life, and life diverting philosophy into lower channels.

Even before this time Tolstóy had never used literature as an amusement for himself or as a means for the amusement of his readers. His literary works were the truthful reproductions of his inner experiences, though, in accordance with the artistic demands of the literary coterie to which he belonged, he clothed these in an artistic form. When the conveyance of his convictions seemed to him to be more urgent than the conveyance of his sensations, as was the case with his pedagogical essays, and much later with his religious and social ideas, he consciously abandoned the artistic form and even neglected the literary norm in his desire to tell the whole truth and nothing but the truth.

He had for a long time dreamed of a happy domestic life, but his marriage, though it gave him everything a man could wish for, failed to allay his doubts, which frequently verged on despair. His associations with the peasants, though they strengthened his dislike for the artificial forms of society, failed to provide him with a ready solution of the problems which had driven him back to the country. His study of history, of Greek, of the drama, to which he had recourse in the desire to widen his mental horizon, only filled him with greater contempt for the self-assertiveness of the sciences and arts, and he set out to search for a new meaning of life, one which would be independent of the vagaries of science. Tormented as he was with an unsatisfied spiritual desire, his earthly bonds evoked before him visions, such as come to the saintly hermit amidst his fasts and devotions : pictures of a happy, innocent youth, the pleasures of manly sport, the din and strife of battle.

It is this titanic inward struggle, this reaching out for a distant and impossible happiness, this clutching and hugging of an irretrievable past, this incorporeal objectivity of thought and concentrated subjectivity of feeling which was going on in him, that Tolstóy externally and internally focused in his two great novels, — externally, in the strange mixture of novel and history, of dialogue and reflection, of calm contemplation and bitter arraignment, and internally, in the strivings of his well-meaning, vacillating, temperamentally unhappy heroes, Pierre and

Levín. *War and Peace* and *Anna Karénin* are not novels
of the ordinary kind, — a plot, a dose of love, a dash of
wickedness, — but records of mental experiences, set off
by a distressing, false, perverted reality. The reader,
guided by the current idea of what constitutes a novel, is
misled into believing that the plot, the love-story, the
delineation of character, are the essential parts of Tolstóy's
narrative, and is apt to look upon the philosophical digres-
sions and the microscopic details of certain scenes as
useless ánd halting incidents in an otherwise grand conception.

But the process of Tolstóy's creation is the very reverse
of the one pursued by the traditional art. Tolstóy is
interested in himself alone, not in the egoistical sense
of self-sufficiency, but as the only safe criterion of the
world outside. His own experiences, his own spiritual
advancement, his own struggle with the flesh, and the
ascertainment of the truth, religious, moral, social, as it
appears to him, are the subjects that have interested him
exclusively from the time he wrote *Childhood*, and it is
only the massive power of his artistic genius, working
within him in spite of himself, that causes him to clothe
his autobiography, considered from various aspects, in the
form of a connected story of novelistic incidents. Regarded as novels merely, *War and Peace* and *Anna
Karénin* lack uniformity and unity of action, but viewed
as annals of life, their artistic setting and the elaboration
of details add vividness and relief to the abstract striving of a searching soul. The novels, like bulbous plants,
consist of a series of superimposed integuments : remove
these one by one, and the pith will be reached, — the
essence, and that will invariably be the author himself.

Let us take *War and Peace.* Its genealogy is interesting : Tolstóy began by investigating the history of the
Decembrists, which, being the history of a revolt, was
eminently adapted to his mood of revolt against the exist-

ing order. He was taken back to the beginnings of this revolt, to the troubled time of the French invasion, and to *The Year 1805*, which logically antedated the incidents he wished to develop. He had intended to work out the history of the national opposition to the political conditions of the first quarter of the nineteenth century, in order to find in them a counterpart or an explanation for his own negative attitude. Instead, he was led to study the great national struggle, the *War*, which gave him the artistic background for his novel; but he soon discovered that in doing so he was drawn away from himself to a world of struggle outside himself, and he felt constrained, after having laboriously brought Pierre, a reflection of his own inner life, out of the tangle and contention of historical forces, to return to the treatment of his inward strife, — to *Peace*. But his own struggles, at the time the novel was ended, were not complete, and so, while *War* furnishes us with a rounded narrative of historical events, *Peace*, like life itself, leaves us in the middle, after bringing us down to the period in the author's life when the literary exigencies of the novel, already overtaxed, demanded an ending.

In *The School at Yásnaya Polyána* Tolstóy tells us of his idea of teaching history in the following words : " I have also made experiments in teaching modern history, and they have been very successful. I told them the history of the Crimean campaign, and the reign of Emperor Nicholas, and the year 1812. All this I told almost in a fairy-tale tone, as a rule, historically incorrect, and with the events grouped about some one person. The greatest success was obtained, as was to have been expected, by the story of the war with Napoleon." Here we have, not only an explanation why the year 1812 was chosen by him as the central event for his novel, but also an exposition of the manner in which he treated historical incidents : they were grouped about some one person and were not necessarily historically correct. This verdict will hold in regard to the historical background of *War and Peace,* where historical accuracy, however cautiously striven after by the author, is not to be looked for, and where incidents are grouped about Napoleon, Alexander I., Kutúzov, Pierre, as persons who are most adapted to the writer's purpose. Tolstóy has been accused of having made a number of historical blunders, and a prominent general has pointed out mistakes of a military character, such as a wrong disposition of the forces at Borodinó. It is quite likely that Tolstóy himself was acquainted with his shortcomings at the time of his writing, but that he preferred occasionally to depart from the historical truth, for the sake of a more artistic and even more philosophical treatment of his subject.[1]

Indeed, many truths are conveyed to us by him that strike us more forcibly and affect us more powerfully than the mere enumeration of actual occurrences. If he describes battles, which stand out with harrowing vividness, he impresses us with the idea that the issue of a battle, the victory or the defeat, is frequently a matter of mere guesswork, that orders are never executed as intended, that battles never take place as planned, that personal bravery counts for little, that officers are seldom distinguished for courage. If the Sevastopol sketches filled us with horror at the recital of the deadly effect of war, the present treatment of war adds contempt for the whole so-called military science and makes us look with pity and disrespect upon the military leaders. Similarly we are made to scale down our regard for the genius of Napoleon, who is represented to us as a man possessed of petty human weaknesses and an exalted opinion of himself. For Napoleon he had the same loathing that later he expressed

---

[1] Only after this chapter was written did the translator discover Tolstóy's own statement concerning *War and Peace* (given in the present volume, p. 181), which corroborates the above mentioned opinion.

for the blasphemers of the Holy Ghost, as he could not help but think of Napoleon as the personification of violence and militarism. He is not even willing to ascribe to him any personal influence upon the eastward and westward movements of the nations, or upon the abandonment and conflagration of Moscow. If in his former sketches war was realistically painted from within, it now is divested of its last trace of usefulness and is deprived of every justification.

In a similar manner he treats the deleterious effects of the governmental power. He heaps equal ridicule upon the municipal regulations of Napoleon during his stay in Moscow and upon quarrelsome, ambitious, selfish Rostopchín, who turns poor Voronhohágin over to the fury of the mob. It is true, he depicts Alexander I. as a generous Tsar, beloved by his subjects; but there is nothing in the picture to indicate that Alexander I. was possessed of any positive characteristics, and the awe inspired by his presence reminds one of that hypnotization which later he put at the base of all governmental power. Diplomacy is by him robbed of all significance, and diplomats are either small-witted gossips or downright fools. Where he is not hampered by the national patriotism, which he, however, does not seem to share, he finds nothing attractive or excusable in the whole governmental machinery: Napoleon is a petty bourgeois, Murat a feeble, pompous prince, and the Emperor of Austria a timid simpleton; councils of war are assemblies of inept generals more concerned about personal preferments and the exactness of their military operations than about beneficial results; and life proceeds fairly well without the protection of the authorities.

In respect to society he assumes the same negative attitude as before. The higher circle which congregated at the house of Madame Scherer, the superficial society which Andréy Bolkónski shuns, the profligate set with whom Pierre associates for a time, the temporizing and fawning Prince Vasíli and his brood of degenerate children, Hélène and her following of debauchees, are all equally intended as deterrents from that artificial world of men who constitute the upper classes of the metropolitan population. As opposed to these, he dwells with sympathy upon the well-meant, mystic activity of the Mason Bazdyéev, though the Masons at large present themselves to him as worldly men who are bent upon the advancement of their own petty purposes, and he can find even some good in the brutally despotic type of the elder Bolkónski, in whom there lies at least the germ of a sterling second generation, represented by Andréy and Márya. Above all, it is the simple-minded family of the Rostóvs, in whom he sees the prototype of his own, that rivets most of his attention.

There is probably nothing in *War and Peace* that surpasses the delicate psychological discrimination with which he depicts family groups. There is certainly an abyss between religiously fervent Márya and self-poised Andréy on the one hand, and their unyielding, tyrannical father on the other, and yet the reader feels constantly that they are the same positive characters, but under changed conditions of time. How absolutely one and the same are Prince Vasíli, with his insinuating pressure of the hand, and unconscionable, half-witted, degenerate Ippolít, and fleshly, vulgar, debauched Hélène! And who does not see the blood identity of the ingenuous family of the Rostóvs, with the good-natured father, the fond and impassioned mother, impetuous and enthusiastic Nikoláy, and childishly frank Pétya, and thoughtless and yet lovable Natásha, who later makes such an excellent mother, and even petulant Vyéra, who, under the influence of her calculating German husband, becomes a somewhat narrow-minded, but yielding wife?

All this splendid setting of history and society serves

only as a background for his hero, Pierre, who is Tolstóy historically removed. But Pierre is not all of Tolstóy. Just as in *Boyhood* and *Youth* Irténev and Nekhlyúdov represent two sides of the same man, so the sterner, more spiritual aspect of the author was depicted in Andréy Bolkónski, whose very death thoughts anticipate the later conceptions of the author himself, just as homely, patient, long-suffering, devoted Márya is an exact reproduction of his mother, of whom he knew only from hearsay. The more earthly, vacillating, helpless, earnestly striving Pierre is Tolstóy with all the complexity of his insoluble questions and contradictory sentiments. He suffers constantly, not only because he sees the vapidity of society life about him and the calamities entailed by war and the wretchedness of the peasants, but also because he vainly strives after religious and moral perfection, under the guidance of his Masonic friends, and is utterly at a loss how to help the peasants, and fails to acquire any definite habits or to find any appropriate field of action for himself. His marriage to Hélène is an utter failure, and he cannot tear himself away from that corrupt society in the meshes of which he is caught by his wife and her family. At last his salvation comes. Natásha, intended for the sterner Andréy, loses him through her own thoughtlessness, and makes a good wife for the less spiritual Pierre. In the bosom of his family, with all its petty cares and its humdrum life, he seeks oblivion from the doubts that have beset him heretofore. The novel ends where Tolstóy's own happy domestic life left him at the time that he completed *War and Peace*.

But the ideal toward which even then Tolstóy tended was neither Pierre nor Andréy, but Platón Karatáev, the simple peasant of the type of Natálya Sávishna, whose life of meekness and submission to fate comes nearest to the Christian ideal preached by the Gospel. So far Platón was still an unattainable perfection, and served for Pierre-

Tolstóy as a court of final appeal in matters of conduct. For woman he establishes as the highest ideal the condition of motherhood, in which all other sides of life are lost sight of and are of little importance. His types of women are, outside of the negligible, corrupt Hélène and her like, of two classes: either the women possess the precise, single-minded, loyal characteristics of Sónya, and then, however attractive they must appear to an Anglo-Saxon, who would invariably choose them for heroines, they are declared by Tolstóy to be "sterile" and are ruthlessly cast aside; or they are temperamentally changeable and unaccountable in their affections, which are generally bestowed upon the wrong persons, but superlatively endowed with the animal instinct of maternity, to which they finally abandon themselves to the exclusion of every other sentiment. Even such is Natásha. As militarism, carnage, death are the harvest of *War*, so domesticity is the apotheosis of *Peace*, — that domesticity which Tolstóy dreamed of in the *Cossacks* and hoped for in *Domestic Happiness*.

Thus *War and Peace* is an enlarged diary of inner experiences and philosophic strivings. The chosen career of a novelist kept Tolstóy within the narrow frame of a novel, and prevented him from expatiating upon his theme in a scientific treatise, which, besides, he could not have done at that period, as his dreams, hopes, and ideas had not yet become sufficiently concrete for such an objective treatment. Viewed from the standpoint of an artistic production, *War and Peace* naturally lacks completeness; but if it is viewed as an elaboration of a diary of inner experiences, these defects vanish, and we are left to admire the many artistic details in which the novel abounds to an extraordinary degree. The vivid narration of battle scenes, the grandeur and awe of Andréy's illness and death, and the deaths of Pétya and Platón, the minute descriptions of natural scenery and of sports, in which he always delights, the exquisite delineation of character, are magnificent mosaics in the great national epic, which throughout bears witness to the author's gigantic genius during the period of tense internal struggle toward self-perfection.

Anna Karénin brings us one step nearer to the author's mental transformation. His domestic happiness had not lost any of its charms and did not cease to give him a full measure of contentment ; but the eternal questions demanded an answer with ever greater persistency, and to this answer Tolstóy felt himself obliged to give utterance in a novel which would represent his own state and the condition of society in a more contemporaneous form than *War and Peace.* The title of the novel is misleading, since it is not Anna Karénin who is the centre of it, but Levín. Indeed, the novel proceeds just as well without Anna as it does with her. Just as *War and Peace* began with *The Year 1805,* so the present novel was evidently intended as a portrayal of manners of society, but, as it proceeded, Tolstóy, as usual, fell back upon himself and his own inner life, which begged for expression, and the story continued to deal with Levín alone, and came to a stop when Tolstóy's own experiences did not warrant any further analysis : it stops with the day when Tolstóy wrote the last chapter, and thus is a valuable contribution to the study of the author's mental state previous to his so-called conversion.

As a mere novel, *Anna Karénin* is more perfect than *War and Peace.* The long disquisitions are avoided, and whatever didacticism there is scattered through its pages is deftly dealt out in the form of conversations. The plot itself is more uniform, and the two elements of which it is composed, the story of the fall of a woman and the autobiography of Levín, are blended together without displaying the sutures as in the older novel. Otherwise it contains the same component parts as before, — the minute description of special incidents, such as the hunt, the races, the field work, the representation of city life as undesirable and of an activity in the country as alone worthy of man, the emphatic contempt for the professions and for so-called science and the laudation of the life of the simple peasant. The treatment of the characters is the same as before, but their modernness brings them nearer to the reader than did the historical background of the first novel.

The plot is unobtrusively told. Anna Karénin, becoming untrue to her marriage vows and allying herself with Vrónski, with whom she becomes infatuated, suffers the natural punishment for her crime, and in a moment of despair commits suicide. But the situations and the denouément are not forced. Anna is more sinned against than sinning, for her cold, precise husband has not been able to foster love in his warm-hearted wife. Anna is not a criminal, and does not rush headlong into the commission of a breach of morality, but is inevitably drawn into the abyss by the force of circumstances. Nor is Vrónski an unconscionable wretch: his education, the levity of the society in which he moves, and his own impassioned nature cause him to enter without any pangs of conscience into a liaison with a married woman; but he is staunch to his love and would fain remain the lover he was, if Anna's jealousy and irritation did not make an understanding impossible. Anna suffers for her crime, not as a just retribution for sinning, but because the crime itself is the punishment, and the end is only the final solution of a protracted period of suffering.

Nor does the author show any greater animus against the other characters who move on a lower stage of life: Stíva Oblónski, with his infidelity to his wife, his desire to pass life without any exertion or labour, his punning in the face of the most serious circumstances, is not at all the bad man we should imagine him to be. Disputatious

Katavásov, liberal Koznyshév, punctilious Karénin, the doctor, the lawyer, though with none of these can the author agree, are delineated with the greatest fairness. As for the women, we have the same types as before: Várenka is a modernized Sónya, Kitty is no other than Natásha, and Dolly is temperamentally exactly like the mother of the Rostóvs. Again it is motherhood that is preached as the highest privilege and virtue of a woman, and the very punishment for Anna's crime consists in her being compelled to relinquish the high office of maternity.

It is, however, Levín, as formerly Pierre, who comes in for the author's fullest share of attention. He knows Levín best, and he is interested in analyzing Levín's state of mind, in order later to revert to another reflection of himself at a more advanced stage of his development. Levín, like Pierre, is awkward, frank, sensitive, fond of domestic life, and in search after truth. But he has proceeded farther in his convictions concerning the futility of participating in political affairs, is more decidedly set against city life, and finally takes refuge against his besetting doubts in faith. He tries to live a truly Christian life, but he is not temperamentally prepared to live up to his own ideals, and there are frequent reversions to his older moods. " Call it faith," he says of his own mental condition, " or not, — I do not know what it is, — but this feeling has just as imperceptibly entered through suffering and has taken up a firm abode in my heart. I shall be as angry with Iván the coachman, shall discuss as before, shall express my thoughts as inappropriately as before ; there will be the same wall between the holy of holies of my soul and others, even my wife ; I shall be accusing her as much because of my own fright, and then shall repent of it ; I shall just as much fail to comprehend through reason why I pray and continue praying, — but my life, my whole life, independently of everything that may happen to me, every minute of it, is now no longer senseless, as it has been, but has an unquestionable meaning from the good, which it is in my power to invest it with."

After such a confession only one of two things could have happened : either Tolstóy would in the future recant his striving after perfection, and then there would be room left for at least another great novel, or he must proceed still farther and higher along the ladder of religious evolution, where religion becomes the all-absorbing subject of his thoughts, and the novel is no longer adequate for a full expression of his profound convictions. It is the latter that has happened.

VII.

A FEW extracts from Tolstóy's letters to Fet during the year 1879 will serve as corroboratives or correctives of the *Confession* which he published in the same year.

"In my last letter I wrote you that I should not like to return to the grave, because there would still be left my relations to God."

"God knows where my *Decembrists* are. I do not even think of them, and if I did think of them, and should write, I flatter myself with the hope that my spirit alone, of which the writing would smack, would be intolerable for those who shoot people for the good of humanity. How right the peasants and you are, in saying that the masters shoot, not for what has been taken away, but because the peasants have been taken away. But I must say, I conscientiously do not read any papers now, and I consider it my duty to turn everybody away from this deleterious habit. There sits an old man, a good fellow, in Vorobévka; he has transfused in his mind two or three pages of Schopenhauer and has sent them forth in Russian, has finished a party at billiards, has killed a snipe, has enjoyed the sight of a colt from Zakrás, and is sitting with his wife drinking delicious tea, smoking, beloved by all and loving all, and suddenly they bring in an ill-smelling, damp sheet, — it pains the hands and the eyes, and in the heart there is a malice of condemnations, a sensation of alienation, a feeling that he does not love any one, and that no one loves him, and he begins to speak, and speaks, and is angry, and suffers. That must be given up. It will be better so."

289

"I have not for a long time enjoyed God's world so much as this year. I stand with mouth wide open, marvelling and afraid to move, for fear of missing something."

"If I am that falcon and if, as follows from the rest, my bold flight consists in this, that I deny real life, I must defend myself. I do not deny real life, nor the labour which is necessary for the support of this life; but it seems to me that a great part of your life and of mine is filled with gratifications, not of natural needs, but of such as are artificially grafted upon us by our education and by needs invented by us and grown into a habit, and that nine-tenths of the labour put by us on the gratification of these needs is idle labour. I should like to be firmly convinced that I give more to men than I receive from them; but as I feel myself very prone to value my own work very highly and the work of others very low, I do not hope by a mere increase of my labour and a choice of harder work to convince myself that others will not be at a disadvantage in squaring up with me (I shall by all means assure myself that the work which I like is the most necessary and difficult); I should like to take as little as possible from others and to work as little as possible for the gratification of my needs, and I think that it would thus be easiest not to blunder."

"I have successfully recommended to you the reading of *The Thousand and One Nights* and Pascal; both have not exactly pleased you, but come up to your taste. Now I intend to offer you a book which no one else has yet read and which I read the other day for the first time and still continue to read and to go into ecstasies over; I hope that this, too, will be to your liking, the more so since it has much in common with Schopenhauer: this is Solomon's Proverbs, Ecclesiastes, and the Book of Wisdom, — it is impossible to find anything more modern than these; but if you read them, read them in Slavic.

I have a modern Russian translation, but it is bad. The English translation is bad, too. If you had a Greek translation, you would see what it is."

A year later, in 1880, he wrote: "Now it is summer, and, as usual, life fills me with transport and I forget to work. This year I have struggled for a long time, but the beauty of the world has conquered me."

By this time *My Confession* was written, and the foundation was laid for the *Critique of Dogmatic Theology* and *The Four Gospels Harmonized and Translated.* In view of the above extracts and of what we have learned from the analysis of Tolstóy's previous life and work, the *Confession* has to be taken with some degree of caution. There is no untruth in it in the main, but the suddenness of the religious conversion, the intensity of his despair, the salvation through faith, are all the result of a retrospective emotional attitude under the influence of the last, most potent illumination. But in reality there is nothing new or unforeseen in his new phase of life. His religiousness was expressed by him in his first production, *Childhood,* and was emphasized again and again in *War and Peace* and in *Anna Karénin.* His suicidal intentions date back to the *Memoirs of a Marker* and are touched upon in the *Cossacks* and further developed in *Anna Karénin.* His negative attitude toward civilization and progress, his opposition to violence in every form, his temperamental contempt for the lie in every shape, have always been the same. What is it, then, that took place in the year 1879 which led to his *Confession* and to the so-called second part of his life and activity that both by him and the critics are assumed to be something quite distinct from the first part?

The answer is found in the dual nature of Tolstóy; he is intensely subjective, unable at any time to get away from himself, analyzing, probing, and chastizing himself continuously, until his whole spiritual being has become

a most delicate instrument for the reception of the most
advanced truths; on the other hand, or, perhaps, on
account of this great receptiveness of his nature, he more
than any one else appears as the product of what is best
in our Christian civilization. Ever since the time of
Christ, to use a paradox, the whole of Europe and the
church Christianity have been vivified by that small
leaven of the Gospel Christianity which through the ages
has kept the world from breaking up into chaos and
which from time to time has borne fruit in the creation
of those dissenting sects that have sought a greater approximation with the Gospel. So, too, the best minds
have constantly striven after that truth which the church
Christianity has vainly tried to banish from the original
precepts of Jesus. Rousseau even, with his return to
Nature and his simplicity of life, represents an element
of that unconscious tendency toward a primitive Christianity.

By dint of his extreme sensitiveness, Tolstóy from his
earliest youth came under the influence of all the factors
that made for a simple Christianity. His constitutional
opposition to all the falseness in society, science, and art,
his strong antipathy to violence in whatever form, his
fervent desire to comprehend the cause of all causes,
his religious strivings and his religious doubts alike, all
of these lay in the direct line of his Christian life, without his being able to see his path ahead of him. And
it is because he was unable to see the unifying principle
of his disjointed thoughts and sentiments that he suffered
and wavered and fell into despair. At times, indeed, it
seemed to him that his opposition to the existing order
was merely temperamental, and that he himself was to
blame for his departures. Whenever he was assailed by
this periodic doubt, he gave vent to his mood in a new
literary production, in every one of which there is depicted that inner struggle which just then was going on

in him. Still he never could be satisfied, for no sooner had he overcome one period of doubt than another overcame him.

And subduing his temporary acute stages of despair, which, as he says, and as we learn indirectly from his earlier writings, led him to the contemplation of suicide, he struggled on and on. Then Schopenhauer gave him some temporary relief, for here he found many things united that in him had lived isolated. And then Solomon's Proverbs and Ecclesiastes and the Book of Wisdom, taken up by mere chance, brought him nearer to the solution of those questions which had tormented him so long. Then his previously acquired knowledge of Greek tempted him to read the Gospel, and the effect, he imagines, was instantaneous. In reality, however, it was merely the completion of the circle of his life and thought. His education, as that of all Europeans, was the result of all the palpable and also of the more remote influences of Christianity; his spiritual life had still more carried him back to the Gospel, and now the reading of the Gospel finished the circle on which he had begun.

It was not the discovery of Christ, a new Christ for him, that produced his conversion, but the discovery of the essential unity of his hopelessly disconnected thoughts. Heretofore we had the various aspects of Tolstóy as Irténev, Nekhlyúdov, Olénin, Pierre, Levín. Now it is Christ-Tolstóy that becomes the final and lasting stage of his spiritual evolution. Beyond this it is impossible to go. Christ's life of humility and brotherly love, His temptation by the devil, His persecution, His love for the lowest of humanity, — that was precisely what Tolstóy, unconscious of the mainspring of his strivings, had before him as the excelsior of his aspirations. The very so-called impracticableness of Christ's abstract truths and His momentary wavering in the garden of Gethsemane were points strikingly in keeping with Tolstóy's own character. In so far as Tolstóy discovered this parallelism between his life and that of the teacher of Christianity, there actually began a new stage of life for him; but it was merely the discovery of what had long ago existed within him, of what gave him the positive conviction that he was marching in the right direction, even though it be toward an inaccessible height. It was this well-moored enthusiasm, this discovery of a staff and stay, this universal, all-permeating, all-true Gospel teaching that urged him on to cast aside the last reserve, to abandon every vestige of the litterateur's art, to speak out frankly and tell without artistic subterfuge what he had been hinting at and saying by implication in all his previous novels.

His career, he thought, began anew, and as *Childhood, Boyhood, and Youth* had ushered in his literary activity, so now *My Confession* was to make tabula rasa of his older life and to lay the foundation for his religious activity. But the two are essentially the same, except for the greater subjectivity, maturity, and straightforwardness of the second. Next it was necessary to do away with that illusive Orthodox theology which had tempted him to fall back upon the belief of the church and which held many men in subjection. This he did in the *Critique of Dogmatic Theology,* a work of little value for those who are convinced of the truth of Gospel Christianity or to the reader at large, but destined some day to become one of the most powerful weapons against the Greek Catholic Church in Russia. Having cleared the way in his own consciousness and having put out of combat the church, he proceeded to reëstablish primitive Christianity from the four Gospels. Flushed with the enthusiasm of the new discovery and with the confidence in his self-acquired knowledge of Greek, Tolstóy set out to subject the Gospel to a thorough scrutiny. The manner in which he proceeded must appear irksome to a student of Gospel criticism. While pretending to avoid interpretation, Tolstóy interprets as much as any commentator, and in the arbitrary rejection of what he assumes to be doubtful material he frequently oversteps the limits of the probable ; nor is his knowledge of Greek such as to warrant an exact analysis of delicate linguistic points. But even then, making allowance for all possible shortcomings, his harmonization and translation of the Gospel remains an important contribution to Gospel criticism.

What Tolstóy interprets out of the Gospel is merely what he brings into it from a whole life of spiritual experiences. The central truth of the Gospel is for him contained in the Sermon on the Mount and in the dicta of Christ Himself. Most of these utterances had long formed the conscious, more frequently the unconscious, principles of his acts and thoughts. Imagining that the coincidence of his ideas with those contained in the Gospel was accidental, whereas his own world-conception had from the very beginning been in various ways influenced by it, he concluded that revelation consisted in this very coincidence of the Gospel truths with the dictates of reason, and in the reasonableness of all such tenets as had been familiar to him from the start he saw an argument for the reasonableness of the few principles which he had not thought of before. Thus, his strong dislike for violence in every form naturally made him hail with delight the simple prohibitions of the Sermon on the Mount against anger and swearing and killing, and to this he added, on the strength of the Gospel alone, the prohibition of adultery in the sense of an absolute chastity, in place of his former glorification of maternity. It is curious to note, in connection with this acceptance of the simple teachings of original Christianity, that the American sect of the Perfectionists, who singularly agree with Tolstóy in almost all his deductions from the Gospel teaching, and have in their communities lived the true Christian life, have rejected this one principle of ultra-chastity and have instead, again on the strength of the Gospel, extended the community of possessions to include community of wives.

Tolstóy is accused of carrying his principles, which, however, are not his, but Christ's, to impossible conclusions. The accusation is unjust. There can be no compromise in the matter of truth, and Tolstóy evolves his ideas to their logical conclusion, quite irrespective of whether they will prove impracticable, in the worldly sense of the word. If they lead to inconveniences, the trouble is not with the truths, but with our perverted life. The truths cannot be truths under certain conditions, and cease to be such when they do not adapt themselves to the present state of affairs. Either Christ's teaching is right or it is wrong. Once the justice of His teaching is admitted, there can be no cavilling with it. One may fall short of the goal, but there can be no compromise. The many opponents of Tolstóy have attacked him on the ground that his own theories are so abstract and so impossible of execution, that he himself has not lived up to them. But the opponents err egregiously. Tolstóy has never claimed to be perfect, and has distinctly pointed out in his letters and diaries that he is not a saint. Man is weak, and the very best will, in the struggle between their strongly entrenched habits and their best thinking, fall below the mark set by their own reason. A contemptible man is he who, in falling, finds a justification for his fall. This Tolstóy has never done: he has with singular courage upheld the supreme and final truth, even though it may tell against his own actions. In fact, in judging of Tolstóy's theories, which, it must never be forgotten, are Christ's and those of many other great religious teachers, we must leave Tolstóy entirely out. His theories must be judged in themselves, and not in connection with the man. They must stand or fall by themselves.

Injudicious persons have now and then addressed Tolstóy, requesting him to give his opinion on this or that aspect of public life, as though Tolstóy had any particular opinion on any particular point. All his views are merely the logical development of the precepts of the Sermon on the Mount, and to this one must turn for the solution of doubtful questions. From this Gospel code all of Tolstóy's principles are naturally and logically deduced. The injunction of loving our neighbour as ourselves in its ultimate application leads to the equality of all men, the freedom from race hatred, the abolition of patriotism, as being a sectional feeling in which the love of our neighbours suffers diminution. "Thou shalt not kill." From this follow the abolition of war and of capital punishment, and vegetarianism. And from this, in conjunction with the prohibition against swearing, there follows the passive opposition to courts of justice and to any and every kind of government. Similarly, Christ's precept of mendicancy and thoughtlessness for the morrow leads to the abolition of private ownership and to the establishment of the Christian commune.

With these principles there can be no compromise, and all the half-measures and palliations are unconditionally rejected. Peace Congresses are abortive endeavours to regulate war; parliaments work hand in hand with the governments, and only perpetuate violence; socialism introduces a new slavery in the place of the old, and anarchism stands self-accused by its use of force to obtain otherwise desirable ends. For the same reason art and literature, as now constituted, are merely implements in the power of the rich, and as such are unconditionally condemned; progress is of questionable value, because it fails to attain the ends of the Christian religion; the professions are all equally to be rejected, for they all fail to aid the masses.

It would seem that Tolstóy in his condemnation includes everything evolved by humanity in the course of history. But this assumption is incorrect: he does not object to the acquisitions of humanity in themselves, but in so far as they act as external means for the attainment of personal well-being. To him the only legitimate purpose of man's life is the establishment of the right relation to God, that is, religion, and of the right relation to humanity at large, which arises from the fundamental principle of religion. This cannot be striven after by any of the human institutions and contrivances, but by an internal perfection, — " The kingdom of God is within you." And it is only through this internal work, through this important function of religion, that all other needs can be supplied and obtain a meaning, — " Seek ye the kingdom of God and His righteousness, and all these things shall be added unto you."

Thus religion, in its broadest sense of man's relation to the cause of all causes, becomes the chief and only criterion of all human acts and activities. Art, science, literature, all the social relations, have a reason to exist only if they comply with this basal demand of religion, and they are all to be condemned in proportion as they depart from this all-embracing and unifying law and serve man for his selfish ends. When art and science and all the other activities shall have become unified and religious, when in the enthronement of all of them not one human being shall suffer physically, morally, or mentally, then there will arrive the time when they will perform the functions which are proper to them, but not until then.

Like the " *Memento mori* " of the Trappist monks, " The kingdom of God is within you " from the time of the *Confession* on becomes the watchword of all of Tolstóy's ideas, and every problem that presents itself to him is answered in the light of this Gospel saying. It is the same old striving after personal perfection which characterizes Tolstóy in his earliest writings. No conversion,

Portrait of Tolstóy, 1893, after Finishing
"The Kingdom of God Is within
You"

Photogravure from a Photograph

no violent change has taken place in the spiritual life of the author; there is not even a new angle of vision in this accentuation of the religious side of life and of a salvation from within. There is only a logical unification of a series of revolts. Of necessity Tolstóy had to arrive in the end at what American thought, itself the issue of a series of revolts, had arrived at before him. It was the American school-books of " Peter Parley," which departed so completely from those current in Europe, that had very early in Tolstóy's career directed his attention to American pedagogical ideas, and these were again supplemented by what he later, by the courtesy of Eugene Schuyler, could glean out of American school-books. So now, when his extreme Gospel Christianity directed his attention to the most advanced revolt, political, social, religious, he found himself peculiarly in agreement with much that had been worked out in America. Indeed, as soon as his first few writings under the influence of his new fervour reached the reading public in the United States, many who felt themselves to be in full agreement with him sent him books, pamphlets, and periodicals, in which identical propositions were advanced. Thus he for the first time discovered the simple Christianity of the Quakers and the Shakers, the religious writings of Channing and of Parker, the non-resistant activity of Garrison and Ballou. Henceforth he again falls under the sway of American thought, accepting from it everything which voices the revolt in its most pronounced form. The difference between him and the American writers is only such as nationally exists between a Russian and an American.

Tolstóy's activity since his *Confession* has been principally directed toward the elucidation of all sides of life in the light of the Gospel teaching. *My Religion, Life, The Christian Teaching,* and a large number of minor articles and letters set forth his views in a more or less detailed form, and special articles are devoted to the elucidation of his ideas concerning particular points, patriotism, morality, non-resistance, the use of a bloodless diet, abstinence from spirituous liquors, continence in the sexual relation, and so forth.   These differ from similar disquisitions by other writers in that not one of them is elaborated by Tolstóy as a separate issue, but as a minor part of the same central idea, — the truth of the Gospel teaching.   For the same reason he cannot find any approximate or partial truths in any of the current attempts at ameliorations, improvements, and advancements, and modern philanthropy, like many other sides of our civilization, is subjected to an incisive criticism and is found wanting in the basal principle of " the kingdom of God is within you."

Naturally Tolstóy became interested in the Russian sects that profess a primitive Christianity, and of these the Dukhobors came in for the greatest share of his attention, as the persecutions to which they were subjected by the government demanded prompt action, to save them from utter destruction.   Chiefly through his instrumentality, the Dukhobors were gathered from the various settlements within and without Russia, and were provided with means of transportation to Canada, where they were given land by the Canadian government.   The letters which Tolstóy wrote concerning the Dukhobors reiterate the general statements concerning the meaning and essence of the Gospel.   The letters to the Dukhobors are interesting in that they evince Tolstóy's solicitude for the practical application of the Gospel teaching, in order to have before him a palpable proof of the truth of his contentions.   Most interesting, however, are his two letters to Verígin, the leader of the Dukhobors, in that they give us an insight into a peculiarity of Tolstóy's character which is generally overlooked by his critics.

When Tolstóy's wholesale condemnation of art, literature, and the sciences had led Verígin to express himself contemptuously in respect to books and the use of modern inventions, Tolstóy felt himself obliged to take Verígin to task and to prove to him the usefulness and necessity of certain acquisitions of modern civilization. This at first sight looks like veering around to a contrary opinion, and similar utterances of his have been made the subject of just such accusations. But there is no contradiction in this. Tolstóy does not object to either science, art, literature, or modern inventions, but to their perversions, to their disregard of the sanctity of life and the equality and liberty of man, to their being used in the service of the few against the many. His wholesale condemnation, carried to its logical conclusion, is meant for the perusal of the thinking and educated, who are used to philosophical reasoning. There are, however, two classes of men who may be misled by his generalizations into outdoing the master, — the slavish imitators and the half-educated. To the latter belongs Verígin, and Tolstóy was compelled to emphasize to him the opposite side, the usefulness of those human acquisitions which, in their present form, he had rejected as a whole. For the same reason, though rejecting every government, he felt himself impelled to address the emperor upon the subject of reforms, by no means in the sense of a compromise, but as a minimum of a possible political platform. How far-sighted Tolstóy can be, when not dwelling upon the logical consequence of his theories, may be seen from the fact that the late Zemstvoist demands almost coincide with Tolstóy's own programme ; but Tolstóy's programme is much more far-reaching, since it is not conceived in the spirit of compromise, but as the first step toward the final consummation of the Christian life.

Of late years Tolstóy has been inclined to look more for possible practical applications of his theories, instead of persisting more especially in the sphere of philosophical deductions. Thus, though he formerly looked askance at Henry George's Single Tax, as being an external means for bringing about the eternal peace, which can originate only from within, he now gives it a more favourable place in his scheme of peasant reforms, which more than any others absorb his attention. For the labour question as a political or sociological problem he has as little use as for the socialistic and anarchistic panacea which are suggested for its solution, but the labourers are again and again addressed by him, and are admonished to rely solely on the internal reform, on the kingdom of God within them, for their future welfare, and they are advised to return to the soil, where alone they can be free. The land question, not political freedom and industrial development, is, therefore, the only burning question of the day in Russia, as it must be everywhere else, if life is to run in normal channels.

Tolstóy has not been able, in spite of his growing dislike for literature, to devote all his time to philosophical disquisitions and to pamphleteering. His artistic nature demanded its due, and at intervals he returned to his artistic productions; but never again did he for a moment forget his one aim of inculcating the truths of the Gospel teaching. His main concern has been to bring the Gospel teaching nearer to the peasants, the simple folk to whom, according to Christ, is given the comprehension of divine truths. Hence he has clothed his thoughts in the form of moral tales, legends, and fairy-tales, employing the simplest and most accessible literary means for the inculcation of Christian virtues. One of these stories, which shows the folly of the use of spirituous drinks, he has even changed into dramatic form, apparently to make it available for representation on a popular stage.

But he also wrote for an enlightened public. The ideas which he held concerning the frequently immoral effect of music combined with his newly emphasized, exaggerated views on the sexual relations led him to present the double question in the form of a powerful psychological analysis of marital relations, with their jealousies and sexual excesses, which culminate in the murder of the guilty wife. This study, *The Kreutzer Sonata*, provoked a storm of indignation from the prudish and the hypocritical, as though Tolstóy in any shape or manner gave food for immoral conceptions. *The Kreutzer Sonata* is about as immoral as is an anatomical theatre or a museum of loathsome diseases, and certainly is as abhorrent as the latter. Besides, the idea of the immoral effect of music is as old as Plato and the Chinese sages, and the insistence on extreme chastity is quite familiar to a certain class of Americans, with whose ideas he was evidently acquainted before writing *The Kreutzer Sonata*. When, under the stress of the many attacks upon him, he wrote an epilogue to this work, he was, indeed, obliged to fall back mainly on the ideas of the American apostles of ultra-chastity. In any case, *The Kreutzer Sonata* can only have a sobering, and not an immoral, effect upon the reader.

Tolstóy's great versatility has been attested in the production of two dramas, both of them complete in themselves and well adapted for the stage. One of these, the comedy, *Fruits of Enlightenment*, is an amusing satire on the superstition of spiritualism, the inanity of society, the pompous pretence and absurdity of modern so-called science. The other drama, *The Power of Darkness*, is a much more serious production. As *The Kreutzer Sonata* depicts the effect of immoral relations upon the men of the upper classes, so *The Power of Darkness* treats with the harrowing effects of improper sexual relations upon the benighted peasantry. But it is not to the plot itself, which is worked out with wonderful realism, that the author wishes to direct the hearer's attention, but to the power of repentance, which leads Nikíta, the adulterer and unwilling accomplice in the murder of his new-born babe, to make a clean breast of his crimes before the Christian people. Still more to the author's liking is Akím, Nikíta's simple-minded father, whose speech is barely articulated and who represents that Christian righteousness which needs no wisdom for its utterance.

Probably no other work of Tolstóy's later period has provoked so much discussion as *What Is Art?* in which he condemns nearly all modern art. The attacks which on this score have been directed against his views could have proceeded only from those who were not acquainted with his previous works, especially those that have been published since his preoccupation with the Gospel. To those who knew Tolstóy from his former writings there could be no doubt as to what his conception of art must be. Naturally religion is by him put at the foundation of art, else there is no criterion for it, just as there is no criterion for any other human activity without a correct understanding as to man's relation to God. Similarly, from Tolstóy's general dislike of everything which lacks sincerity and simplicity, it follows that he can have no use for those manifestations of the creative powers which by his canon must be considered as mere adulterations of art. That in his sweeping arraignment of modern art he may have included some really deserving productions, or may have here and there overlooked some worthy artist, does not invalidate the fact that Tolstóy has given a consistent and healthy criterion for man's higher activities, which artists would do well to keep constantly before them as their guide.

A no lesser sensation was caused among the reading public by Tolstóy's *Resurrection*, in which the author, according to the critics, outdid himself in realism and in extravagant arraignment of modern society. But that is only so on the surface. There is nothing new in his latest portrayal of the black sides of the legal system, of the state church, of penal institutions, of the government, except that this time it is all represented in the form of a novel and that he has for the first time limned characters from the society of intellectuals, of men and women belonging to the student class, instead of delineating types from the narrower circle to which he himself belonged and from the peasant class which he knew so well. The heroine, Katyúsha, who after being seduced by Nekhlyúdov falls lower and lower, and while being an inmate of a house of ill repute is falsely accused of murder and deported to Siberia, is drawn with the same delicacy which the author has bestowed upon his best types of women in his former writings. Nekhlyúdov, the same autobiographic reflection as before, accidentally sits as a juror in the court trying Katyúsha for her supposed murder. He is tormented by remorse, wishes to expiate his guilt toward her by marrying her, becomes aware of the many wrongs created in the name of civilization, of the futility of legal justice, of the criminality of private ownership, of the vapidity of society, of the indissolubleness of the marriage ties. He undergoes hardships and privations in his desire to be near Katyúsha, whom he wishes to help, and, in spite of his occasional lapses into his aristocratic habits, moves steadily toward a higher, unified world-conception. In short, Nekhlyúdov is again a form of Tolstóy, and, like Tolstóy, he finally arrives at the solution of all his doubts in the right comprehension of the Gospel teaching.

Tolstóy's private life in the last twenty-five years need not arrest us long. He has tried to live the simple religious life, a life of hard labour. A number of ill-intentioned critics have ever been ready to find flaws in Tolstóy's private life, in order to prove the impossibility of realizing Tolstóy's precepts. But it has already been pointed out that Tolstóy has never claimed himself to be perfect, and that he merely declines to make compromises with his own conscience, even though his own practices may not be in agreement with his better knowledge. Similarly we can dismiss the accusation preferred against Tolstóy that, in turning over his property to his wife, who also collects the royalties upon his works, he is guilty of duplicity. If he could see a better solution, he would be the first to live up to it. As it is, we must admire the man who, in spite of the eternal contradictions with which he is surrounded, still maintains the infallibility of the dictates of reason. There have, no doubt, been men who have been able much better to harmonize their daily acts with their reason, but it must be borne in mind that Tolstóy's struggle is one of gigantic proportions, since with the unbending spirit of non-compromise he unites an utter helplessness in matters of practical application, both of which are characteristic of the whole of Russian life. Nor need we dwell on the external facts of his excommunication by the Greek Catholic Church, upon the fact that but a very few of his own family follow his precepts or agree with him in theory, or upon his relations to a large number of private individuals, as these in no way alter the judgment we have so far formed concerning his life and thoughts from his writings and his previous life experiences. If Tolstóy's life was even in the first half of his literary activity fully reflected in his literary productions, it has now, since his *Confession*, been even more completely recorded in his written work. It is, indeed, the most remarkable characteristic of his maturer years that his thoughts do not belong to any one individual or to any one time, but are the eternal truths again and again repeated through the ages.

Our task is done. We have analyzed half a century of Tolstóy's activity, and have found it singularly consistent and steadily advancing toward the primitive Christianity by which it has unconsciously been influenced from the very start. Tolstóy's faults are many : he lacks the cautious training which makes a man wary and balanced in his judgments; he frequently shocks people by his abruptness of thought and neglect of style and traditional literary forms; he antagonizes and frets and is restless. But through and above all this shine brightly the sincerity and earnestness of purpose, the broadest sympathy with humankind, the greatest altruism, an unbounded faith in the ultimate divine ends of man, a fervent religious sentiment, a titanic artistic nature, a wonderful insight into the workings of the human mind, a fearlessness which even a despotic government has not dared to challenge, though the church has anathematized him. The name of his admirers is legion, but the number of his followers is very restricted, not because his theories, that is, Christ's precepts, are difficult of execution, but because the world at large has not yet outgrown the hope and desire of an external salvation. None the less, Tolstóy is recognized as the spiritual guide of the New Russia which is to rise from the ashes of the Old, and his popularity abroad is bound to grow with the growth of brotherly love and universal peace and good-will to all men upon earth. It is said that Dante more than any other author represents the highest flower of our Christian civilization. With equal justice it may be said that Tolstóy stands for the highest aspirations of Christ's teaching, to which the world is gradually returning after nearly two millenniums.

CHRONOLOGICAL TABLE OF EVENTS IN THE LIFE OF LEV TOLSTÓY

CHRONOLOGICAL TABLE OF EVENTS IN THE LIFE OF LEV TOLSTÓY

1828. August 28 O. S.[1] Count L. N. Tolstóy born.
1831. Death of his mother.
1837. Father's death. Journey to Moscow. Return to Yásnaya Polyána, under the guardianship of Countess A. I. Ósten Sáken.
1840. Death of Countess Ósten Sáken, and settlement in Kazán, in the house of his aunt P. I. Yúshkov.
1843. Tolstóy enters the Philological Department of Kazán University.
1845. Leaves Kazán University, and returns to Yásnaya Polyána. Goes to St. Petersburg and again returns to Yásnaya Polyána.
1848. Goes to St. Petersburg for his candidate's examination at the university.
1851. Goes to the Caucasus, and in the fall there enters the army as yunker in the light artillery.
1852. July 9. "Childhood" finished.
Writes "A Morning of a Landed Proprietor," "The Incursion," "Boyhood."
September 6. "Childhood" published, in the *Contemporary*.
October 18. Writes plan of "Cossacks."
1853. "The Incursion," published in the *Contemporary*.

[1] Dates are given in old style. Dates of writing have in this chronology been corrected according to the best information obtainable.

311

Winter. Returns to Yásnaya Polyána.
December. Arrives at the Danube, where he joins the army.

1854. " Boyhood " published, in the *Contemporary*.
November. Arrival at Sevastopol.

1855. " Memoirs of a Marker," published in the *Contemporary*.
" Sevastopol in December, 1854, and in May, 1855," published in the *Contemporary*.
Takes part in the battle at the Chérnaya.
" The Cutting of the Forest " (dedicated to I. S. Turgénev), published in the *Contemporary*.
Helps writing " The 4th of August."
Sent as courier to St. Petersburg, after the storming of the Malákhov Hill.
First signing of his name in an address of leading literary men.

1856. " Sevastopol in August, 1855," published in the *Contemporary*.
Publication of his collected Military Stories.
" The Snow-storm," published in the *Contemporary*.
" Two Hussars," published in the *Contemporary*.
" A Morning of a Landed Proprietor," published in *Memoirs of the Fatherland*.
" Meeting a Moscow Acquaintance at the Front," published in *Library for Reading*.
First picture in a group of literary men (with Grigoróvich, Goncharóv, Druzhínin, Turgénev, and Ostróvski).
" Youth " finished in November.

1857. " Youth," published in the *Contemporary*.
First journey abroad (February — in Germany and Paris ; April and May — in Italy ; June and July — in Switzerland ; July 7th — in Lucerne).
" Lucerne," published in the *Contemporary*.
August. Back to Yásnaya Polyána.
October and November. In St. Petersburg and Moscow.
Second journey abroad, to Paris and Dijon.
" Albert " written at Dijon.
Back to Russia.

1858. " Albert," published in the *Contemporary*.
" Three Deaths " written.
Opinion of 105 members of the Túla gentry concerning the allotment of land to the peasants, in the *Contemporary*, signed also by Tolstóy.

1859. " Three Deaths," published in the *Library for Reading*.

"Domestic Happiness," published in the *Russian Messenger*.

1860. Third journey abroad.
Meeting with Berthold Auerbach and Julius Fröbel.
Death of his brother, Nikoláy.
"Polikúshka" written.
1861. Visit to Italy, Paris, and London.
Meeting of Proudhon and Lelewel at Brussels, and of Diesterweg at Berlin.
April 25. Back to St. Petersburg.
May 10. Back to Yásnaya Polyána.
May 12. Petitioning the government to be permitted to open a school.
Acting as Mediator of the Peace.
"The Cossacks" finished.
July. Announcement of the publication of *Yásnaya Polyána*.
1862. Publication of the *Yásnaya Polyána*, containing:
"On Popular Education."
"On Methods of Teaching the Rudiments."
"A Project of a General Plan for the Establishment of Popular Schools."
"Education and Culture."
"Are the Peasant Children to Learn to Write from Us?"
"The School at Yásnaya Polyána."
Lives among the Bashkirs.
September 23. Marriage.
"Childhood and Youth," translated into English.
1863. Last of *Yásnaya Polyána*, containing:
"Progress and the Definition of Education."
"The Cossacks," published in the *Russian Messenger*.
"Polikúshka," published in the *Russian Messenger*.
"The Linen-Measurer" written.
"The Decembrists" begun.
1864. First publication of his Collected Works.
"War and Peace" begun.
1865. First part of "War and Peace" under the name of "The Year of 1805," published in the *Russian Messenger*.
1866. Views the Field of Borodinó.
1868. "A Few Words Concerning the Book 'War and Peace.'"
1869. "War and Peace" finished.
Begins studying Greek.
"The Primer" begun.
1871. Journey to Samára.

"Primer," first book, printed.
1872. "The Primer" printed. (It contains the *Stories for Children, God Sees the Truth, The Prisoner of the Caucasus,* etc.)
1873. "Anna Karénin" begun.
1874. "On Popular Education," in *Memoirs of the Fatherland.* Russian and Church-Slavic "Primers" printed.
1875. "New Primer" printed.
"First four Readers" printed.
1877. "Anna Karénin" finished.
1878. "The Decembrists" abandoned.
"First Recollections."
1879–82. "My Confession" (printed abroad).
1880–82. "Critique of Dogmatic Theology" (printed abroad).
"The Four Gospels Harmonized and Translated" (printed abroad).
1881. "What Men Live By."
1882. "On the Moscow Census."
"Short Exposition of the Gospel" (printed abroad).
"Church and State" (printed abroad).
"Letter to N. N." (printed abroad).
1884. "My Religion" (printed abroad).
"Introduction to T. M. Bondarév's Teaching" (printed abroad).
1884–86. "What Shall We Do Then?" (printed abroad in separate parts as "What Is My Life? and "Money").
"The Death of Iván Ilích."
1885. "Neglect the Fire."
"The Candle."
"The Two Old Men."
"Where Love Is, There God Is Also."
Texts for Chapbook Illustrations.
"Iván the Fool."
1886. "The Power of Darkness."
"Nicholas Stick" (printed abroad).
"What a Christian May Do."
"Popular Legends."
"The First Distiller."
"To N. N. Ge's Painting."
"Letter to a Revolutionist." [1]

[1] Henceforth the publication of Tolstóy's works follows soon after they are written, and with but a very few exceptions only those that are published abroad are reliable.

1887. " On Life."
" What Is the Truth in Art ? "
" The Three Sons."
" To the Dear Youth."
1888. " Linen-Measurer " printed.
" Walk in the Light, While Ye Have Light."
" Letter to a Frenchman."
1889. " The Kreutzer Sonata."
" Fruits of Enlightenment."
" The Holiday of Enlightenment."
" Letter to A. V. Vlásov."
1890. " Epilogue to the Kreutzer Sonata."
" On the Relation between the Sexes."
" On Non-Resistance to Evil."
" Why People become Intoxicated."
" Introduction to A. Stockham's Tokology."
" Apropos of A. L. Ershóv's Book."
1891. " The Coffee-house of Surat " (translated from the French
of B. de St. Pierre).
Tolstóy's family goes to the Famine district.
September 19. Tolstóy grants permission to translate and
reprint his works.
1891-93. " Articles and Reports on the Famine."
1892. " The First Step."
1893. " The Kingdom of God Is within You."
" The Non-Acting " (printed abroad).
" Introduction to Amiel's Diary."
1894. " Karma " (translated from the English).
" Introduction to S. T. Seménov's Peasant Stories."
" Introduction to the Works of Guy de Maupassant."
" Christianity and Patriotism " (printed abroad).
" Religion and Morality."
" Mazzini on Immortality " (translated).
" Letter to the Editor of the Daily Chronicle."
1895. " Epilogue to Drózhzhin's Life and Death."
" Master and Workman."
" Reason and Religion."
" Three Parables."
" Letter to a Pole."
" Relation to the Government and the Existing Order."
" God or Mammon ? "
" Shame ! "
" Persecution of Christians in Russia."
" Letter to P. V. Verígin."

"A Message to the American People."
"Three Letters on Reason, Faith, and Prayer."
"To the Tsar and His Associates."
"Three Letters concerning Shopov."
"The Tolstóy Society of Manchester."
1902. "What Is Religion?"
"To the Working People."
"On Religious Toleration."

INDEX

To Life and Works of Tolstóy

INDEX

To Life and Works of Tolstóy

ON THE PRONUNCIATION OF
RUSSIAN WORDS

ON THE PRONUNCIATION OF RUSSIAN WORDS

———◆———

THE transliteration of Russian words in the present translation is strictly etymological, that is, the words are rendered precisely as they are spelled in Russian, without any reference to their pronunciation. This method is the only rational one, as it is quite impossible in most cases to give a precise idea of the original pronunciation, while in some cases we get uncouth forms, such as the preposterous ending *off*, in which some translators revel. The only exception has been made in the case of the name *Peter*, which in Russian is spelled *Petr*, to avoid the puzzling ending.

Russian pronunciation generally follows the spelling so closely that the reader will come very near the correct form if he shall give the vowels the Continental values (*a* like *a* in *far*, *e* like *e* in *bet*, *i* like *i* in *hit*, *o* like *a* in *all*, *u* like *u* in put, *y*, if not followed or preceded by a vowel, like *y* in pity), and the consonants their English values (*g* as in *get*, *kh* as *ch* in German *ach*, *zh* as *z* in *azure*, *y* before and after a vowel as *y* in *yet*).

Those who want to approximate the correct pronunciation more closely must observe these additional rules:

1. *E* and *i* sound *ye* and *yi* respectively after *d, t, l, r,* and *n,* and *e* sounds also *ye* after *b, p, m,* and *f.*

2. *E* beginning a syllable and in the beginning of a word
is always *ye.*

3. *E* when accented generally sounds *yo,* but *o* after *sh*
and *ch* (the index will indicate all the cases when *e* is to
be read *yo* or *o*).

4. *O* before the accent sounds like short *ah.*

5. Final consonants sound hard, that is, *g* like *k, d* like
t, b like *p, v* like *f, z* like *s, zh* like *sh.*

Thus *Andréy* sounds *Andr-yéy* (Engl. *yea*), by 1; *Rostóv*
— *Rastof,* by 4, 5; *Raévski* — *Ra-yéf-ski,* by 2, 5; *Ko-
novnítsyn* — *Ka-navn-yí-tsin,* by 4, 4, 1; *Arakchéev* —
A-rak-ché-yef, by 2, 5. For this reason *Tolstóy's* name is
approximately *Tahl-stóy,* while *Lev* is *L-yef,* though popu-
larly this, by 3, may be *L-yof,* and *Nikoláevich* is *N-yi-
ka-lá-ye-vich.*

It may be mentioned here that the middle name generally ending in *vich* (sometimes in *ich* or *ych*) for men, and
in *vna* for women, is a patronymic, meaning as much as
" son of," or " daughter of," the name to which the ending
is attached. It is proper form to address persons we
know, not by their family names, with Mr., Mrs., or Miss
attached to them, but simply by their given name and
patronymic. Peasants and servants are addressed by their
first name only, but if they are advanced in years, they
are generally known by their patronymic alone.

The accent is in Russian quite irregular, and in proper
nouns frequently puzzling. In the index the accents, now
and then divergent in the text, have been given according
to the best information obtainable, and in the few cases
where the index differs from the text, it is the first that
should be given preference.

INDEX
To Thoughts and Names in Tolstóy's Works

INDEX

To Thoughts and Names in Tolstóy's Works

335

398 INDEX

BIBLIOGRAPHY

Of Works and Articles on Tolstóy in English,
German, and French

BIBLIOGRAPHY

Of Works and Articles on Tolstóy in English,
German, and French

———•———

In 1903, the seventy-fifth year of L. N. Tolstóy's life,
there were published in Russia two bibliographical works
dealing with the popularity of the great Russian author.
The first, *Count L. N. Tolstóy as a Universal Author,
and the Diffusion of His Works in Russia and Abroad*,
published in St. Petersburg by P. D. Dragánov, Assistant
Librarian of the Imperial Public Library, claims to be
only an extract from a larger work to be published in the
future, which will treat of the translations of Tolstóy into
forty-five languages. The second, *Count L. Tolstóy in
Literature and Art. A Thorough Bibliographical Index
to the Russian and the Foreign Literatures concerning
Count L. N. Tolstóy*, by Yúri Bítovt (Moscow), which
apparently intends to be complete, gives in all 4,002
numbers. This latter work, though interesting as regards
the information given from Russian sources, is very far
from being either exact or complete. Thus, instead of
the nearly 250 numbers of German works and articles on
Tolstóy and his works, collected by me, only twenty are
given; a large number of translations into English, which
have appeared in periodicals and cheap editions, are not
mentioned; many translations into Slovak and Judeo-
German personally known to me are unknown to the

author. From these facts it may be assumed that even now it would not be difficult to bring together ten thousand numbers, if not much more.

But even with the insufficient material at hand it is possible to establish certain important and curious points in the popularity of the greatest Russian prose writer. He has been translated into all the literary languages of Europe, including Karelian, Esthonian, Lettish, Lithuanian, Turkish, and Georgian. Some of his works are to be found in Arabic, Sart, Kazano-Tartar, Perso-Tartar, Cheremis, Chinese, Japanese, Armenian, Hebrew, Judeo-German, and even Esperanto. The English language leads in the number of separate pieces translated : though only 262 are given by Bítovt, it may safely be assumed that there are more than three hundred of them.

Up to the year 1900 there appeared 304 separate pieces, either complete editions, or whole works, or separate articles, in Russia alone, most of these in St. Petersburg and Moscow. Of the eighteen so-called complete editions, sixteen have been published in Moscow. These Russian publications contain all the early productions fairly complete, and, since 1880, only a few of the later works, nearly all of them curtailed and corrupted by the censor. The uncensored works frequently coursed in Russia in lithographic copies and found their way abroad, where the best texts, though not always reliable, were published by M. Elpidin in Carouge-Genève ; since 1896 correct texts have been printed in England, at first in London and later in Christchurch, by Vladímir Chertkóv (Tchertkoff), Tolstóy's foreign representative. The works published abroad comprise more than half of all of Tolstóy's writings.

The present collection of works on Tolstóy, in English, German, and French, is fairly complete for the first two, less so for the French, as the bibliographies in that language are very unsatisfactory. Readers are requested

to communicate to the translator any omissions they may
observe.

I. ENGLISH

1 A., M. R. Tolstoi Maltreated, in *Nation 71*, 287.

2 A TALK ABOUT T.; INTERVIEW WITH MR. TCHERTKOFF,
in *Young Man 13*, 80.

3 A VISIT TO COUNT T., in *Cornhill 18*, 597.

4 ABOUT T., in *Independent 55*, 2419.

5 ADAMS, M. Ethics of T. and Nietzsche, in *International
Journal of Ethics 11*, 82.

6 ANNA KARENINA, in *Literary World 17*, 127.

7 ARNOLD, M. L. Tolstoi, in *Fortnightly Review 48*, 783,
Critic 12, 22, and *Living Age 176*, 82.

8 ———. L. Tolstoi, in his *Essays in Criticism*, 2d series,
London, 1889.

9 AUSTIN, L. F. L. T. as Critic of Maupassant, in *Academy
53*, 180, and *Current Literature 23*, 397.

10 BARTOL, C. A. "Kreutzer Sonata," in *Forum 10*, 204.

11 BASCOM, J. T.'s Christian Teaching, in *Dial 28*, 19.

12 BEHRS, C. A. Recollections of L. T., transl. from the Russian by C. E. Turner, London, 1893.

13 BENNETT, J. T.'s "What Is Art?" in *Musical Times 41*,
169, 231, 446.

14 BENTZON, TH. Recent Interview with T., in *Critic* n.s. *41*, 570.

15 BERENSON, B. Writings of T., in *Harvard Magazine 3*, 138.

16 BERNSTEIN, J. T.'s Objections to Socialism, in *Metaphysical
Magazine 16*, 161.

17 BEVERIDGE, A. J. The Russian Advance, New York and
London, 1903.

18 BIENSTOCK, J. W. T.'s Recent Literary Activity, in *Independent 54*, 2891.

19 BIRD, F. M. Lapse of T., in *Lippincott's Magazine 46*, 273.

20 BIXBY, J. T. T. and the New Quakerism, in *Arena 28*, 133.

21 BJERREGAARD, C. H. A. On T.'s "Resurrection," in *Ideal
Review 12*, 127.

22 BOGLIETTI, G. On T., in *Review of Reviews* (Eng.) *4*, 284.

23 BRINTON, C. T. under Ban of the Church, in *Critic 37*, 231.

24 CAHAN, A. Mantle of Tolstoi, in *Bookman 16*, 590.

25 CALDERON, G. L. The Wrong T., in *Monthly Review 3*, 129, and *Living Age 229*, 819.

26 CARPENTER, BISHOP B. Reply to " The Kingdom of God Is within You," in *New Review 10*, 186.

27 CELEBRATION OF T.'s 70TH BIRTHDAY, in *Bookman 8*, 106.

28 CHAT ABOUT T., in *Critic 34*, 10.

29 CHESTERTON, G. K. T. and the Cult of Simplicity, in his *Twelve Types*, London, 1902, and in his *Varied Types*, New York, 1903.

30 CHESTERTON, G. K., PERRIS, G. H., AND GARNETT, E. Leo Tolstoy, New York and London, 1903.

31 CHILDHOOD, BOYHOOD, AND YOUTH, in *Spectator 62*, 762.

32 CHRISTIAN TEACHING, in *Public Opinion 25*, 569.

33 COLBRON, G. I. Essays, Letters, and Miscellanies, in *Bookman 13*, 182.

34 CRAWFORD, V. M. " War and Peace," in her *Studies in Foreign Literature*, Boston, 1899.

35 CREELMAN, J. The Avatar of Count T., and, T. and his People, in his *On the Great Highway*, New York, 1901.

36 CROSBY, E. H. T.'s Philosophy of Life, in *Arena 15*, 279.

37 ———. T. as Philosopher, Prophet, and Man, *ib. 25*, 429.

38 ———. T. and his Message, *ib. 30*, 660, and New York, 1903.

39 ———. Two Days with Count T., in *Progressive Review 2*, 407.

40 ———. Answer to the Riddle of Life, in *Open Court 17*, 708.

41 ———. T. and Non-resistance, in *Outlook 54*, 52.

42 ———. T. as a Schoolmaster, a series of five articles in *Complete Education*, of Toledo, Ohio (afterward included in his book of the same name).

43 ———. Count T., His Philosophy, a series of six articles in *Facts and Fiction*, Chicago, Jan. — June, 1897 (substantially included in his book " Tolstoy and His Message ").

44 ———. Count T. at Home, in *Leslie's Weekly*, Nov. 10, 1898.

45 ———. T.'s Gospel of Love and Self-denial, in *Christian Herald*, N. Y., Jan. 9, 1901.

46 ———. Count T., the Peasant Nobleman, in *The Pilgrim*, Michigan, June, 1901.

47 ———. Seventieth Birthday of the Grand Old Man of Russia, in *Social Gospel*, Commonwealth, Ga., 1898.

48 ———. Snap-shots at Tolstoy, in *The Whim*, Newark, N. J., July, 1901.

49 ———. A True Story, in *The Whim*, Nov., 1901 (now forming a chapter in "Tolstoy as a Schoolmaster").

50 ———. T. and His Message, London and N. Y.

51 ———. T. as a Schoolmaster, Chicago, 1905.

52 CUFFE, H. O. T.'s Book "The Kingdom of God Is within You"; Christianity according to T., in *Lucifer 19*, 330.

53 DAWSON, W. J. The Man and His Message, in *Young Man 9*, 397.

54 DEATH OF IVAN ILYITCH, transl. by C. Garnett, in *Athenæum*, 1902, 2, 680.

55 DECREE OF T.'s EXCOMMUNICATION, in *Current Literature 31*, 232.

56 DESCHAMPS, G. T.'s "Resurrection"; A Review (*Balzac Library*, No. 3), New York, 1900.

57 DICAST. Failure of T.'s Religion, in *Independent 53*, 725.

58 DILLON, E. J. Work of T. in the Famine Districts, in *Review of Reviews* (N. Y.) 5, 29.

59 ———. Count T.'s Faith and Practice, *ib.* (Eng.) 5, 35.

60 ———. T.'s Disciples and Traducers, *ib.* (Eng.) 5, 414.

61 DINNER IN HONOR OF T.'s 70TH BIRTHDAY, in *Critic 33*, 276.

62 DIRCKS, W. On T.'s "Resurrection," in *Dome 5*, 217.

63 DOLE, N. H. Sketch of T., in *Bookbuyer 17*, 89.

64 ———. T.'s Astronomy, in *Athenæum*, 1902, 1, 436.

65 DOUMIC, R. T.'s Theory of Art, in *Living Age 218*, 607.

66 ———. "Resurrection," in *Eclectic Magazine 135*, 86, and *Living Age 225*, 529.

67 DOVIDOFF, MAD. L. T. Count L. T., in *Cosmopolitan 12*, 719.

68 DOWD, J. T.'s Criticism of Modern Art, in *Public Opinion 26*, 149.

69 DOWNES, R. P. Tolstoi, in *Great Thoughts 8*, 104.

70 DUPUY, E. Great Masters of Russian Literature, trans. by N. H. Dole, New York, 1886.

71 EDWARDS, G. C.   Leo Tolstoi, in *Sewanee Quarterly Review* *9*, 457.

72 EGGLESTON, F. O.   T. and Problem of Life, in *Unitarian Review 34*, 79.

73 ELLIS, H.   The New Spirit, London, 1890.

74 ETHICS OF L. T., in *Overland Monthly* n. s. *13*, 651.

75 EVANS, MRS. E. E.   A Nearer View of T., in *Open Court 16*, 396.

76 EXCOMMUNICATION OF T., in *Outlook 67*, 84.

77 ———, in *Independent 52*, 2401.

78 FARRAR, F. W.   Leo Tolstoi, in *Forum 6*, 109.

79 ———.   Religion of T., *ib. 6*, 337.

80 FAVILLE, J.   T. on Immortality, in *Andover Review 9*, 499.

81 FINDLATER, J. H.   T. as a War Novelist, in *Living Age 230*, 494.

82 FLOWER, B. O.   On May A. Ward's "Prophets of the Nineteenth Century," in *Arena 24*, 552.

83 ———.   Review of T.'s Plays, *ib. 32*, 671.

84 G., J. L.   How the Russian Novelist Lives and Works, in *Critic 34*, 417.

85 GANZ, H.   The Land of Riddles, from the German, by H. Rosenthal, New York, 1904.

86 GARNETT, C. AND E.   T. and "Resurrection," in *North American Review 172*, 504.

87 GARNETT, E.   Merejkowski's "T. as Man and Artist," in *Bookman 17*, 95.

88 ———.   T.'s Place in European Literature, *ib. 19*, 184.

89 GAY, S. E.   "The Kreutzer Sonata," in *Modern Review 2*, 99.

90 GIBSON, A. E.   The Message of T.'s "Resurrection," in *Metaphysical Magazine 14*, 317.

91 GOSSE, E. W.   Count L. T., in *Critical Kit-kats*, London, 1896.

92 GRIERSON, F.   Modern Mysticism and Other Essays, London, 1899.

93 GRISWOLD, H. T.   Personal Sketches of Recent Authors, Chicago, 1898.

94 GROTE, PROF. Moral Systems of T. and Nietzsche, in *Public Opinion 14*, 621.

95 GUNNING, W. D. T. and Primitive Christianity, in *Open Court 1*, 398.

96 HALE, E. E. Leo Tolstoi, in *Cosmopolitan 7*, 415.

97 HALPÉRINE - KAMINSKY, E. T. on the Music of Wagner, in *Music 14*, 345.

98 HANDLEY, F. L. Tolstoy, in *Our Day 15*, 71.

99 HAPGOOD, I. F. T. at Home, in *Atlantic Monthly 68*, 596.

100 ———. T. and the Public Censor, in *Fortnightly Review 60*, 57.

101 ———. T. as He Is, in *Munsey's Magazine 15*, 555.

102 ———. Gabriele D'Annunzio and T., in *Bookman 3*, 227.

103 ———. T. and Turgeneff, in *Nation 42*, 388.

104 ———. Christian Name of T., *ib. 46*, 237.

105 ———. "Kreutzer Sonata," *ib. 50*, 313.

106 ———. Maude's " T. and His Problems," *ib. 73*, 420.

107 HAPGOOD, N. Ethics of L. T., in *Harvard Monthly 8*, 191.

108 HEATH, R. L. Tolstoi, in *Leisure Hours 38*, 158.

109 HENDERSON, C. R. Slavery of Our Times, in *Dial 30*, 401.

110 HENLEY, W. E. Views and Reviews, New York, 1890.

111 HORNDLOW, A. T.'s Denunciation of Contemporary Art, in *Bookman 12*, 382.

112 HORTON, S. On T., in *Primitive Methodist Quarterly Review 33*, 37.

113 HOUGHTON, R. C. L. Tolstoi, in *Methodist Review 49*, 377.

114 HOWELLS, W. D. My Literary Passions, New York, 1895.

115 ———. Leo Tolstoi, in *Warner Library 25*, 14,985.

116 HOWELLS AND M. THOMPSON ON T., in *Literary World 18*, 233.

117 HUBBARD, E. Interpretation Done in Little, in *Cosmopolitan 34*, 442.

118 ———. Confession of T., in *Dial 8*, 125.

119 HUYBERS, E. A. " What Is Art ?" in *Literature 3*, 116.

120 HYDE, G. M. T.'s Theory of Art, in *Bookman 8*, 148.

121 IMITATION OF TOLSTOY, in *Cornhill Magazine 62*, 376, and *Living Age 198*, 407.

122 IMPORTANT AND THE TRIVIAL IN ART, in *Independent 52*, 1656 and 1711.

123 INGERSOLL, R. G. "Kreutzer Sonata," in *North American Review 151*, 289.

124 JOHNSTON, C. Quarrel between L. Tolstoy and Ivan Turgenief, in *Academy 38*, 392.

125 ———. T. at Home, in *Arena 20*, 480.

126 ———. How T. Writes, *ib. 21*, 269.

127 JUTTEN, D. B. Religion of T., in *Baptist Review 10*, 307.

128 KENNAN, G. A Visit to Tolstoy, in *Century Magazine 12*, 252.

129 KENWORTHY, J. C. Pilgrimage to T.: Letters from Russia to the *New Age*, Jan., 1896, London, 1900.

130 ———. T.: His Life and Works, London, 1902.

131 ———. A Visit to Count T., in *Humane Review 1*, 262.

132 ———. T.'s "What Is Art?" in *St. George 1*, 67.

133 ———. Thoughts on a Recent Visit to Count T., *ib. 3*, 191.

134 KENWORTHY'S T., in *Athenæum*, 1902, *2*, 309.

135 KIRKLAND, J. Count L. T., in *Dial 7*, 79.

136 KNOWLSON, T. S. T.'s "My Confession," the Confession of an Inquiring Spirit, in *Great Thoughts 5*, 263.

137 KRAUSKOPF, RABBI J. T., the Apostle of Russia, Philadelphia, 1896.

138 KREUTZER SONATA, in *Review of Reviews 1*, 330.

139 KROCKOW, COUNTESS VON. Seuron's Life of T., in *Independent 48*, 26.

140 L., A. F. Remarkable Phenomena in Connection with the Portraits of Count T., in *Outlook 69*, 950.

141 LANGEL, A. "Anna Karenina," and "War and Peace," in *Nation 40*, 70.

142 ———. "My Religion," *ib. 41*, 298.

143 ———. T. Souvenirs, *ib. 42*, 234.

144 ———. T. on Patriotism, *ib. 59*, 171.

145 ———. T.'s Theory of Art, *ib. 67*, 275 and 308.

146 LAUGHLIN, J. L. Reply to T.'s "On Money," in *Open Court 14*, 221.

147 LEROY-BEAULIEU, A. Theories of T., in *Chautauquan 9*, 149.

148 LIFE AND TEACHINGS OF L. T., ed. by G. H. Perris, in *Athenæum*, 1902, *1*, 330.

149 LIST OF T., in *Literary World 18*, 321.

150 LONG, R. E. C. T. in Thought and Action, in *Review of Reviews* (Eng.) *23*, 433, and (N. Y.) *24*, 33, and (Aust.) *18*, 653.

151 LYNCH, MISS H. "Kreutzer Sonata" vs. Zola's "Fécondité," in *Fortnightly Review 67*, 69, and in *Balzac Library*, No. 2, New York, 1900.

152 MACQUEEN, P. Tolstoi on America, an Interview, in *Frank Leslie's Popular Monthly 52*, 610.

153 MACY, J. A. Tolstoi's Moral Theory of Art, in *Century Magazine 62*, 298.

154 MALLET, MRSS E. M. The Theosophy of Count T., in *Theosophical Review 26*, 48.

155 MARVIN, F. S. T.'s "What Is Art?" in *Positivist Review 7*, 110.

156 MASSINGHAM, H. W. The Philosophy of a Saint, in *Contemporary Review 78*, 809.

157 MAUDE, A. The Teaching of T., Manchester, 1900.

158 ———. T. and His Problems: Essays, London and New York, 1901.

159 ———. Essays on Art: I. An Introduction to "What Is Art?" II. T.'s View of Art. London, 1902.

160 ———. T.'s Theory of Art, in *Contemporary Review 77*, 241.

161 ———. The Later Work of T., in *Bookman 11*, 359.

162 ———. Misinterpretation of T., in *Open Court 16*, 590.

163 ———. A Talk with Miss Jane Addams and L. T., in *Humane Review 3*, 203.

164 ———. Talks with Count T., in *New Century Review 7*, 404.

165 MAUDE'S "T. AND HIS PROBLEMS," in *Athenæum*, 1901, *1*, 787.

166 MAYO, I. F. The Philanthropist of the Russian Famine, in *Victorian Magazine 1*, 307.

167 McDougall, E. M. L. On L. T., in *Sunday Magazine 21*, 706.

168 Merejkowski, D. T. as Man and Artist; with an Essay on Dostoïevski, New York and London, 1902. Reviewed, in *Bookman 17*, 95.

169 Moore, G. Impressions of T., in *Lippincott's Magazine 72*, 608. Work of T., *ib. 72*, 697.

170 More, P. E. Shelburne Essays, New York, 1904.

171 ———. T.'s Theory of Art, in *Atlantic Review 218*, 607.

172 ———. The Ancient Feud between Philosophy and Art, in *Atlantic Monthly 86*, 337.

173 My Religion, in *Literary World 17*, 238.

174 Newmarch, R. Tchaikovsky and Tolstoi, in *Contemporary Review 83*, 112, and *Literary Age 237*, 58.

175 Newton, W. W. A Run through Russia; the Story of a Visit to Count T., Hartford, 1894.

176 Nicchia. My Last Memory of T., in *Craftsman 4*, 45.

177 Nordau, M. Tolstoism, in his *Degeneration*, New York, 1895.

178 Norman, H. T. at Home, in *Scribner's Monthly 28*, 299.

179 ———. Count T. at Home and Abroad, in his *All the Russias*, New York, 1902.

180 Norton, G. T. and Montaigne, in *Nation 42*, 335.

181 Novels of T., in *Saturday Review 63*, 22.

182 P., C. S. The Teachings of Count T., in *Theosophical Review 27*, 155.

183 Panin, I. N. Lectures on Russian Literature : Pushkin, Gogol, Turgenef, Tolstoy, New York, 1889.

184 Paulding, J. K. T. at the Berlin Theatre, in *Nation 72*, 47.

185 Payne, W. M. Review of T.'s "Resurrection," in *Dial 28*, 401.

186 Peck, H. T. Review of T.'s "Resurrection," in *Bookman 11*, 176.

187 Perris, G. H. Russia of T., in *Forum 29*, 751.

188 ———. L. T., the Grand Mujik, a Study in Personal Evolution, London, 1898.

189 ———. T.'s "What Is Art?" in *Architectural Review 4*, 213.

190 ———. L. T. as Writer, in *Bookman 19*, 180.

191 ———. T.'s Home Life, in *The Daily Chronicle*, August 6, 1904.

192 PERRIS'S L. T., reviewed in *Outlook* (Eng.) *2*, 54.

193 ———, *Academy 54*, 139.

194 ———, *Literature 3*, 147.

195 ———, *Critic 30*, 184.

196 ———, *Athenœum*, 1898, *2*, 382.

197 PHYSIOLOGY OF WAR, in *Nation 46*, 345.

198 PHYTHIAN, J. E. T.'s "What Is Art?" in *Manchester Quarterly 20*, 184.

199 POWER OF DARKNESS, in *Literary World 18*, 297.

200 PRESCOTT, D. Our T. Club, in *Century Magazine 21*, 761.

201 PUBLICATION OF "RESURRECTION," in *Academy 56*, 806.

202 R., A. I. A True Theosophist Count Tolstoi, in *Theosophical Tract Series*, Bombay, 1890.

203 RAGG, A. E. To Count T., a Poem, in *Canadian Magazine 17*, 44.

204 RALSTON, W. R. S. Novels of Count L. T., in *Nineteenth Century 5*, 650, and *Living Age 141*, 409.

205 READE, R. H. L. Tolstoi, in *Good Words 33*, 448.

206 REGENERATION, A REPLY TO MAX NORDAU, with Introduction by N. M. Butler, New York, 1896.

207 RELIGION OF T., in *New England Magazine 40*, 140.

208 RESURRECTION, in *Academy 57*, 255.

209 RICKABY, J. Reply to "The Kingdom of God Is within You," in *New Review 10*, 195.

210 ROBERTSON, J. M. T. and the Ethics of Jesus, in *Free Review 4*, 214.

211 ROD, E. L. Tolstoi, in *Eclectic Magazine 133*, 585, and *Living Age 222*, 629.

212 ROGERS, J. G. Reply to "The Kingdom of God Is within You," in *New Review 10*, 198.

213 ROSEGGER, P. G. "Kreutzer Sonata," in *Open Court 5*, 2795.

214 ROYCE, J. T. and the Unseen Moral Order, in *Liber Scriptorum*, New York, 1893.

215 SAINTSBURY, G. Literary Prophets of the Later Nineteenth Century, in *Independent 54*, 3023.

216 SCHINZ, A. Count T. and E. Rod, in *Bookman 17*, 645.

217 SCHUYLER, E. Count T. Twenty Years Ago, in *Scribner's Magazine 5*, 537 and 732, and in his *Selected Essays*, New York, 1901.

218 SEDGWICK, H. D. T.'s Life and Work, in *World's Work 3*, 1953.

219 SERGYEENKO, P. A. How Count L. N. T. Lives and Works, trans. by I. F. Hapgood, New York and Boston, 1899.

220 ———. Reviewed in *Literary World 30*, 151.

221 ———. Reviewed in *Dial 26*, 346.

222 ———. Reviewed in *Athenæum*, 1900, *1*, 145.

223 SEVASTOPOL AND OTHER MILITARY TALES, trans. by L. Maude and A. Maude, reviewed in *Athenæum*, 1901, *2*, 871.

224 SHARP, W. "Work While Ye Have the Light," in *Academy 39*, 109.

225 SHELDON, W. L. T. from an Ethical Standpoint, in *Ethical Record 2*, 65.

226 SINCLAIR, ARCHDEACON. Reply to "The Kingdom of God Is within You," in *New Review 10*, 188.

227 SKETCH OF T., in *Harper's Weekly 45*, 696.

228 SMITH, J. H. T.'s "Childhood, Boyhood, and Youth," in *Journal of Education 17*, 220 and 262.

229 SOISSONS, COUNT DE. On T.'s "Resurrection," in *Humanitarian 17*, 403.

230 SOME OF THE WORDS OF A FREE MAN, in *Current Literature 31*, 402.

231 SPEECHES AT THE DINNER GIVEN IN HONOUR OF HIS 70TH BIRTHDAY, in *Critic 30*, 276.

232 SPIELMANN, M. H. "What Is Art?" in *Literature 3*, 77.

233 STADLING, J. With T. in the Russian Famine, in *Century Magazine 46*, 249, 560.

234 STEAD, W. T. Count T. and His Gospel, in his *Truth about Russia*, London, 1888.

235 STEINER, E. A. Visit to T.'s Home, in *Chautauquan 36*, 581.

236 ———. Count T.'s Sociological Views, in *Bibliotheca Sacra* *58*, 179.

237 ———. Interview with T., in *Outlook 66*, 828.

238 ———. T. To-day, *ib. 75*, 35.

239 ———. T.'s Marriage and Family Life, *ib. 75*, 267.

240 ———. T. in the Heart of Russia, *ib. 75*, 537.

241 ———. Tolstoy the Man, New York, 1904.

242 STEUART, J. A. Letters to Living Authors, London, 1890.

243 STEVENS, T. With Count T., in his *Through Russia on a Mustang*, New York, 1891.

244 STOCKHAM, MRS. A. B. T., a Man of Peace. The New Spirit, by H. H. Ellis, Chicago, 1900.

245 STODDARD, F. H. L. T. and Matthew Arnold, in *Andover Review 10*, 359, and *Congregational Review 3*, 20.

246 STRACHEY, L. Merejkowski's "T. as Man and Artist," reviewed in *Critic* n. s. *42*, 270.

247 STREET, A. E. The Realities of War: Count T. and M. Verestchagin, in his *Critical Sketches*, London, 1894.

248 SYMONS, A. "What Is Art?" in *Saturday Review 86*, 148.

249 ———. T.'s Plots not Adapted to Dramatization, *ib. 95*, 227.

250 TALES FROM TOLSTOI, trans. by R. N. Bain, reviewed in *Athenæum*, 1901, *2*, 871.

251 "THE GOSPEL IN BRIEF," reviewed in *Saturday Review 83*, 448; *Biblical World 9*, 231.

252 THEORIES OF T., in *Critic 33*, 184.

253 THOMPSON, M. L. Tolstoi, in *Book News 6*, 9.

254 THOMPSON ON T., in *Literary World 18*, 281.

255 LEO TOLSTOI, in *Westminster Review 130*, 278.

256 ———, *National Magazine 14*, 579.

257 ———, *Edinburgh Review 194*, 49.

258 ———, *Book Buyer 3*, 296.

259 ———, *Book News 7*, 268.

260 ———, *Academy 54*, 139.

261 ———, *Dial 25*, 121.

262 L. T. AND F. DOSTOIEFFSKY, in *London Quarterly 70*, 49.

263 T. AND HIS FAMILY ESTATE, in *Review of Reviews 19*, 490.

264 T. AND KOROLENKO, in *Nation* *46*, 203.

265 T. AND NIETZSCHE, in *Review of Reviews* *22*, 614.

266 T. AND THE CHURCH, in *Current Literature* *30*, 5.

267 T. AND THE CZAR, in *Outlook* *61*, 209.

268 T. AND THE DOCTRINE OF HENRY GEORGE, in *Review of Reviews* (Am.) *17*, 73.

269 T. AND THE DORPAT UNIVERSITY, in *Outlook* *75*, 525.

270 T. AND THE GOSPELS, in *Public Opinion* *19*, 51.

271 T. AND THE RUSSIAN CENSORS, in *Outlook* *69*, 694.

272 T. AS A DRAMATIST, in *Academy* *64*, 407.

273 T. COMPARED WITH IBSEN, in *Chautauquan* *31*, 329.

274 T. INTERVIEWED, in *World Literature* *1*, 109.

275 T. ON ART, in *Nation* *67*, 308.

276 T. ON EDUCATION AND INSTRUCTION, in *Review of Reviews* *26*, 233.

277 T. ON MONEY, in *Open Court* *14*, 193.

278 T. ON THE OFFICE OF A PRIEST, *ib.* *25*, 616.

279 T.'s "ANNA KARENINA," trans. by C. Garnett, reviewed in *Athenæum*, 1901, *2*, 871.

280 ———, *Nation* *72*, 404.

281 T.'s BOOK, "THE KINGDOM OF GOD IS WITHIN US,"— CHRISTIAN ANARCHISM, in *Review of Reviews* *9*, 306.

282 T.'s DAILY LIFE, in *Critic* n. s. *39*, 105.

283 T.'s DEFIANCE TO THE RUSSIAN CHURCH, in *Independent* *53*, 1693.

284 T.'s DEVICE FOR PEACE, in *Independent* *51*, 1036.

285 T.'s ESSAYS, LETTERS, AND MISCELLANIES, reviewed in *Literary World* *31*, 216.

286 T.'s EXCOMMUNICATION, in *Independent* *53*, 1662.

287 ———, *Outlook* *67*, 841.

288 T.'s HOME LIFE, in *Current Literature* *26*, 308.

289 T.'s HORROR OF WAR, in *Independent* *55*, 889.

290 T.'s ILLNESS, in *Critic* *40*, 290.

291 T.'s METHOD OF WORK, in *Current Literature* *30*, 665.

292 T.'s PLAN OF REDEMPTION, in *Living Age* *219*, 386.

293 T.'s "RESURRECTION," trans. by Maude, reviewed in *Independent* *52*, 779.

294 ———, *Public Opinion 28*, 409.

295 ———, *Review of Reviews 21*, 167.

296 ———, *Critic 36*, 355.

297 ———, *Athenæum*, 1900, *1*, 431.

298 ———, *Chautauquan 31*, 111.

299 ———, *Nation 70*, 345.

300 T.'s " Resurrection," dramatized by H. Bataille, reviewed in *Athenæum*, 1903, *1*, 251.

301 ———, *Harper's Weekly 47*, 418.

302 ———, *Independent 55*, 744.

303 T.'s Seventy-fifth Birthday, in *World's Work 7*, 4061.

304 T.'s " The Four Gospels Harmonized and Translated," in *Review of Reviews* (Eng.) *11*, 371, and (Aust.) *6*, 565.

305 T.'s Theory of Art, in *Quarterly Review 191*, 359.

306 T.'s Translator Defended, in *Nation 61*, 365.

307 T.'s Views of Art, in *Review of Reviews 22*, 91.

308 T.'s Work, in *Dial 25*, 121.

309 ———, *Literature 3*, 73.

310 T., the Statesman, in *Independent 53*, 1930.

311 T. through French Eyes, in *Review of Reviews 26*, 48.

312 Triggs, O. L. An Instance of Conversion, in *Open Court 16*, 69.

313 Tyler, M. F. Novels of T., in *New England Magazine 46*, 193.

314 Unpublished Letters from Tolstoi, in *Athenæum*, 1902, *2*, 451.

315 Van Ness, T. A Visit to Tolstoi, in *Literary World 20*, 56.

316 Visit to T., in *Cornhill 65*, 597, and *Living Age 194*, 210 ; *Literary World 28*, 160.

317 Vittum, E. M. T. and the Modern Church, in *New England Magazine 48*, 54.

318 Walker, J. B. Discontinuance of Count Tolstoi's Novel, in *Cosmopolitan 27*, 447.

319 "WAR AND PEACE," in *Literary World 17*, 348.

320 ———, *Spectator 60*, 202.

321 WARD, M. A.   Prophets of the Nineteenth Century: Carlyle, Ruskin, Tolstoy, Boston, 1900.

322 WEDGWOOD, C. C.   Leo Tolstoi, in *Contemporary Review 52*, 249 ; *Eclectic Magazine 109*, 634.

323 WENTZ.   Maude's "T. and His Problems," reviewed in *Book Buyer 23*, 243.

324 WESTRUM, S. VAN.   Review of Sergyeenko's "How Count T. Lives and Works," and of T.'s "Resurrection," in *Book Buyer 20*, 230.

325 "WHAT IS ART?" in *Bibliotheca Sacra 55*, 772.

326 ———, *Literary World 29*, 277.

327 ———, *Nation 67*, 226.

328 ———, *Nation 67*, 275.

329 ———, *Outlook 60*, 87.

330 ———, *Popular Science Monthly 53*, 553.

331 ———, *Public Opinion 25*, 249.

332 "WHAT TO DO?" in *Literary World 18*, 315.

333 WHEELER, W.   The Social and Religious Teachings of T., in *Primitive Methodist Quarterly Review 21*, 601.

334 WHIPPLE, C. K.   "Kreutzer Sonata," in *Open Court 5*, 2796.

335 WHITE, A. D.   Walks and Talks with T., in *McClure's Magazine 16*, 507, and *Idler 19*, 479.

336 WHITE, W. H.   T.'s Astronomy, in *Athenæum*, 1901, *2*, 879.

337 WILKINSON, W. C.   Tolstoi, in *Homiletic Review*, pp. 16–27, 107–116, 1889.

338 WOLKONSKY, S.   Negations of T., in *Living Age 213*, 771.

339 ———.   Pictures of Russian History and Russian Literature, Boston, 1897.

340 WOOD, H.   "What to Do?" in *New Science Review 1*, 184.

341 WORCESTER, J. H., JR.   L. T. as a Reformer, in *Presbyterian and Reformed Review 2*, 459.

342 WRONG T., in *Review of Reviews 23*, 727.

343 WYCKOFF, G. P.   Maude's "T. and His Problems," in *Dial 32*, 46.

344 YARROS, V. S.   Decline of T.'s Philosophy, in *Chautauquan*
     38, 703.

345 ———.   Review of Maude's translation of " What Is Art? "
     in *Dial 24*, 249.

346 Z. Z.   " What Is Art? " in *Outlook 2*, 52.

II. GERMAN

347 ACHELIS, TH.   Leo Tolstoi, in *Neues Wiener Tagblatt*, No.
     248, 1899.

348 ———, in *Magazin für Litteratur*, Nos. 37, 38, 1901.

349 ———, in *Hamburger Correspondent*, No. 18, 1901.

350 ———.   Graf L. T., in *Der Lotse*, No. 7, 1901.

351 ———.   Leo N. Tolstoi, Berlin, 1902.

352 ACHER, M.   Tolstoj's "Auferstehung," in *Zeit*, No. 283,
     1900.

353 ADELUNG, SOPHIE VON.   Ein Vorläufer L. T.'s, in *Deutsche
     Rundschau*, Febr., pp. 294–305, 1906.

354 AMYNTOR, G.   Die Cis-moll-Sonate, Leipzig, 1891.

355 ———.   Russische Dichtung und Kultur, in *Cosmopolis*,
     1897.

356 ANDREAS-SALOMÉ, LOU.   L. T., unser Zeitgenosse, in
     Neue Deutsche Rundschau, No. 9, 1899.

357 AUS T.'S LEBEN (aus P. Sergejenko's Buch), in *Deutsches
     Wochenblatt*, pp. 244–47, 1899.

358 AXELROD, E. L.   T.'s Weltanschauung und ihre Entwicklung,
     Stuttgart, 1902.

359 ———.   Die Grundidee von T.'s "Auferstehung," in *Die
     neue Zeit*, Nos. 49–51, 1901.

360 B., W.   Tolstoi und Turgenjew, in *Unterhaltungsbeilage der
     Täglichen Rundschau*, No. 220, 1893.

361 BAHR, H.   Gegen Tolstoi, in *Zeit*, No. 205, 1898.

362 BARTELS, A.   T.'s "Auferstehung," in *Der Kunstwart*, No.
     13, 1900.

363 BAUER, E.   Graf L. T. als Plagiator, in *Gegenwart*, No. 49,
     1896.

364 BEAUNIER, A.   T. und die Kunst, in *Allgemeine Zeitung*,
     No. 68, 1901.

365 BECK, H.   Noch einmal die Kreutzersonate vom Standpunkt des Irrenarztes, Leipzig, 1898.

366 BEHRS, C.   Leo Tolstoi, in *Westermann's illustrierte deutsche Monatshefte*, Juni, pp. 282–99 and Juli, pp. 407–26, 1899.

367 BERG, L.   T. und die Kunst, in *Die Umschau*, No. 37, 1898.

368 BERGER, A. FRHR. VON.   T.'s Kreutzersonate, in *Bohemia*, No. 75, 1892.

369 BERNECKER, E.   Graf Leo Tolstoj, in *Biographische Volksbücher*, Nos. 108–111, Leipzig, 1901.

370 BETTELHEIM, A.   Bücher und Kritik von L. T., in *Nation*, No. 11, 1902.

371 BIEDENKAPP, K.   Nietzsche und Tolstoi, in *Allgemeine Zeitung*, No. 164, 1897.

372 BIEDENKAPP, Z.   T. als Politiker, in *Nordeutsche allgemeine Zeitung*, No. 243, 1902.

373 BLENNERHASSETT, LADY.   T.'s " Auferstehung," in *Deutsche Rundschau*, pp. 472–4, 1900.

374 BODE, W.   Die Lehren T.'s, Weimar, 1900.

375 ———.   Tolstoi-Konitz-Sternberg, in *Ethische Kultur*, No. 3, 1901.

376 ———.   Der Erzbischof gegen die Tolstoianer, in *Das freie Wort*, No. 4, 1901.

377 ———.   Was ist T.? *ib.*, pp. 11–16, 1902.

378 ———.   T.'s Stellung zur Kunst, in *Gegenwart*, No. 21, 1900.

379 ———.   Exkommuniziert, *ib.*, No. 15, 1901.

380 ———.   T.'s Antwort auf die soziale Frage, *ib.*, No. 52, 1901.

381 ———.   T.'s Stellung zu den Landfragen, in *Das Land*, pp. 49–51, 104–5, 1901.

382 ———.   T.'s Lehre vom Glück, in *Der Lotse*, No. 37, 1902.

383 BONUS, A.   Tolstoi, in *Der Kunstwart*, No. 13, 1902.

384 BRANDES, G.   Menschen und Essays, Frankfurt a. M., 1893.

385 ———.   Menschen und Werke, Frankfurt a. M., 1894.

386 BRAUN, E. B.   Graf T. und Bernardin de St. Pierre, in *Zeitschrift für vergleichende Litteraturgeschichte*, No. 10, 1896.

387 BRAUSEWETTER.   Religiöses Problem u. T., in *Deutschland*, Mai und Juni, 1903.

388 BRÜGGEN, E. VON DER.   R. Kipling und T., in *Die Grenzboten*, No. 14, 1901.

389 Brückner, A. Leo Tolstoj, in *Deutsche Litteraturzeitung*, No. 5, 1887.

390 Carrière, M. Natur und Kunst, in *Nord und Süd*, No. 55, 1890.

391 Conrad, M. G. T., die Kunst und wir, in *Die Gesellschaft*, IV., pp. 331–4, 1898.

392 Crome, H. T.'s Stellung zu Staat und Gesellschaft, in *Der alte Glaube*, No. 9–12, 1901.

393 Crüwell, G. A. T.'s " Auferstehung," in *Über Land und Meer*, No. 51, 1899.

394 Czumikow, W. Antichristen, in *Zukunft*, pp. 229–33, 1901.

395 Daab, Fr. Graf Leo Tolstoj, in *Das Land*, pp. 382–4, 1901.

396 Dreydorff. Die grosse Frage (nach unseres Lebens Sinn und Bedeutung, bezüglich auf Nietzsche, Strauss, Tolstoi), in *Deutsches Protestantenblatt*, Nos. 31, 32, 1901.

397 Dreyfus, A. Der Künstler Tolstoi, in *Frankfurter Zeitung*, No. 134, 1000.

398 Driesmans, H. "Die Macht der Finsterniss" und die Ballettänzerin, in *Versöhnung*, No. 28, 1899.

399 Dukmeyer, Fr. Die Deutschen in T.'s Schilderung, in *Beilage zur allgemeinen Zeitung*, No. 111, 1902.

400 Dukmeyer, Won. Tolstoi, Prophet oder Popanz, Berlin, 1895.

401 Ehrenfels, Chr. Frhr. von. Die Wertschätzung der Kunst bei Wagner, Ibsen und Tolstoi, Prag, 1901.

402 Eiche, H. T.'s Ethik und die moderne Kultur, in *Gegenwart*, No. 8, 1902.

403 Eine Tolstoikolonie in Holland, in *Die Reformation*, No. 18, 1902.

404 Ein Tag bei Tolstoi, in *Psychologische Arbeiten*, No. 39, 1899.

405 Eltzbacher, P. Rechtsphilosophie T.'s, in *Preussische Jahrbücher*, pp. 266–82, 1900.

406 Ephron, H. Wie T. lebt und arbeitet, in *Wiener Rundschau*, pp. 564–6, 1899.

407 EREMITA. " Macht der Finsterniss," in *Kirchliche Wochen-schrift für evangelische Christen*, No. 18, 1901.

408 ERNST, P. L. T. und der slavische Roman, in *Deutsche litterarische Volkshefte*, No. 32, Berlin, 1889.

409 ———. Kunst und Seele, in *Magazin für Litteratur des Inn-und Auslandes*, No. 67, 1899.

410 ———. Leo Tolstoi, in *Magazin für Litteratur*, pp. 321-3, 1902.

411 ETTLINGER, A. Leo Tolstoj, eine Skizze seines Lebens und Wirkens, in *Forschungen zur neueren Litteraturgeschichte*, X., Berlin, 1899.

412 FINGER, B. Tolstoi'sches Christentum, in *Zeitfragen des christlichen Volkslebens*, No. 207, 1902.

413 FISCHER, H. T.'s " Auferstehung," in *Christliche Welt*, Nos. 6, 7, 1900.

414 FRANK, H. Zwei wunderliche Heilige (T., Bruder Iwan von Kronstadt), in *Nord und Süd*, Feb. 209-16, 1901.

415 FRÖBEL, J. E. Lebenslauf, Aufzeichnungen, Erinnerungen und Bekenntnisse (Meeting of Tolstoy and Fröbel, Vol. II., pp. 74 ff.), Stuttgart, 1890, 1891.

416 FUCHS, O. T.'s " Macht der Finsterniss," in *Die Wage*, No. 30, 1899.

417 GADEBUSCH, A. "Macht der Finsterniss," in *Illustrierte Zeitung*, No. 3016, 1901.

418 GALITZIN, FÜRST D. Du sollst nicht töten! Erwiderung auf Graf L. T.'s Kreutzersonate, deutsch von A. Berger, Berlin, 1891.

419 GANZ, H. T. oder Göthe, in *Neue freie Presse*, No. 12,215, 1898.

420 ———. T.'s " Auferstehung," *ib.*, V. No. 25, 1900.

421 GERSCHMANN, H. Studien über den modernen Roman, in *Programm des Realgymnasiums*, Königsberg, 1894.

422 GESPRÄCH MIT T., in *Heimgarten*, pp. 146-8, 1901.

423 GIESSLER, W. Das Mitleid in der neueren Ethik, mit besonderer Rücksicht auf F. Nietzsche, R. Wagner u. L. T., Halle a. S., 1903.

424 GLASENAPP, G. VON. Kosmopolitische Studien zu Poesie, Philosophie und Religionsgeschichte, Riga, 1899.

425 GLEICHEN - RUSSWURM, A. VON. T. und die Theosophen, in *Magdeburger Zeitung*, April 15, 1903.
426 GLOGAU, G. Graf L. T., ein russischer Reformator. Ein Beitrag zur Religionsphilosophie, Kiel, 1893.
427 GNADE, E. Zur modernen Litteratur, in *Gegenwart*, No. 40, 1890.
428 GOLANT, N. Zu Graf T.'s 70. Geburtstag, in *Die Wage*, No. 1, 1898.
429 GOLDENWEISER, A. Das Verbrechen als Strafe und die Strafe als Verbrechen — Leitmotive in T.'s " Auferstehung," Berlin, 1904.
430 GOLDSCHMIDT, A. T.'s " Moderne Sklaverei," in *Die Gesellschaft*, pp. 303–10, 1901.
431 GROT, N. Nietzsche und T., in *Zukunft*, No. 21, 1897.
432 ———. Nietzsche und T. Aus dem Russischen von Alexis Markow, Berlin, 1898.
433 GROTTHUSS, J. E. Probleme und Charakterköpfe, Stuttgart, 1898, 4th ed., 1902.
434 GYURKOVECHKY, VICT VON. Warum T. Liebe verachtet und Aerzte hasst? Wien, 1892.

435 HALPÉRINE - KAMINSKY, E. Die Rolle der Kunst. Antwort europäischer Schriftsteller und Künstler an T., in *Deutsche Revue*, Feb., pp. 227–47, 1899.
436 HANSSON, O. F. Nietzsche und der Naturalismus, in *Gegenwart*, No. 39, 1890.
437 HARDEN, M. T.'s " Auferstehung," in *Zukunft*, pp. 49–57, 1900.
438 HARNACK, O. T. als Modeschriftsteller, in his *Essays und Studien zur Litteraturgeschichte*, pp. 330–45, Braunschweig, 1899.
439 HARTMANN, A. VON. T.'s sittliche Weltanschauung, in *Preussische Jahrbücher*, No. 112, 1903.
440 HASSEL, U. VON. T. und sein Verhältniss zu Kirche und Staat, in *Monatschrift für Stadt und Land*, pp. 515–22, 1901.
441 HEIDENSTAM, V. VON. Die Aesthetick T.'s, in *Wiener Rundschau*, pp. 497–500, 1899.
442 HEILBORN, E. " Die Macht der Finsterniss," in *Nation*, No. 6, 1901.

443 HEIMANN, M.   T.'s " Auferstehung," in *Deutsche Rundschau*, pp. 291–303, 1900.

444 HENCKEL, W.   Graf L. T. und die Duchoborzen, in *Wiener Rundschau*, No. 3, 1899.

445 HERBERT, M.   T. als Moralist und als Künstler, in *Litterarische Warte*, No. 2, 1901.

446 HEY, S.   " Macht der Finsterniss," in *Die Gesellschaft*, pp. 204–10, 1901.

447 HÖBER, E.   Neues von und über T., in *Das litterarische Echo*, col. 1262, 6, 1901.

448 HOPFEN - VEVEY, O. H.   T. und die Keuschheit, in *Der Lotse*, No. 30, 1902.

449 HORNEMANN, F.   L. T.'s Glaube, in *Kirchliche Gegenwart*, pp. 247–50, 263–6, 279–83, 295–8, 313–5, 1902.

450 HÜRNER, A.   T.'s " Auferstehung," in *Schweizerische Reformblätter*, Nos. 32–4, 1901.

451 IGNOTUS.   Tolstoj, seine Widersacher und die Hungersnot, in *Magazin für Litteratur des Inn- und Auslandes*, No. 61, 1892.

452 JENTSCH, K.   Hat Tolstoj recht ? in *Zeit*, No. 335, 1901.

453 JEROGOW, W.   Neues von und über L. T., in *Gegenwart*, No. 44, 1893.

454 KALKSCHMIDT, E.   Tolstoi's " Auferstehung," in *Internationale Litteraturberichte*, pp. 145–6, 1900.

455 KARROTOM, A.   L. T. als Sektierer, in *Das neue Jahrhundert*, No. 20, 1899.

456 KAUTSKY, K.   T. und Brentano, in *Die neue Zeit*, No. 27, 1901.

457 KÖBER, R. VON.   L. T. und sein unkirchliches Christentum, Braunschweig, 1890.

458 ———.   T. über Wissenschaft und Kunst, in *Sphinx*, No. 15, 1892.

459 ———.   Neues von und über T., *ib.*, No. 17, 1893.

460 KRAUS, E.   Die kleinen Menschlichkeiten des Grafen T., in *Magazin für Litteratur des Inn- und Auslandes*, pp. 337–40, 1895.

461 KREBS, R. Reformgedanken des Grafen L. T., Erfurt, 1900.

462 ———. Turgenjew und Tolstoi, Berlin, 1893.

463 KÜHNEMANN, E. Noch einmal die kleinen Menschlichkeiten des Grafen T., in *Magazin für Litteratur des Inn- und Auslandes*, pp. 433-5, 1895.

464 ———. Leo Tolstoi, in *Westermann's Monatshefte*, 1899 and 1900.

465 ———. T.'s "Auferstehung," *ib.*, pp. 697-701, 1901.

466 KÜLPE, E. Antitolstoi, in *Der alte Glaube*, No. 31, 1903.

467 LAMMERMAYER, F. L. N. Tolstoi, in *Blätter für litterarische Unterhaltung*, pp. 801-3, 1892.

468 LANDAU, M. Ein Plagiat des Grafen T., in *Zeitschrift für vergleichende Litteraturgeschichte*, No. 9, 1896.

469 LEIXNER, O. VON. Kann T. dem deutschen Volke ein Führer sein? in *Deutsche Monatsschrift für das gesamte Leben der Gegenwart*, Dec., p. 336, 1904.

470 LEMKE, H. Pädagogische Wanderungen durch T.'s Werke, in *Pädagogische Zeitung*, No. 88, 1902.

471 LEWINSKY, J. T. und das russische Theater, in *Deutsche Revue*, Vol. IV., pp. 17-30, 1897.

472 ———. Das russische Theater. Mein 2. Besuch Russlands, *ib.*, Jan., pp. 34-44, 1899.

473 LIENHARD, F. T.'s "Auferstehung," in *Der Thürmer*, April, pp. 45-7, 1900.

474 LÖBL, E. T.'s "Auferstehung," in *Wiener Zeitung*, No. 39, 1000.

475 LOMBROSO, C. Mein Besuch bei T., in *Das freie Wort*, pp. 391-7, 1901.

476 LORENZ, M. Leo Tolstoi, in *Preussische Jahrbücher*, pp. 503-9, 1900.

477 LÖWENFELD, R. Gespräche über und mit T., Berlin, 1891, und Leipzig, 1901.

478 ———. L. N. T., sein Leben, seine Werke, seine Weltanschauung. I. Th., Berlin, 1892.

479 ———. T.'s neuestes Werk, in *Magazin für Litteratur des Inn- und Auslandes*, No. 62, 1893.

480 ———. Exkommuniziert, in *Die Wage*, No. 15, 1901, and in *Deutsches Kolonialblatt*, No. 18, 1901.

481 MARHOLM, L. Wir Frauen und unsere Dichter, Leipzig, 1895.

482 MAURENBRECHER. Probleme des Sozialismus in Russland, in *Die Hilfe*, No. 19, 1901.

483 MEERHEIMB, H. VON. Gedanken über T. Ein Beitrag zur Verständniss seines Charakters und seiner Schriften, in *Monatsblätter für deutsche Litteratur*, pp. 544–54, 1901.

484 MEYER-BENFEY, H. T.'s " Auferstehung," in *Gegenwart*, No. 25, 1900.

485 MÜLLER, G. Mehr Licht in uns, Welt! Ein Beitrag zur Klärung schwankender Begriffe und Anschauungen im Anschluss an Graf T.'s " Christliche Gesinnung und Patriotismus," Leipzig, 1895.

486 MÜNCHHAUSEN, M. VON. Tolstoi, in *Deutsche Zeitschrift*, No. 16, 1901.

487 MÜNZ, B. Schriften über und von T., in *Blätter für litterarische Unterhaltung*, pp. 586–8, 1894.

488 ———. Russische Litteratur, *ib.*, pp. 168–70, 651–3, 1896.

489 MYSTISCHER SOZIALISMUS, in *Neue Bahnen*, pp. 175–84, 228–37, 1902.

490 NEHRING, W. R. Löwenfeld, Tolstoi, in *Deutsche Litteraturzeitung*, pp. 459–60, 1893.

491 NERUDA, E. Ein Präludium Chopin's, in *Magazin für Litteratur*, No. 51, 1898.

492 NETTER, O. Tolstoi-Konitz-Sternberg, in *Ethische Kultur*, No. 9, 1901.

493 NICOLAIDES, C. T.'s Stellung zu der Religion, in *Beilage zur Allgemeinen Zeitung*, No. 217, 1902.

494 NORDAU, M. Der Tolstoismus, in *Entartung*, Vol. I., Berlin, 1893.

495 NORDEN, J. Zum 70. Geburtstage T.'s, in *Illustrierte Zeitung*, No. 111, 1899.

496 NOTOVICH, O. K. Ein wenig Philosophie. Sophismen und Paradoxe. Anlässlich der religiös-philosophischen Schriften des Grafen L. N. T., aus dem russischen, Berlin, 1887.

497 OPPENHEIMER, F. Tolstoi als Bodenreformer, in *Der Tag*, 25. Juni, 1903.

498 PANTENIUS, TH. H. Graf Leo Tolstoj, in *Daheim*, No. 9, 1901.

499 PANTHIÈRE, A. DE. Offener Brief an den Grafen T., in *Freie Bühne für modernes Leben*, No. 4, 1893.

500 PEZOLD, TH. Westeuropäische Einflüsse auf den Entwicklungsgang der neuern russischen Litteratur, in *Baltische Monatsschriften*, No. 45, 1899.

501 POBJEDONOSTSEW, T. UND DER STUNDISMUS, in *Deutsche evangelische Kirchenzeitung*, Nos. 32–4, 1901.

502 POLONSKY, G. Gewissen, Ehre und Verantwortung bei T., München, 1898.

503 ———. T.'s " Auferstehung," in *Sozialistische Monatshefte*, pp. 414–22, 1901, and *Beilage zur Allgemeinen Zeitung*, No. 147, 1901.

504 POPPENBURG, F. "Die Auferstehung," in *Nation*, No. 30, 1900.

505 PORUCK, J. Die Religion der Zukunft, Berlin, 1894.

506 RADE. Exkommuniziert, in *Christliche Welt*, No. 14, 1901.

507 RAUDER, A. Die Lehre von Victor Hugo, Leo Tolstoi, und Emil Zola über die Aufgaben des Lebens, vom biologischen Standpunkte aus betrachtet, Jurjeff, 1896.

508 REICHEL, H. Der Leipziger T.-Prozess, in *Christliche Welt*, No. 31, 1902, and in *Deutsche Zeitung für Kirchenrecht*, pp. 104–24, 1903.

509 REPKE, J. Tolstoi und der Patriotismus, in *Zeitfragen des christlichen Volkslebens*, No. 198, Stuttgart, 1901.

510 RITTER, C. Tolstoi, in *Christliche Welt*, No. 26, 1902.

511 RÖCKEL, M. T. als Mensch, in *Gegenwart*, No. 42, 1901.

512 RODEF. T. und Dostojewskij, in *Wiener Fremdenblatt*, No. 68, 1903.

513 ROISSET, E. Das "Doppel-ich" in der neuesten französischen Litteratur, in *Nord und Süd*, No. 64, 1893.

514 SAITSCHIK, R. Die Weltanschauung H. Ibsens, in *Neue Zeit*, No. 11, 1893.

515 ———. Die Weltanschauung Dostoevski's und Tolstoi's, Neuwied, 1893.

516 SALOMON, L. L. Tolstoi, in *Illustrierte Zeitung*, No. 3094, 1902.

517 Samson - Himmelstjerna, H. von. Anti-Tolstoi, Berlin, 1902.

518 Samtleben, G. Jesus Christus und sein Evangelium nach T.

519 Schering, E. T.'s "Auferstehung," in *Die Umschau*, No. 9, 1900.

520 Schmidt, W. Ethische Fragen, in *Neue kirchliche Zeitschrift*, pp. 390–412, 1901.

521 ———. Graf L. T.'s Glaube und Verständniss des Christentums, in *Der Beweis des Glaubens*, pp. 209–25, 261–78, 1901.

522 Schmitt, E. H. Der Entwicklungsgang L. T.'s, in *Wiener Rundschau*, No. 4, 1899.

523 ———. L. T. und seine Bedeutung für unsere Kultur, Leipzig, 1901.

524 ———. L. T. als Gnostiker, in *Neue Bahnen*, pp. 139–43, 1902.

525 Schön, S. T. und die Aerzte, Wien, 1891.

526 Schröder, L. von. T.'s "Auferstehung," in *Baltische Monatsschriften*, pp. 280–6, 1900.

527 ———. T.'s Weltanschauung, in *Beilage zur Allgemeinen Zeitung*, No. 142, 1901.

528 ———. T. und seine Weltanschauung, in *Die Zeit*, No. 341, 1901.

529 Schroeder, F. Der Tolstoismus, übersetzt aus dem französischen, Dresden, 1899.

530 Schultze, S. Die Zeitseele in der modernen Sitte und Kunst, Halle, 1899.

531 Schur, E. Gedanken über T., Berlin, 1902.

532 Schütz, F. Ein Tag bei L. T., in *Neue freie Presse*, Nos. 11,408–9, 1896.

533 Schweichel, R. T.'s "Auferstehung," in *Die neue Zeit*, No. 28, 1900.

534 Selnah. Tolstoi, in *Katholische Zeitschrift für Erziehung und Unterricht*, pp. 251–8, 1902.

535 Sergejenko, P. Wie L. T. lebt und arbeitet. Deutsch von H. Stümcke, Leipzig, 1898.

536 Seuron, A. Graf L. T. Intimes aus seinem Leben, Berlin, 1895.

537 SINCERUS, A. Tolstoi, in *Deutscher Hausschatz in Wort und Bild*, Nos. 22, 23, 1902.

538 SSOLOGUB, F. Die Welt T.'s, in *Deutsche Worte*, No. 206, 1898.

539 SPIELHAGEN, F. Musste es sein? Ein offener Brief an den Grafen L. T., in *Am Wege*, Leipzig, 1903.

540 SPIELMANN - WIESBADEN, C. Die Dichtung und das Volk, in *Das Dichterheim*, No. 12, 1892.

541 STANGE, C. Das Problem T.'s in *Allgemeine evangelisch-lutherische Kirchenzeitung*, Nos. 11, 12, 1903.

542 STEIGER, E. T.'s " Auferstehung," in *Das litterarische Echo*, No. 10, 1900.

543 STEIN, P. Der Einsiedler von Jasnaja-Poljana, in *Berliner illustrierte Zeitung*, No. 36, 1899.

544 STEINER, R. T. und Nietzsche, in *Magazin für Litteratur*, No. 46, 1901.

545 STELLMACHER, K. T.'s " Gegen die Kunst," in *Ethische Kultur*, No. 34, 1901.

546 STERN, A. Studien zur Litteratur der Gegenwart, Dresden, 1895.

547 STERN, M. R. VON. Ein Besuch in Kilchberg, in *Berliner Tageblatt*, No. 172, 1892.

548 STÖCKER, A. Herausgabe der Werke T.'s, in *Der Thürmer*, No. 22, 1902.

549 STOCKHAM, A. B. Bei T., in *Neue metaphysische Rundschau*, pp. 101–7, 1902.

550 STÜMCKE, H. T.'s " Macht der Finsterniss," in *Bühne und Welt*, pp. 1128–30, 1899.

551 TEICHERT, A. Besuch bei Tolstoi, in *Neue freie Presse*, d. 3. Sept. 1902.

552 TEWS, J. T. als Erzieher, in *Ethische Kultur*, No. 45, 1902.

553 THESEN ZUM LEIPZIGER T. - PROZESS, in *Beilage zur Allgemeinen Zeitung*, No. 40, 1902.

554 TOLSTOI, L., in *Der christliche Herold*, pp. 235–6, 250–2, 1899.

555 TOLSTOI AUS DER ORTHODOXEN KIRCHE AUSGESTOSSEN, in *Der Volksanwalt*, pp. 62–4, 1901.

556 TOLSTOI : DIE MACHT DER FINSTERNISS, in *Heimat*, No. 9, 1901.

557 Tolstoi gegen Tolstoi, in *Die Wahrheit*, No. 61, 1899.

558 Tolstoi, L., über die Kunst, in *Signale für die musikalische Welt*, No. 8, 1898.

559 Tolstoi in der Weltlitteratur, in *Börsenblatt für deutschen Buchhandel*, No. 266, 1901.

560 Tolstoi und seine Richter, in *Der Lotse*, No. 27, 1901.

561 Tolstois Antwort an den heiligen Synod, in *Christliche Welt*, No. 5, 1902.

562 Tolstois Kritik der Glaubenslehre, in *Deutsches Protestanteblatt*, No. 39, 1901.

563 Trepplin, G. Zur T.-Litteratur, in *Die Gesellschaft*, I., pp. 327–9, 1902.

564 Tschertkoff, W. Ein T.-Jünger, in *Weltrundschau*, pp. 229–32, 1903.

565 Tschudi, H. von. Kunst und Publikum, Berlin, 1899.

566 Uhse, M. Die Ethik von T.'s " Auferstehung," in *Leipziger Tageblatt und Anzeiger*, No. 109, 1900.

567 Waldersee, E. T.'s Darstellung des Evangeliums, in *Evangelische Volkschule*, Nos. 24, 25, 1903.

568 Weber - Lutkow, H. L. T.'s sozial-politisches Hauptwerk "Was sollen wir thun?" in *Neue Bahnen*, pp. 259–63, 1903, und *Ostdeutsche Rundschau*, d. 24. Mai, 1903.

569 Weis - Ulmenried, A. T. — Prophet oder Charlatan? in *Gegenwart*, No. 8, 1903.

570 Wenck. T.'s Testament, in *Die Hilfe*, No. 22, 1900.

571 ———. T.'s Weltanschauung, *ib.*, No. 25, 1900.

572 Wergun, Dmitry. Ein neues Buch T.'s "Die Knechtschaft unserer Zeit," in *Zeit*, No. 320, 1901.

573 Wesendonck, H. Der modern-religiöse Wahnsinn oder Christlehre keine göttliche Lehre, Graf Leo Tolstoi's Evangelium-Narrheit, Leipzig, 1891.

574 Widmann, J. V. Zu L. T.'s 70. Geburtstag, in *Nation*, No. 50, 1898.

575 Wie T. lebt und arbeitet, in *Der Thürmer*, pp. 315–9, 1901.

576 Wohlbruck, O. Bei L. T., in *Die Woche*, No. 6, 1900.

577 ZABEL, E. Litterarische Streifzüge durch Russland, Berlin, 1885.

578 ———. Russische Litteraturbilder, Berlin, 1899.

579 ———. Dichter und Darsteller. L. N. Tolstoj, Leipzig, 1901.

580 ZABEL, E., ÜBER TOLSTOI, in Die Umschau, No. 8, 1901.

581 ZAGOSKIN, N. Die Familie T., in Zukunft, pp. 480–4, 1898.

582 ZACHARIAS, F. T.'s Moral, in Zürcher Diskussionen, No. 12, 1898.

583 ZIEGLER, L. L. T. und Religion der Wiedergeburt, in Süd-west-deutsche Rundschau, pp. 248–65, 1902.

584 ZILLMANN, P. Zur T.-Litteratur, in Neue metaphysische Rundschau, pp. 97–100, 148–54, 236–42, 1902.

585 ZUM FALLE TOLSTOI, in Illustrierte Zeitung, No. 3014, 1901.

III. FRENCH

586 ADAM, MME. (JULIETTE LAMBERT). Introduction à l'évangile du comte Léon Tolstoï, in Nouvelle Revue, Vol. XXIII., 15 Juill., 1883.

587 ANGOT DES ROTOURS, J. Morale du cœur, Paris, 1893.

588 A PROPOS DE L'EXCOMMUNICATION DU COMTE T., in Revue des études franco-russes, p. 56, 1901.

589 A PROPOS D'UNE LETTRE DE T., in L'Européen, Mai 9, 1903.

590 BADIN, A. Un roman du comte Tolstoï, avec préface de M. Ivan Tourguéneff, in Nouvelle Revue, Vol. XI., 15 Août, 1891.

591 BEAUPUY, C. DE. Qu'est-ce que l'art? in Etudes, Vol. XIV., pp. 337–42, 1899.

592 BENTZON, T. Autour de T., in Revue des deux mondes, Août 15, 1902.

593 BESNARD, L. L'œuvre dramatique de L. T., in Revue d'art dramatique, Mai et Juin, 1899.

594 BIENSTOCK, J. W. Colonie de Tolstoïens en Angleterre, in Revue des Revues, Vol. XXXVIII., p. 38, 1901.

595 ———. T. et les Doukhobors, Paris, 1902.

596 BLANC, MME. T. Promenades en Russie, Paris, 1903.

597 BONET-MAURY, G. T. et les essais de socialisme chrétien en Russie, in Revue chrétienne, pp. 119–23, 1898.

598 BOURDEAU, J. Les maîtres de la pensée contemporaine
    3ᵉ ed., Paris, 1904.

599 BOURDON, G. En écoutant T., entretiens sur la guerre et
    quelques autres sujets, Paris, 1905.

600 CALIPPE, ABBÉ CH. Tolstoï et l'œuvre sociale des moines,
    in *Association catholique*, Mars, pp. 226–37, 1899.

601 COURRIÈRE, C. Mœurs intimes. Une visite au comte L. T.,
    in *Revue Britannique*, Fév., 1899.

602 CROSBY, E. H. T. et ses traducteurs, in *Humanité nouvelle*,
    Août, 1900.

603 CYON, E. DE. Un pessimiste russe, in *Nouvelle Revue*, Vol.
    XXXIV., 1ᵉʳ Juin, 1885.

604 DE LA QUESTION SEXUELLE D'APRÈS T., in *Revue des études
    franco-russes*, p. 24, 1902.

605 DOUMIC, R. Les idées du comte Tolstoï sur l'art, in *Etudes
    sur la littérature française*, 3ᵉ série, Paris, 1899.

606 ———. " Resurrection " du comte T., *ib.*, 4ᵉ série, 1901.

607 DRAGOMIROF, M. I. " Guerre et Paix " de T. au point de
    vue militaire (traduit du russe par le commandant Moulin),
    Paris, 1896.

608 ———. Etude du roman " La guerre et la paix " au point
    de vue militaire, in *Nouvelle Revue*, Vol. IC., 1896.

609 DUC - QUERCY, MME. A. L. T. chez lui, in *Revue des
    Revues*, Vol. XXXVIII., p. 620, 1899.

610 DUMAS, G. T. et la philosophie de l'amour, Paris, 1893.

611 DUPUY, E. Les grands maîtres de la littérature russe,
    Paris, 1897.

612 FAGUET, E. Tolstoï " Qu'est ce que l'art ? " in his *Propos
    littéraires*, 1ᵉ série, Paris, 1902.

613 FELGÈRES, CH. Essais d'histoire et de littérature, Paris,
    1896.

614 GAUTIER, J. DE. Tolstoï, in *Revue blanche*, No. 127, 1898.

615 GOLDENWEISER, A. S. Le crime comme peine, la peine
    comme crime ; analyse du roman du comte L. T. " Resur-
    rection," tr. du russe par J. de Joukovsky, Paris, 1904.

616 HALPÉRINE - KAMINSKY, E. "La puissance des ténèbres" du comte L. T. sur la scène française, in *Nouvelle Revue*, 1ᵉʳ Février, 1888.

617 ———. Le rôle de l'art. Réponses à T. (H. Fiérens-Gevaert, Paul Adam, Jules Case, etc.), in *Grande Revue*, Fév. et Mars, 1899.

618 ———. Une autre "Resurrection," in *Revue blanche*, Jan. 3, 1903.

619 HENNEQUIN, E. Les écrivains francisés, Paris, 1889.

620 ———. Le comte L. T., in *Nouvelle Revue*, 1ᵉʳ Oct., 1888.

621 JEANROY - FELIX, F. Ecrivains célèbres, Paris, 1900.

622 KOVALEVSKI, M. M. La morale de Tolstoï, in *Morale sociale*, pp. 162–91, 1899.

623 KUFFERATH, M. Musiciens et philosophes: Tolstoï, Schopenhauer, Nietzsche, Richard Wagner, Paris, 1899.

624 LA VIE ET LA DOCTRINE DE JÉSUS, in *Revue bleue*, Juin 22 et Juillet 6.

625 LABADIE - LAGRAVE, G. T. et les Russes, in *La Revue hebdomadaire*, Nov. 29, 1902.

626 LAMY, M. E. A propos d'alliance russe, in *Revue des deux mondes*, Août, 1894.

627 LEMAITRE, J. Impressions de théatre, v. 1, Paris, 1888.

628 LE NÉO - CHRISTIANISME, in *Bibliothèque universelle et Revue suisse*, No. 59, 1893.

629 LÉON TOLSTOÏ, in *Revue des Revues*, II., p. 8, 1891.

630 LES ÉCRIVAINS RUSSES CONTEMPORAINS, in *Revue des deux mondes*, 15 Juillet, 1884.

631 LIONNET, J. L'évolution des idées chez quelques uns de nos contemporains, Paris, 1903.

632 LOURIÉ, O. Une conversation avec T., in *Revue encyclopédique*, No. 261, 1898.

633 ———. Pensées de T., in *Revue sociale*, No. 162, 1898.

634 ———. T. et l'art, in *Revue philosophique*, No. 1, 1899.

635 ———. T. et la question sociale, in *Revue sociale*, pp. 300–18, 435–51, 1899.

636 LOYSON, P. H. L'investiture de T., in *Revue franco-allemande*, v. 5, 1901.

637 MAFFRE, P. Le Tolstoïsme et le christianisme, Montauban, 1896.

638 MANACÉINE. L'anarchie passive et le comte L. T., Paris, 1894.

639 MARIE, D. T. et Dostoïevsky, in *Revue des études franco-russes*, p. 316, 1903.

640 MAURY, L. Pensées de T., in *Revue encyclopédique*, No. 261, 1898.

641 MEREJKOWSKY, D. Le christianisme de T. et de Dostoïevsky, in *Revue bleue*, Dec. 27, 1902.

642 ———. T. et Dostoïevsky, traduit par le comte Prozor et S. Persky, Paris, 1904.

643 MONTJOYARD, VICOMTE DE. Mystique militante, in *Nederlandsche Gids*, No. 82, 1893.

644 MÜNTZ, E. T. et la mission sociale de l'art, in *Gazette des Beaux Arts*, No. 500, 1899.

645 MURET, M. T. intime, in *Bibliotheque universelle*, 4e pér. vol. 4, 1894.

646 NESVOY. Chez le comte L. T., in *L'Européen*, Nov. 21, 1903.

647 ———. Les doctrines de T. en Italie, *ib.*, Feb. 28, 1903.

648 ———. Lettre de Russie : le Tolstoïsme, *ib.*, Mars 14, 1903.

649 NORDAU, M. Le Tolstoïsme, in *Dégénérescence*, Paris, 1895.

650 PASSY, F. Une thèse de T., in *Institute de France, Académie des sciences morales et politiques, Séances et travaux* n. s. V. 57, pp. 232–241.

651 ———. Le rayons de l'aube, in *Le journal des économistes*, Juin, 1901.

652 PELISSIER, G. " Resurrection " par T., in his *Etudes de litterature contemporaine*, v. 2, 1901.

653 ROD, E. Les idées morales du temps présent, Paris, 1891.

654 SCHROEDER, F. Le Tolstoïsme, Paris, 1893.

655 SOREL, A. Lectures historiques, Paris, 1894.

656 STRANNIK, I. La pensée russe contemporaine, Paris, 1903.

657 Strauss, E. " Resurrection " de T., in *La Critique*, Dec. 5, 1902.

658 Suarés. Tolstoï, Paris (1899).

659 Tolstoï et la critique russe, in *Revue des études franco-russes*, p. 40, 1901.

660 Vessiot, A. Pages de pédagogie (T. éducateur), Paris, 1895.

661 Vogüé, Vicomte E. de. Le comte L. T., in *Revue des deux mondes*, No. 7, 1884.

662 ———. " La puissance des ténèbres," reflexions d'un spectateur, in *Revue des deux mondes*, Mars 15, 1888.

663 ———. Le roman russe, Paris, 1897.

664 ———. Le Tolstoïsme et l'anarchie, Paris, 1900.

665 Wyzewa, T. de. Ecrivains étrangers, Paris, 1896.

666 ———. Tolstoiana, in *Ecrivains étrangers*, 3e série, Paris, 1900.

THE END.

ERRATA[1]

Vol. IV., p. 41, l. 16, change "psaltery" to "psalter."
Vol. IV., p. 221, l. 24, change "gives" to "give."
Vol. IV., p. 303, l. 36, change "goslings" to "kids."
Vol. IV., p. 304, l. 1, change "goslings" to "kids."
Vol. IV., p. 336, l. 2, change "Medans" to "Medes."
Vol. V., p. 148, l. 1, change "one but the last" to "last but one."
Vol. VII., p. 204, l. 8, change "princes" to "prince."
Vol. XIX., p. 110, the last sentence in par. 7 to read, "They are catching fire," etc.
Vol. XIX., p. 111, l. 4 in par. 9, change "surely renders" to "surrenders."
Vol. XIX., p. 185, l. 2 in par. 8, change "question" to "life."
Vol. XIX., p. 243, l. 5, add "while" before "the proprietors."

Errata in proper names are corrected in the index.

[1] Readers are requested to communicate to the translator any errata they may notice.